LANGUAGE AND PHILOSOPHY

LANGUAGE
AND
PHILOSOPHY

A SYMPOSIUM

Edited by Sidney Hook

New York University Press   1969
University of London Press

The contents of this volume comprise the proceedings of the ninth annual New York University Institute of Philosophy, held at Washington Square, New York, April 12–13, 1968. Previous volumes in the series, also edited by Sidney Hook, are:

Determinism and Freedom in the Age of Modern Science
Psychoanalysis, Scientific Method, and Philosophy
Dimensions of Mind
Religious Experience and Truth
Philosophy and History
Law and Philosophy
Art and Philosophy
Human Values and Economic Policy

Contents

Introduction

The "revolution in philosophy," about which so much has been written describing contemporary philosophical developments, may be said to have begun with the discovery of the central importance of the word, of language habits and language games, of the meanings of "meaning." Although not professionally interested in language, or the study of comparative languages, many philosophers concluded that the perennial problems of philosophy resulted from failure to understand the logical grammar or rules of language and that when proper distinctions were made there was no such thing as philosophical knowledge or truth. Philosophy was an activity of analysis or insight into the aberrant uses of language. It unlocked no mysteries, provided no key to the understanding of nature and human nature. At most, it emancipated thought from "the tyranny of words." Genuine thought and knowledge about the world, on this view, could only be acquired by the empirical methods of scientific inquiry. The basic syntax of language and grammar did not reflect the metaphysical structure of the world, as had once been believed; nor was it the source of any truth or knowledge independent of experience. It was acquired through the same processes of experience by which skills, habits, techniques, and knowledge are learned.

There now occurred an interesting development. Some professional students of linguistics, notably Noam Chomsky, have challenged these conclusions on the basis of comparative linguistic studies and a study of the way any language is learned. They assert that there is a universal grammar common to all languages of which the child has an unconscious but perfect knowledge. They believe that only such a hypothesis can account for the ability of the learner to grasp an indefinitely large number of sentences, once he has been introduced to a few, and constantly to *create* new, well-formed sentences. Unless we assume that men are endowed with "innate ideas" and specific "mental faculties," on this view, we cannot understand the science of linguistics or the wondrous ability of the child of tender years to learn how to speak.

It is this "counter-revolution" in philosophy which claims that the empirical tradition in knowledge from Locke down is false and the rationalistic tradition of Leibniz is sound — that is the chief topic of debate in these interesting exchanges between philosopher, linguist, and anthropologist. The facts are not in dispute but their philosophical interpretations are. A great deal may depend upon the upshot. Linguistic analysis has claimed to dissolve the problems of philosophy. The science of linguistics, according to some of its practitioners, claims to reinstate them; and not only to reinstate them but to solve them or at least some of them.

A little knowledge of the surface grammar of language seems to have brought traditional philosophy into disrepute. Will further knowledge of depth grammar reinstate philosophy as an independent discipline? The issue is squarely joined in this volume. Perhaps we are not dealing with a "counter-revolution" in philosophy so much as with a renaissance.

The discussion of language and culture in the first part of the volume also bears on the central issue. If the hypothesis of Whorf is true, and basic linguistic categories are derived from social organization, the significance of universal constants in language, if any, would not necessarily reflect innate ideas but certain empirical uniformities in social life and the conditional necessities of human communication. This conclusion might be defended independently of the specific form of Whorf's doctrines.

In the third part of the volume, some contributions on

the relation between logic and language pose an allied problem. Does logic as a language or a form of language give us knowledge about the world, and if so, what kind and about what? More specifically, is it concerned with necessary truths about states of affairs, and if so, what kind of affairs?

It is hoped that the contributions will suggest something of the verve and liveliness that characterized the proceedings of the Institute.

Sidney Hook

PART I

Language and Culture

A

Language and Culture

FLOYD G. LOUNSBURY
Yale University

I HAVE TO SAY at the outset that I approach this subject — that of the relation of language to culture — with some misgivings. Although it is a topic of perennial interest among anthropologists, whose profession I must represent here, I fear that what our hosts and the other participants in this meeting might be most interested in having from an anthropologist on this subject is precisely what I am least prepared to make very definite statements about; and that what I do feel prepared to be definite about, which can be seen as falling within the range of this broad topic, is of such a restricted and specialized concern that it is least likely to be of much interest to philosophers of language, theorists of grammar, or logicians. Under these circumstances, I have come to the conclusion that I might as well present something of both — something vague and indefinite about what perhaps may be of most interest, and something more definite and technical in a limited domain of language-and-culture problems that may not be of such general interest. Also I must caution, and plead for indulgence on these grounds, that I feel I can only speak as someone more or less committed to a certain tradition of cultural and social anthropology, and similarly of linguistics. I am not a philosopher. Some people think I am not much of a linguist. And for that matter, there are a lot of anthropologists who are in vehement disagreement with me too.

When I made myself face squarely the question of what,

3

precisely, anthropology (or 'linguistic anthropology,' or 'anthropological linguistics') has to offer on the subject of the relations between language and culture, between language and thought, and on related problems, the answer seemed to reduce to this: it has offered a long line of interesting and insightful speculative hypotheses, often eloquently expressed, frequently appraised as 'brilliant,' usually anecdotally illustrated — *but no proofs*. Until fairly recently, perhaps. I would argue that in recent work we have been able to approximate a little more closely to 'proofs'; but these are at best proofs of very restricted propositions about special kinds of subject matter within the larger domain of language-and-culture relationships. The more general propositions — those that would be of widest interest — are still in that limbo of speculative hypotheses.

It has seemed to me then that perhaps the best thing I might do with this assignment is to make it an occasion for showing *how difficult it is* to establish or to reach general agreement on language-and-culture hypotheses. And it seems also that the best — or at least the easiest — way of showing this would be to turn this into a historical review of sorts, relating something of the history of the endeavor.

There is, in fact, quite a long history of this subject. The speculations on the relation between language and thought, of course, go back to ancient times. More recently in European intellectual history, the same question — that of the relation of language to thought — was in the forefront of that long and many-sided debate about 'the origin of language' which engaged the minds and pens of philosophers, theologians, and philologists almost continuously from the middle of the eighteenth century till close to the end of the nineteenth century. The espoused issue throughout the history of that debate was usually a theological one: that of a natural or a supernatural origin of language. But though this was the professed issue at stake, it was argued out in terms of other issues: e.g., (*a*) whether the elementary ideas, necessary for language, understanding, thought, and reason, are an innate endowment of the

mind, or whether they are acquired through sense experience;
(*b*) whether thought is, or is not, possible without language —
i.e., whether language should be regarded as an instrument for
the expression of thought, or whether thought is in essence a
linguistic phenomenon, thinking being dependent on speaking,
this including of course 'internal speech'; (*c*) whether the cir-
cumstance that caused man to need and to develop speech — if
this indeed was his doing — was primarily 'psychological' (innate necessity for self-expression, in vocal as well as other
forms), or 'sociological' (needs arising in social contacts, coop-
eration, etc.); (*d*) whether the first root vocables may have
been derived from natural cries of the organism, or from imita-
tion of the sounds of things in nature, or from vocal 'gesture'
(vocal accompaniments to pointing and other gestural behavior); and (*e*) how a transition might have been made from
any of these natural, iconic, or indexical signs to a language
whose root elements consist almost entirely of arbitrary signs.
Though it is customary to dismiss this extensive literature as
absurd — as being about the 'pooh-pooh' theory, the 'ding-dong'
theory, and the 'bow-wow' theory of the origin of language — it
is of interest to note that some of the primary issues in that debate were issues that had a long and respectable ancient history, and that — more important — have survived this particular context of argument and are still with us in other contexts in
linguistics and in the philosophy and psychology of language
(note in particular the first two of those mentioned).

Along a different line, speculations about the relation of
language 'type' to the development of thought patterns and to
stages of social and cultural evolution were prominent in the
long history of the 'nineteenth-century linguistic typology.'
This is a history that extends from 1808 until quite recent
times, and during which the interpretations of the psychological and cultural significance of language types underwent a
number of striking reversals. The matter is still taken seriously
by some. Only last year I listened to a lecture by a distinguished philosopher, who was visiting some universities in this
country, in which he argued that there are — and can be — only

three types of languages (essentially Schleicher's Hegelian argument), which he correlated with three basically different types of thinking, and which he then sought to illustrate with the interestingly different influences on modern literature in his country that have been contributed by writers coming from different ethnic segments of the population, and representing different linguistic and cultural backgrounds.

Yet another line of hypotheses — a more recent one — about the relations of culture to language and of language to thought, and not tied to such gross categorizations as the three (or four, or five) 'types' of the nineteenth-century typology, is that contained in the so-called 'hypothesis of linguistic relativity' — as foreshadowed to a certain extent in the writings of Boas, but as expressed in a far more radical form in certain of the later writings of Sapir and in those of Whorf. Boas, Sapir, and Whorf could report their 'findings' (or 'the findings of linguists') about the relationships between language, thought, and culture in apparent confidence that these ushered in new understandings of the human mind, dispelling popular prescientific errors. But these findings and the conclusions drawn from them were more in the nature of proclamations than of proofs. And of course, what any given inquirer into language 'finds' in language may be in part determined by what he has been alerted to look for there; and this can be influenced by the intellectual climate of the times, or more importantly in the case of these innovators, in reaction against such climates of opinion.

The 'Whorf hypothesis' was, and still is, widely appealing to anthropologists, and it attracted a fair amount of attention from psychologists, philosophers, and linguists as well. But the questions raised in that hypothesis are by no means satisfactorily answered as yet. At the present time there is a tendency, at least among some linguists, to see the pertinent issues in a rather different light from that which seemed to be implied in the statements of Sapir and Whorf, and to conclude that the hypothesis of linguistic relativity is untenable, and that Sapir and Whorf may not really have believed everything they seemed to be saying.

Among anthropologists recently there has been something of a revival of interest in questions about language as a manifestation of culture and as potential evidence for theories of cognition. This has been concurrent with a search for new ways of determining the meanings of crucial native terms (often baffling at first) that are encountered in ethnographic field work, and for new ways also of expressing the semantic structure of sets of terms and concepts. Attention has been shifted rather away from grammar and toward the semantics of lexicon. This has been accompanied also by a shift of emphasis in the understanding of the concept of 'culture,' which is what anthropology is supposed to be mainly about.

As noted earlier, it was felt that a paper on the announced subject of "Language and Culture" might best accomplish its aim by sketching something of the history of anthropological opinion on the relationship referred to in the title. And it will be recalled that a particular aim of the paper was also to be to show how difficult it has been to reach agreement on the nature of this relationship. A number of different topics in the history of thought on this subject have been referred to in this "Introductory Note." Each of them might be treated at length. The earlier topics, however, can perhaps be passed over, in order to come immediately to the 'linguistic-relativity' hypothesis. Following this, I want to refer to more recent work in lexical semantics, and to illustrate, by means of a case history, the difficulties in reaching agreement on what the semantic structure of a language is (or what the semantic structure of even a small portion of the lexicon of a language is), and on what the cultural and psychological facts really are that are expressed in that structure.

The task of an ethnographer set down in a strange society has often been likened to that of a cryptanalyst. He must observe goings-on whose meanings and motivations he cannot fathom. His job is to deduce, in whatever way he can, what they mean to the people who are involved in them. Even seemingly familiar kinds of behavior may be deceptive, in that they may carry an import wholly different from that which he, extrapolating from his own system of social signs and meanings, would ascribe to it. The ethnographer, then, must construct a new set of concepts and alert himself to a new set of meaning-conveying signals before he can comprehend, at least in an intellectual way, what goes on around him in the strange milieu. Emotional comprehension of another people's behavior may be still harder. That requires internalizing a new set of values as well. However, that is not an essential part of the ethnographer's task. If it were, and if success were really attained, his ethnography might never get written. Or it might be quite a different sort of document from what the profession expects.

But the analogy with cryptanalysis is not quite perfect. A cryptanalyst at least can assume that, when a cipher is cracked, the hidden message will become understandable and translatable. Anthropologists have been rather less sure about this in their ethnographic analogue. To the contrary, the more extreme cultural relativists among them have become quite convinced of the nonequivalence and untranslatability of concepts that derive from different social and cultural systems.

An ethnographer has to work pretty much through the medium of the language spoken by the people he studies. Even where bilingualism makes possible the use of an intermediary language for certain phases of social contact and for getting certain kinds of information, the conceptual world of a people can hardly be penetrated without recourse to their own language. And the relativity of culture has its analogue, or correlate, in a relativity of the meaning content of language.

I have made reference above to anthropologists whom I termed "the more extreme cultural relativists." This wording suggests that there must also be some less extreme adherents of that position. Such indeed is the case. One can recognize considerable differences of degree in the relativist position, whether it be in the interpretation of matters of culture or of those more strictly of language. The crucial issue — a point of disagreement that differentiates the position of 'complete relativists' from that of 'limited relativists' — is the supposition of *incommensurability* between different systems, and the interpretation that is placed on this notion. Sapir introduced this term rather casually into one of his articles. Whether or not he meant it to be taken literally can of course be argued; but in any case the notion is there and it has been taken quite seriously by some. This statement of his (a brief note in *Science* in 1931, which has been much quoted since) is an expression of a quite thoroughgoing linguistic relativism. It was here that Sapir spoke of "the tyrannical hold that linguistic form has upon our orientation in the world," and where he said of language that it "not only refers to experience largely acquired without its help but actually defines experience for us . . . because of our unconscious projection of its implicit expectations into the field of experience." The notion of incommensurability was brought in by Sapir as follows: "Inasmuch as languages differ very widely in their systematization of fundamental concepts, they tend to be only loosely equivalent to each other as symbolic devices and are, as a matter of fact, incommensurable in the sense in which two systems of points in a plane are, on the whole, incommensurable to each other if they are plotted out with reference to differing systems of coordinates." The implication here is of a noncomparability of concepts expressed by different languages when these are from historically separate cultural traditions. (It should be noted that he appended the qualification that "the point of view urged in this paper becomes entirely clear only when one compares languages of extremely different structures, as in the case of our Indo-European languages, native American Indian languages, and native languages of Africa.") Sapir's metaphor further implies that the noncomparability results from categorizations of experience in terms of *unlike* prime categories in diverse linguistic systems.[1] This makes experience itself noncomparable, for according to the statement just quoted, "language actually

defines experience for us." The fundamental issue, then, is that
of the ultimate prime categories, i.e., whether or not there are
common factors in the concepts peculiar to different cultural
and linguistic systems.

This 1931 statement to which I have made reference apparently represents something of a turning point in Sapir's outlook, or else it is a crystallization of a point of view which had
only gradually been taking shape. His earlier writings hardly
support the position that he announced here. Rather, they are
more reminiscent of the position of Boas, who may be said to
have anticipated a 'limited relativist' position, recognizing variability in language and in culture, and a dependence of these
on the special histories of different peoples, but at the same
time stressing the universality of fundamental factors and common starting points. But this later formulation of Sapir's is the
one that Whorf took over and expressed so vividly and persua-
sively to such a wide audience. Anthropologists in particular
seem to have found the view congenial. This is hardly to be
wondered at, considering the bewildering variety of cultural
and social forms with which they are confronted.

Not all linguists or cultural anthropologists however, either in Sapir's and Whorf's time or now, have been willing to
see the common bases of human experience and the 'psychological unity of mankind' so subordinated to the superstruc-
tures of social, cultural, and linguistic systems that they are denied an identification as fundamental and universal starting
points for all such systems. The 'limited-relativist' position admits of these as common factors that introduce a sizable degree of commensurability, comparability, and even translat-
ability between systems. It may still properly be termed a
'relativist' position, however, inasmuch as it recognizes the
nonuniversality of higher-order concepts and the variability
and relativity of virtually everything in a cultural or linguistic
system above the level of the ultimate primes.

Historically there are a number of independent sources for
the ideas of cultural and linguistic relativity. Although the influences of Sapir and Whorf have been strongly felt in Ameri-

can anthropology and linguistics, there are separate sources and more or less parallel traditions in Europe. The legacy of Humboldt and the influence of Weisgerber and Trier have been felt for some time in European linguistics, and a rather extreme relativist position has developed in some of British social anthropology in recent years.

Carried to its logical conclusion in cultural and social anthropology, the complete-relativist position implies the invalidity of the classic 'comparative method' of that discipline — a conclusion that has been proclaimed on more than one occasion. Thus, for example, whereas some anthropologists have undertaken to make comparative studies of such social institutions as 'marriage,' 'kinship,' 'the incest taboo,' etc., and, while searching out the variable features of these and their possible conditioning factors, have at the same time also focused on the identification of constant features and have sought to frame universal, cross-culturally valid definitions of these concepts, other anthropologists of a different persuasion — more extreme relativists — have shown much skepticism concerning the possibility of there being any universal defining features for such institutions. In this 'complete-relativist' view, a universally valid conjunctive definition of such an institution — as say 'marriage,' or 'kinship' — is not possible. But beyond this, in the extreme form of this position, even a disjunctive definition is logically an impossibility — unless it contain as many alternatives as there are societies whose institutions or concepts of so-called 'marriage,' or 'kinship,' are to be defined. Each is a thing unto itself. Not only are the essential features variable from one case to the next, but they cannot — in this extreme view — even be supposed to be genuinely comparable, i.e., 'commensurable.' Each such institution, it is held, must be studied in the context of the social system of which it is a part, and derives its meaning and its definition from its relations to all of the other components of that particular system, rather than from some universal conceptual component. (This statement, about the meaning of an institution being derived from its relations to all of the other components of the system, is also one of the cardinal tenets of the 'structuralist' position in social anthropology. It should be noted, however, that this structuralist notion does not necessarily entail acceptance of the more extreme form of the relativist position. Some structuralists, in fact, are 'limited relativists' and are professed universalists in regard to the most fundamental features of human society and culture, as also of language, even while recognizing the great variability in the elaborations of the primary concepts, in the metaphoric extensions to these, in the various secondary accretions to them, and in their consequently different 'structural' or systemic values.)

Now, however much anthropologists may have thought about questions of cultural or linguistic relativism, they are wary of discussing such matters *in abstracto* as general issues. Above all, they are empiricists in outlook — or at least they picture themselves so — and they prefer to draw their conclusions from the study of data and in the context of particular substantive problems. And as for holding to any general position on the question of relativism, one might actually espouse a complete relativist position — or contrariwise, a universalist position — in regard to some particular area of subject matter, without necessarily taking a similar position in regard to problems in some other area of his subject matter, or without claiming adherence to such a position as a matter of principle. Supposedly one is guided by his data.

Although the concerns of Sapir and Whorf were not limited to any one aspect of language, it was nonetheless grammar that interested them most. Sapir especially seemed rather disdainful of the subject of vocabulary, so far as the possibility of finding anything of general linguistic or cultural interest was concerned. The relations of language to culture that could be found in vocabulary he seems to have regarded as of a rather trivial order. ("It goes without saying that the mere content of language is intimately related to culture. A society that has no knowledge of theosophy need have no name for it . . . But this superficial and extraneous kind of parallelism is of no real interest to the linguist . . . The linguistic student should never make the mistake of identifying a language with its dictionary."²) This has been a fairly general attitude — and to a large extent still is — among linguists, and many have expressed themselves in similar vein. (E.g.: "The vocabulary of a people reflects their experiences and interests. It is here that we find the most reliable and the dullest correlations between the rest of culture and language."³) Whorf, it is true, defined grammar in a somewhat broader sense, so that in his hands it dealt with at least some properties of words that were related to their semantic structure. But it was still grammatical categories that were the focus of his attention. Anthropologists today, however, are turning more and more toward the study of meaning in vocabulary. They are not finding it a dull or a trivial matter as it was formerly assumed to be. Rather, they are uncovering semantic structures in lexicon that are nonobvious and of considerable intricacy and complexity (so that it is challenging and interesting to work on them) and also of first-ranking importance for the understanding of the culture of a people (so that, given the aims of the profession, it is worth doing). They are only now learning how to reveal the structure of meaning that is in the lexical component of language. This is something that for a long time previous had been held by linguists to be hopeless (if indeed there was anything much there to be discovered at all), or to be beyond the proper concern of linguistics. But many of those working in the anthropological field at present are finding the semantic structures in vocabulary to be more interesting, and more profitable for cultural anthropology than the formerly popular attempt to discern world view from grammatical categories.

I want to turn now to one particular substantive problem involving language in relation to culture. It is one among many such language-and-culture problems on which anthropologists disagree, some being led to a completely relativist interpretation, and others to a position of limited relativism, i.e., universalist so far as the fundamental prime concepts are concerned. It has to do with a segment of vocabulary rather than with grammar. Its subject matter is the linguistic representation of concepts of kinship. This happens to be a subject much studied in social anthropology, since the concepts and institutions of kinship play an unusually large role in the life of the simpler societies.

The fact that I have just used a term, 'kinship,' to designate a particular area of vocabulary in a language (i.e., in *any* language, or *all* languages) implies that there must be — or that I, or anthropologists in general, think there must be — a universal phenomenon of this sort, definable for all societies, and recognized and conceptualized as such in all societies, to which this term can unambiguously be applied. I will have to admit here that I incline to just such an opinion (being a limited relativist on this matter); but if I were attempting to speak for anthropologists in general, I would have to hedge on this point or deny it altogether. For the leading social anthropologists of today incline far more in the direction of complete relativism in their outlook and conclusions on this matter.

On first glance it looks as though this might be a question of some interest to philosophy: whether or not we have here a concept that can be regarded as a universal mental construct. When we begin to inquire into it in the anthropological manner, however, it reduces to an empirical question — one that may be of interest for a natural science having to do with human social, cultural, and linguistic phenomena, but probably not one that is of inherent interest for philosophy. But it also reduces to a problem of definition. And beyond this, since anthropologists have not been able to reach agreement on this question through their professedly objective and empirical methods, and in fact still hotly disagree on it, it may be asked whether it is in fact a question that *can* be answered by empirical methods. Both the observational problem and the interpretive problem assume increased magnitude. It may be that the field worker's expectations so influence what he looks for, asks for, and gets, that whatever view he enters the field with is self-reinforcing. And it may be that approaches to interpretation are as much influenced by intellectual fashions and philosophical movements that affect all of academia and even wider circles from time to time as they are by 'objective' observation or 'analysis' of data.

Dictionaries usually define the word 'kinship,' in its narrower sense, as a relationship by blood, or, in a broader sense of the term, as relationship by blood or by marriage. Even the most modern dictionaries still employ the folk notion of 'blood' in their definitions, as a metaphor for what is of essence in the concept, viz., whatever of physical substance two people have in common, or whatever special physical likenesses they have, as their heritage from one or more common biological ancestors. It is our common understanding (in our folk culture as well as in our scientific culture) that one's 'blood' — or whatever that metaphor stands for — derives directly and most immediately, and on the average more or less equally, from his two biological parents, and, at a second degree of removal, from the four biological grandparents, and so forth. Our question about whether a concept of 'kinship' is universal in human culture might then be expected to reduce to this empirical question: Is it or is it not the case that people in all societies understand at least this much about the biology of procreation and heredity (however they may express it metaphorically), and that they have a notion of 'relationship' that is derived from this prior understanding and that is defined in terms of it?

If this is the form of the question, then there are some problems raised by ethnographic data that must be taken into consideration. Certainly not all people conceive of one's biological inheritance as deriving more or less equally from two parents. There are reported to be societies in which people believe that one's physical being comes entirely from one's mother, and that one's 'father' in no way contributes to his substance. (He only 'opens the way,' and is not even absolutely necessary.) It is reported, moreover, that in at least one such society a person therefore does not consider his father to be a 'kinsman,' but only an 'affine' — a relative by marriage. It is as if they had no concept of 'father,' but only one of 'stepfather' ('mother's husband'). And then there is reported to be also a society in which people, in precisely the contrary manner, suppose that one's physical being comes entirely from one's father (one's mother is only the garden where the father's seed was planted). In such a society one's own mother is supposed not to be physically 'kin,' but only related through marriage and fosterage. More common, however, are societies in which it is believed that both of one's biological parents contribute something to his essence, but properties of unlike nature. Thus, one's body may derive from one's mother, but one's soul from one's father; or one's flesh may come from one's mother, and one's bone from one's father; or one's flesh and bone (solid substances) from one's mother, and one's blood (or bodily fluids in general) from one's father; and so on. Further, the contribution of one parent may be stronger or more enduring than that of the other. For example, in the last mentioned case, the flesh (which is transmitted only in the female line) endures forever, undiminished and undiluted no matter how many generations (in the female line) may have passed, while the blood (which is transmitted only in the male line) extinguishes itself in two generations. Finally, there are societies in which one is understood to have one biological mother but several biological fathers. Every man who has had relations with a woman during the period of her pregnancy (there are normally several such) has contributed substance for the building up of the foetus in the womb, and is consequently conceived to be, in a physical sense, one of the 'fathers' of the child.

Now if we discount the ethnographic observational problem and suppose all such accounts to be essentially correct, then there is a definitional problem that must be met. This doesn't present too serious an obstacle, however. What we may say that people in all societies understand about the biological basis for the concept of kinship is that one's being is derived from one or more parents (of at most two kinds),[4] and that through common derivation of such sort different individuals are 'kin' to each other and have special qualities of their personal essence in common.

I think there is hardly an anthropologist [5] who, after reading or hearing this much of our account, would not be ready to cry out that all this business about biological connection utterly misses the point, and that biology (however understood) is essentially irrelevant for understanding the concept of 'kinship' — that 'kinship' is a *social* relation, which in the general case (our own may be an exception) is not premised on a concept of biological connection. Social anthropologists have made a big issue of this, and the position has pretty well hardened into dogma in recent decades. It has been argued over and over that 'kinship' is not a matter of genealogy, but one of relative statuses (with correlated role expectations) between members of different *social categories* in whose definition the biological connections of individuals are not necessarily relevant. What, you may ask, can have led anthropologists to such a view? The 'data' backing for this view are numerous and varied. One item, for example, is the frequent and autochthonously recognized discrepancy between physical paternity (or presumptive physical paternity) and ascribed social fatherhood (*pater $\neq$ genitor*), and even between physical maternity and social motherhood. Such discrepancies arise not only through extramarital license (sanctioned or unsanctioned) and fraternal-polyandrous and leviratic practices (whereby a man begets children in his brother's name), or through the practice of adoption (as in cases of illegitimacy, orphanhood, or other circumstances of hardship, need, or fancy), which in some societies assumes staggering proportions, but also through any of a wide variety of customs or laws, such as that whereby the first child begotten of a marriage becomes the legal 'son' or 'daughter' of the man who put up the principal portion of the bride-price in the husband's behalf, or who was on hand and ready with the necessary wherewithal to pay the midwife for delivery of the child, etc. A second kind of data taken to support the position that 'kinship' is not premised on notions of biology or genealogy, but on social categorizations, has been found in the use of the words denoting relationships in the languages of peoples that anthropologists have studied.

Consider some examples of this latter kind of data. A term that is applied to maternal uncles in some society and that might therefore be thought to *mean* 'maternal uncle' turns out on further investigation to refer in fact to a rather large category of persons, say men of some senior-age grade (but not *too* senior) and who belong to a particular clan or come from a particular locale (the one from which one's mother came). Similarly, a term that a naïve anthropologist might suppose to mean 'a man's sororal nephew' turns out in fact to be applicable to a large number of persons besides the children of a man's sisters. It is thus concluded, as one anthropologist has written, that "kinship terms are not the names of genealogical connections, even though they may be associated with such connections; they are the names of categories, sometimes groups, of people, socially defined. And the anthropologist's task is essentially to understand other people's social categories, not uncritically to impose his own." And so (to quote further the same writer), "kinship can no more be reduced to a set of statements about genealogical connexion than, say, an enquiry into the social significance of funerary feasting can be reduced to a set of statements about the physiology of human metabolism." [6] Or to take another example, a Trobriand word that Malinowski took to mean (homonymously) 'grandparent' and 'father's sister,' [7] a later social anthropologist has reinterpreted as "a general term, undifferentiated as to age or sex, comprising the whole broad category of potentially 'hostile' outsiders." [8] Thus the definitions of particular concepts of so-called kinship (such as those just referred to, and others), as well as the notion of kinship in general, become relative and special to each particular society. It is held to be a mistake of ethnocentrism to gloss such terms from other societies with English words like father, mother, maternal uncle, brother, etc.

The need for brevity prevents me from doing justice to the arguments in support of this extreme relativist view of kinship. It also prevents me from doing justice to the arguments that I would offer (some of which I have offered elsewhere [9]) in rebuttal of this position. I will only remark that I think this view is wrong, and that it derives from an erroneous conception of the nature of the structure of meaning in natural languages, as well as from a failure to penetrate very far under the surface of the most easily observable 'social facts,' and that this view furthermore has been nurtured by the prevailing intellectual atmosphere of extreme relativism in the past several decades of linguistics and cultural and social anthropology.

With this said, I would like now to turn to a somewhat more detailed consideration of the kind of linguistic evidence for concepts of kinship with which ethnographers are faced, and which they must account for somehow in their treatments of this subject. Consider the case of a hypothetic ethnographer who, as in the old ethnocentric days, supposes that 'kinship' terms are literally kinship terms, denoting and classifying the various kinds of genealogical connections that may exist between people. And so, proceeding on this assumption, he collects from his informants a full schedule of the terms for several hundred different types of genealogically expressed relationships, checks them out for consistency of reciprocal relationships, agreement of informants, use of alternatives, and so on, and resolves whatever discrepancies may have first entered into his data through misunderstandings or miscalculations. Suppose now that he collects together all of the particular types of relationship that were denoted by one single term, and that he continues in this way and does it for all of the terms that were given him. Now, finally, suppose that amongst these terms was one (*Term X*) that was used to denote the following types of relationship: father; father's brother; father's sister's son; father's mother's sister's son; father's sister's daughter's son; father's father's brother's son; and father's father's sister's son's son; not to mention others that may have been included if he had flung his net far enough. But suppose that on further inquiry and careful observation he finds that the same term is used not only for these types of genealogically con-

nected relatives, but also for all members of a certain matrilineal clan to which some of these (though not all of them)
belong,[10] who are more or less of a parental or junior-to-
parental age range, but excluding those who might be considered as more than a generation-span older than oneself. And
suppose that this usage prevails although no actual genealogical relationship is traceable to such individuals. And then there
was another (*Term Y*) that was found to denote the following
types of relationship: both grandmothers (i.e., father's mother,
and mother's mother); also father's sister; father's sister's
daughter; father's mother's sister's daughter; father's sister's
daughter's daughter; father's father's brother's daughter; and
father's father's sister's son's daughter; not to mention others.
But then suppose he learns also that this same term is used to
denote any and all *old* women (of whatever clan), as well as
any women or girls (of whatever age) belonging to certain
particular clans (such as one's father's, one's father's father's,
or one's mother's father's). These are but samples of his data.
He may end up with upwards of two dozen such relationship
terms, each denoting a motley assortment of genealogically
typed relatives, as well as certain categories of people to whom
it is not possible to trace any genealogical connections. His
problem now is to understand the concepts of kinship held by
the people he has undertaken to study.

Some anthropologists have been led to the point of view
that whatever regularity there is in the assignment of particular genealogical types to a particular kinship category is, as it
were, accidental ('accidental' in the logical sense) — that properties of the genealogical chain are not the distinctive features
in the meanings of such categories. They just "happen" to be
correlated with them to a certain degree; but the distinctive
features of such concepts are something else: features such as
group membership or exclusion, age grading, one or another
kind of contractual arrangement, etc. Some anthropologists
even consider that the genealogical frame of reference is one
of the greatest sources of error in the collection of data for the

social anthropological study of 'kinship.' All of this leads quite naturally to a position of complete relativism.

I do not think, however, that this is the only position one can be led to by such data. In fact, if one makes some contrary initial assumption about semantic structure in languages, one can be led to just the opposite position; and one may find support — even in such data — for an assumption of universality for the *prime concepts* of kinship.

One of the assumptions about semantic structure that is at stake here concerns the validity of the total-category approach to the meanings of words. It is often assumed that the meaning of a word is, as it were, the highest common factor (product of common features) in all of its denotations. And so one looks for common, distinctive features of reference that are shared by all the denotata of the term. This has been called the 'common-feature' method. It is the basis for what has come to be known as componential analysis of meaning. If it be assumed that all of the denotata of a word are actually to be comprehended under a single sense, then *all* of these denotata must be taken into consideration when attempting to isolate common factors for the definition of the meaning of the term. This is the 'total-category' assumption. It is a frequent assumption in attempts to treat of kinship terms. In the total-category approach every denotatum of a term is thus taken to be on a par with every other, as if all were denotata of that term by equal right, and as if there were no distinction that could be drawn between primary referents and secondary referents, or between a central meaning and marginal meanings, or a primary sense and extended senses — as if the definition given must hold once and for all, embracing *all* particular referents of a term under a single definition, all being taken as tokens of the same type or representatives of the same concept. It seems to me that this is a wholly unrealistic view of the meanings of kinship terms, just as it is for most other words in a language. I would assume rather that for kinship terms, as for the majority of other words, a term may have a primary sense (or more than one primary sense if homonymy is involved) and various extended senses. For heuristic purposes, we might even go further in the case of kinship terms and say that the primary sense of each kinship term is to be found in its reference to the genealogically closest type of relationship which is found amongst the referents of the term. Following this line of thought, we might assume, again tentatively, that other more distant referents of a term represent extensions [11] of its meaning and involve therefore an attenuation of that meaning. One may suppose also that, as with other words, there may be more than one path of extension or expansion of the scope of a term. So, there may be several attentuated senses of a term, with overlapping denotations. Now, it may or may not be possible to subsume all the referents of a kinship term under one single conjunctive definition, as a product of some set of essential features.[12] If it is possible, then we may assume, in line with this view of things, that such a definition represents only the most attentuated sense, or the broadest sense, that the term may have. But surely we need not assume that it is its only meaning, or its primary or 'literal' meaning. Now, if we have reason to suspect, either from circumstantial evidence that turns up in observation of the use of a kinship term, or simply on an a priori basis, that some particular referent represents its primary sense, then we can tentatively define the primary sense (the "focal" meaning) in terms of that referent. We still have the other referents to account for, however. To account for these, we need to find a rationale of extension that will predict them.

It is a curious fact in the history of anthropology that although Malinowski was an avowed extensionist in kinship theory, more recent theorists have abandoned that view in favor of the total-category approach to the meanings of kinship terms. I want to illustrate here, however, what can be done under the assumptions of the extensionist theory.[13] This can be illustrated by accounting for the data given under the two terms X and Y above. (These data, incidentally, are not fictitious assemblages. Identical or similar sets have been encountered more than once by anthropologists, and in different parts of the world. In fact, they represent a single recurrent type of kinship terminology. The Seminole of Oklahoma and Florida, and some of the other Muskogean tribes, have such a system. So do the Trobriand Islanders described by Malinowski.[14] This particular variety, together with other similar varieties that differ in certain crucial details, constitute subtypes of what is commonly known as the 'Crow type' of kinship terminology.)

For purposes of argument, and in line with an assumption that the primary sense of a kinship term may correspond to its genealogically closest referent, let us specify the primary sense of *Term X* as 'father,' and the primary sense of *Term Y* as 'grandmother.' Now, these terms for the primary senses, namely 'father' and 'grandmother,' may be taken as designating precisely the same genealogical relationships as they do in English. (Note the *commensurability* that such an equation would introduce!)

Starting from these primary senses, or focal referents, it requires positing just three principles of extension to account for all of the other referents of the terms *X* and *Y*. These can be phrased as rules of equivalence between certain of the elementary genealogical kin-types. They are the following:

1) an equivalence between a man's sister and his mother;
2) an equivalence between siblings of the same sex; and
3) an equivalence between half-siblings and full-siblings.

The word 'equivalence' calls for a note of explanation. We are speaking here only of equivalences as links in a genealogical chain for purposes of determining assignment to terminological kinship categories. Of course, one should expect to find sociological correlates to these equivalence rules; but the cultural content of these varies from case to case, and it is not with these that we are concerned at the moment. Further, the equivalences of which we speak are limited equivalences, bound by certain restrictions of context. They are not context-free rules. We need not go into this matter here, except to note that variations in context restrictions on these rules account for the variations in assignment of kin-types to terminological categories in the various subvarieties of the so-called 'Crow-type' systems,[15] and that not only the equivalence rules, but their context restrictions also, are usually found to have sociological correlates. Finally, it should be noted that these rules are fundamental to the system; they account not only for the extensions of the 'father' and 'grandmother' terms of this type of system (as will be shown immediately), but also for the extensions of all of the other terms. In other words, they may be said to generate the extended system from a small set of primes that give some evidence of being universal concepts.

The equivalence rules stated above may be applied as reduction rules, to reduce more distant genealogical types to the focal types to which they are terminologically equivalent. Thus, for the referents of *Term X:*

    (*a*) Father [primary sense, focal kin-type]

    (*b*) Father's brother
        ⟶ Father [by rule 2]

    (*c*) Father's sister's son
        ⟶ Father's mother's son [rule 1]
        ⟶ Father's brother [rule 3]
        ⟶ Father [rule 2, as in *b* above]

    (*d*) Father's mother's sister's son
        ⟶ Father's mother's son [rule 2]
        ⟶ Father's brother [rule 3]
        ⟶ Father [rule 2, as in *b* above]

    (*e*) Father's sister's daughter's son
        ⟶ Father's mother's daughter's son [rule 1]
        ⟶ Father's sister's son [rule 3]
        ⟶ Father [rules 1, 3, and 2, as in *c* above]

    (*f*) Father's father's brother's son
        ⟶ Father's father's son [rule 2]
        ⟶ Father's brother [rule 3]
        ⟶ Father [rule 2, as in *b* above]

    (*g*) Father's father's sister's son's son
        ⟶ Father's father's mother's son's son [rule 1]
        ⟶ Father's father's brother's son [rule 3]
        ⟶ Father [rules 2, 3, and 2, as in *f* above]

It will suffice to give a single example for the referents of *Term Y*. Thus:

> Father's sister's daughter
> ⟶ Father's mother's daughter [rule 1]
> ⟶ Father's sister [rule 3]
> ⟶ Father's mother [rule 1]
> ⟶ 'Grandmother' [by definition]

The others follow suit. And as noted above, the entire system of reference is generated in this way, so far as genealogically defined relationships are involved.

The extensions beyond traceable genealogy are of two sorts. The one involves expansion of referential scope by successively dropping component features from the definition of the primary sense. For example, consider the 'grandmother' term here, whose primary sense can be defined as *lineal female consanguine relative of second ascending generation*. An expansion to a commonly attested wider sense of such a term is obtained by broadening the generation specification to *second or higher ascending generation*. Another expansion, to include step- and in-law types, is obtained by dropping the specification *consanguine*. Still another common one, to include collateral types, is obtained by dropping the specification *lineal*. With these three expansions of the range of reference of the term, and corresponding attentuations of its meaning, we have the wider sense of *female relative of second-or-higher ascending generation*. But its meaning may be still further attenuated by dropping even the component *relative*, as is common in the use of the term as a courtesy form of address. At this point it may apply to any and all old women, related in any of the previous ways or not, the generation component becoming an 'as if' one. But the component *relative* has really not been dropped in such usage, for the effect of using the term depends on making a pretense of relationship. The component is still there, but it too has taken on an 'as if' character. In other words, the term has become a metaphor. Polysemy of this sort is common in vocabulary. Its appearance in kinship vocabulary is nothing new, and it should not cause one to lose sight of the primary senses of words.

The other kind of extragenealogical extension in our present example, whereby the 'grandmother' term is applied to any woman or girl, regardless of her generation or age, in one's father's matrilineal clan (or father's father's or mother's father's clan), involves no new principle at all, but only the native presumption that people of such a clan are indeed matrilineally related, whether the specific links are known to one or not. Thus, any female of one's father's clan is presumed to be one's father's mother's mother's . . . mother's daughter's daughter's . . . daughter (FM^mD^n). The insertion of additional ascending and/or descending female links in the genealogical chain, where a preceding link is *male* (as in the father's clan, the father's father's clan, or the mother's father's clan), has no effect on the end result of the reduction. This is a generalization readily apparent even to one's native subjects, though they have other ways of expressing it.

Earlier in this paper it was noted that some social anthropologists (possibly the majority, and in any case some of the most distinguished) have regarded *non*genealogical criteria as the essential attributes of the meanings of kinship terms, and the genealogical criteria, such as given in the above examples, only as 'accidental' attributes of certain of the possible referents of such terms. It has even been denied that the so-called kinship terms are *kinship* terms by virtue of a significant overlap of their field of denotation with the field of genealogical specifications. (This leaves one, of course, with the difficult problem of trying to explain just what it is that kinship terms are, that other relation-designating words in a language are not.) I have ended up attempting to make out a case for precisely the opposite point of view (an older view now commonly regarded as ethnocentric and sociologically naïve), according to which one would take the genealogical criteria as essential for the primary senses, as well as for all of the non-metaphoric expanded senses, and the other-than-genealogical attributes of kinship categories as the accidental ones. One may still raise a legitimate question, however, as to whether or not it is realistic, or valid from a psychological point of view, to draw the Aristotelian distinction between essential and accidental attributes at all. If it is not, then may not both of these positions be equally valid? May not different senses of a word — both the logically or historically prior senses and the derived secondary senses — be psychologically equally salient and equally 'primary' so far as the users of a language are concerned? I think that in the case of kinship terms the answer is *No*. But the relevant kind of evidence is at present sparse, and to present the arguments would require another paper.

Boas regarded ethnology as a "science dealing with the mental phenomena of the peoples of the world," and he wrote that if ethnology be so understood, then "human language, one of the most important manifestations of mental life, would seem to belong naturally to the field of work of ethnology." [16] He outlined a theory 'classification' in language, and suggested a pragmatic connection between phenomena of experience, their mental representations, and their linguistic classification. Many problems of importance to anthropology are presented in this form in language. But the interpretation of the linguistic evidence has given rise to almost as many disputes. Some of the disagreements about interpretation stem from the different philosophical biases of the interpreters. Inclination to different versions of the theories of cultural and linguistic relativity have been responsible for some of these. I have chosen one particular language-and-culture problem here — a problem of 'classification' such as Boas spoke of — for purposes of illustration. I have also attempted to point out the difference between a position that can be characterized as 'complete relativism' and one that can be characterized as 'limited relativism.' The question of 'incommensurability' is involved in this difference. Partiality to one or another of these views may considerably influence both one's field observations and one's interpretations of data, and thus one's conclusions, on this particular problem of culture, mental life, and language. Perhaps this may be true also in regard to other such problems.

NOTES

1. "*Incommensurable* . . . : having no common measure [quantities are incommensurable when no third Quantity can be found that is an aliquot part of each]" (*Webster's Third New International Dictionary*).

2. E. Sapir, *Language* (New York, 1939), p. 234.

3. C. F. Hockett, "Chinese versus English: An Exploration of the Whorfian Thesis," in *Language in Culture* (H. Hoijer, ed.; American Anthropological Association, Memoir No. 79, 1954), p. 108.

4. To simplify the problem and not go too far afield here, we restrict the definition to human 'parents.' We shall pass over the matter of the superhuman agents in procreation and contributors of essential attributes to one's being. These may be animal spirits that make visitations, supernaturally highly charged things or places that a woman gets exposed to, ancestral spirits that enter a woman through her forehead, etc., in almost endless variety. The question of whether these are 'parents,' or whether 'kinship' can be reckoned through them, can be answered, but not here.

5. This is a bit of an exaggeration. There are some. But in the prevailing climate of opinion they mostly incline to silence.

6. J. H. M. Beattie, "Kinship and Social Anthropology," *Man,* LXIV (July–August 1964), art. 130.

7. B. Malinowski, *The Sexual Life of Savages in North-Western Melanesia* (London, 1929; 3rd ed., 1932); *Coral Gardens and Their Magic*, II (London, 1935). In the first of these books Malinowski's interpretation of the word in question was apparently that it was a case of polysemy; in the second it was treated as a case of homonymy. The terms that he used for these two notions were, respectively, 'cognate homonyms,' and 'fortuitous (or accidental) homonyms.'

8. E. R. Leach, "Concerning Trobriand Clans and the Kinship Category *Tabu*," in *Cambridge Papers in Social Anthropology,* no. 1 (J. Goody, ed.; Cambridge, 1958), pp. 120–45.

9. F. G. Lounsbury, "A Formal Account of the Crow- and

Omaha-type Kinship Terminologies," in *Explorations in Cultural Anthropology: Essays Presented to George Peter Murdock* (W. H. Goodenough, ed.; New York, 1964), pp. 351–93; "Another View of the Trobriand Kinship Categories," *American Anthropologist,* LXVII, no. 5, pt. 2 (1965), 142–85.

10. The last two named types would not in general belong to the clan in question.

11. The word *extension* in English is, unhappily, polysemous. I am not using it here in the sense that it has in the theory of logical semantics, but rather in the sense that it has when one speaks of a metaphoric extension, an extension of meaning, the extension of sentiments, etc.

12. One likes to assume that it is possible, and then see if one can actually carry through with it. The following are examples: W. H. Goodenough, "Componential Analysis and the Study of Meaning," *Language,* XXXII (1956), 195–216; F. G. Lounsbury, "The Structural Analysis of Kinship Semantics," in *Proceedings of the Ninth International Congress of Linguists* (H. Lunt, ed.; The Hague, 1964), pp. 1073–93. The problem is like that outlined by Carnap for the determination of intensions. R. Carnap: "Meaning and Synonymy in Natural Languages," *Meaning and Necessity,* Supplement D (Chicago, 1956).

13. Malinowski, as noted, assumed the extensionist hypothesis; but although he argued eloquently for it, he was not able to demonstrate its utility and validity in application either to social life or to kinship terminology — at least not sufficiently well to have convinced his students and successors. But see the items referred to in note 7 above, and also his article "Kinship" in the *Encyclopaedia Britannica,* 14th ed., 1st printing (1929).

14. The Trobriand equivalent of *Term Y* is like this, but covers a still broader category though lacking a sex distinction and being self-reciprocal. It embraces the composite domain covered usually by three terms of systems of this type.

15. The matter of context restrictions has been treated in the items referred to in note 12, especially in the second of those papers.

16. F. Boas, "Introduction," *Handbook of American Indian Languages,* Bureau of American Ethnology (Smithsonian Institution), Bulletin 30, Vol. I (Washington, D.C., 1911).

B

Some Troubles with Whorfianism

MAX BLACK

Cornell University

THE CHIEF TROUBLE is to find out what is being claimed. A sufficiently comprehensive formula might run somewhat as follows: *Language, or some aspects of it, partially controls mental life*. Here there is plenty of room for plainer talk and further specification.

(1) In place of "language" (*langue*), we might think of
substituting "speech" (*parole*). If emphasis upon the social
product, *langue*, is intended — as with most Whorfians —
separate consideration should be given to the roles of lexicon,
syntax, and semantics.

(2) "Mental life" might be further specified as perception, concept-formation, commitment to dominant principles
or presuppositions (a "metaphysics" or world-view), and in
other obvious ways. Some Whorfians prefer to stress the social
aspects of the right-hand term, replacing my deliberately
vague "mental life," with its suggestions of individual activity,
by "*culture*."

(3) The imputed relationship between the two terms is
equally elusive. Usually it is conceived as running from left to
right in some "master-slave" fashion. But whether determination in some strong sense is to be expected or, in less ambitious
versions, something as weak as "correlation" or "reflection," is
commonly left unsettled.

Altogether, an enterprising Ph.D. candidate would have
no trouble in producing at least 108 versions of Whorfianism.
(But it is to be hoped that he would be less than satisfied with

my cavalier use of "semantics," "perception," and "culture.")

The most plausible versions of Whorfianism might be those that hope to find in *speech,* rather than in a language, a clue to something else, whether the mental life of the individual or the shared culture of the group. The speech behavior of hippies — to take them as an example — is plainly consonant with their general style of life. No doubt something similar holds for squarer speakers and writers. (Henry James's later style must tell us *something* about him, apart from the fact that he found it congenial, but *what?*)

The difficulty here is to convert an inoffensive banality about the connection between speech patterns and style of life into something sufficiently precise to generate falsifiable empirical hypotheses. Here, as elsewhere, Whorfianism constantly runs the risk of degenerating into blank tautology. If speech behavior, or some aspect of it, is recognized to be itself part of culture, there can be little interest in claiming that it "reflects" or "determines" culture. One might as well say that a man's facial expression reflects or determines something about his whole bodily posture. Speech behavior, one is inclined to say, is a *part* of culture — and there's an end on't. The two terms of the Whorfian relationship must be logically independent if anything of interest is to be in question.

In any event, the practical difficulties of faithfully observing and recording the speech behavior of any group (hippies, poor Appalachian whites, or Oxford dons) are formidable. And if we had the raw material, what could we do with it? How and in what ways should characteristic intonation patterns be regarded as clues to *something else?*

Leaving these questions for bolder spirits to tackle, let us turn to versions of Whorfianism that stress language rather than speech.

One of the most striking features of an alien language, especially if it happens to be "exotic," is divergence from one's native lexical inventory. Differences in vocabulary may take at least the following forms: (1) Novel specifications of familiar concepts (such as the Eskimos' abundant descriptions for various forms of snow); new names for unfamiliar objects, concepts, or attitudes (*potlatch, Schadenfreude, on* in Japanese, *philotimo* in Greek); absence of provision for familiar concepts (the celebrated inability of the Bororo of Brazil to name the shared features of parrots); (4) eccentric boundaries for familiar concepts (absence of discrimination between blue and green in Navaho, and recognition of two kinds of black).

Such facts are engaging, but the proper moral is hard to draw. It would certainly be overhasty to leap, like some writers of romantic tendency, to any thesis of radical untranslatability. For it all depends, not to shirk the obvious, on what we demand of translation. The full pattern of connotation, suggestion, allusion, and the like, can hardly be transmitted. But still, Shakespeare has been translated with some success into German, even if Pushkin still eludes the English — and Lewis Carroll, I understand, has been Frenchified.

In general, semantic mismatches of the first three kinds present no more than temporary obstacles to understanding. Learning to recognize and name varieties of snow is no harder in principle than mastering the technical dialects of biology or any other science. When Nabokov devotes some fascinating pages in his little book on Gogol to explaining the allegedly untranslatable Russian word *poshlost* (roughly: complacent self-satisfaction with vulgar or banal values), he does manage, by skillful use of paradigm instances and commentary, to explain it. *Poshlost,* indeed, may be no harder to assimilate into current English than *camp.* The most that could reasonably be expected would be that *ready* availability of a single word or a well-tailored idiom might facilitate emergence of the associated concept or attitude. (Cf. Stendhal's hero: "If the word love arises between them I am lost.")

Such lexical variations, fascinating as they are to the linguist or the literary critic, seem to raise no profound psychological or philosophical issues. It is altogether intelligible that the special interests of Eskimos, acoustic engineers, or logicians should generate a corresponding proliferation of lexical items. The temptation, which I also feel, to jump to picturesque conclusions about "different forms of life" should be resisted. A point too easily overlooked is that the *use* of a vocabulary invariably required the practice of a vast number of associated preverbal and nonverbal skills. (Cf. Wittgenstein in the *Tractatus* on the complex "tacit adjustments" needed in using ordinary language.) We readily detect and discriminate between thousands of colors for which we have no distinctive names, and the same is true of the Navahos and others who may draw color boundaries in different places. Concepts central to a culture may be excluded from the public vocabulary by social or religious taboos (*Yahveh* in Hebrew, *kiva* in Hopi, forbidden sexual designations in European languages), but that is far from proving their ineffectiveness in the culture. Altogether, inferences from vocabulary to mental life or to culture seem highly precarious, though one cannot help feeling that some interesting discoveries are waiting to be made.

The most tantalizing form of Whorfianism equates the use of a language with commitment to a philosophical position. Whorf said that every language crystallizes "the basic postulates of an unformulated philosophy" and "conceals a METAPHYSICS." D. D. Lee said: "Grammar contains in crystallized form the accumulated and accumulating experience, the Weltanschauung of a people." Lichtenberg said: "Our false philosophy is incorporated in our whole language; we cannot reason without, so to speak, reasoning wrongly. We overlook the fact that speaking, no matter of what, is itself a philosophy." Wittgenstein's views about "idling language" and the "cramps" induced by distorted preconceptions concerning language are too well known to bear repetition. Philosophical laments about the malign influence of language upon thought stretch from Aristotle to Korzybski and beyond.

What are we to make of such sweeping *dicta?* That there is something important to which they point can hardly be doubted. But difficulties immediately press upon us. There is the embarrassment (*pace* Quine) of knowing *what* the ontological commitments of a language or a particular style of discourse really are. For example: what significance, if any, attaches to difficulty of nominalization in a given language — or, in an extreme case, its impossibility. (If ready nominalization encourages a proliferation of fictitious substances, does constraint against such nominalization inhibit the admission of substance as an ultimate ontological category?) There is the ever present danger, especially acute for sophisticated non-native speakers, of fancifully projecting metaphysical significance by reading more into the syntactical structure than its users ever notice. (Or are we ready to postulate an *unconscious* influence of grammar?) Many languages have notably irregular systems of numeration: Japanese has parallel but distinct systems of numerals for categories of objects that to a westerner must seem capriciously segregated. It would surely be absurd to impute some metaphysical significance to such archaic survivals or to suppose that Japanese find difficulty in conceiving of arithmetic as a unified system. (Or do they? And how should we find out?) But if the Whorfian is allowed to *select* his grammatical candidates for metaphysical import, it is quite unclear as to which criteria of choice are relevant.

Another capital difficulty is in identifying the cognitive structures (metaphysics, Weltanschauung, or something more restricted) with which the favored grammatical features allegedly connect. For the only "thoughts" presented will themselves necessarily be expressed in words, and in the Whorfian's own language to boot. Is the metalanguage used by the Whorfian itself irretrievably tainted by preconceived metaphysics? If not, how was it purified? (Does language contain the seeds of its own redemption?) Are some languages, from a metaphysical point of view, really superior to others? And how is this to be shown except by unashamedly *metaphysical* investigation? I leave these questions to those who are more confident than I am about what they mean, with the hope that they will sometime explain how we are to proceed in attempting to answer them.

Given the extraordinary elusiveness of the cluster of ideas I have called Whorfianism, it is hard to account for their perennial allure. One reason may be the current disrepute of the ancient conception of language as a mere garment or neutral medium for the expression of independently existing thought. If thought must necessarily be expressed in language or, at least, in some substitute symbolism anchored in language, the case for Whorfianism may easily come to look almost self-evident.

Another, less determinate, reason may be the charm that attaches to a picture of radically disparate ways of perceiving the world, enforced by the very medium in which thought must be expressed. We are all pluralists nowadays, consciously rejecting older and oversimplified conceptions of Human Nature, Reason, Thought, Language, and all the other capitalized abstractions. As we stumble toward a single world order, there is all the more nostalgic attraction in crying "Vive les differences."

Whatever the reasons, the persistence of Whorfianism might well interest a historian of ideas. Professor Floyd Lounsbury said, in his paper, that "The 'Whorf hypothesis' was, and still is, widely appealing to anthropologists." I find it striking that what has appealed so widely should remain so nebulous.

C

Language and Culture

HARVEY PITKIN

Columbia University

AS AN ANTHROPOLOGICAL LINGUIST with no pretensions to being a philosopher, I cannot but be extremely enthusiastic about Lounsbury's paper. The relations of language and culture, as explored in his exposition, are precisely, it would seem to me, what such a topic demands to have considered at this date. No facile pronouncements, nor reiterations of speculation or eloquently proclaimed hypotheses, are appropriate any longer in discussions of this relationship. And while those who are not anthropological linguists may be disappointed at the lack of titillation offered by such a reasoned and mature avoidance of partisanship for the most naïve and extremist positions, a perspective on this question is much better provided by a historical résumé of the ideas of the last centuries that recounts the repetition of the same points of view in their various guises and with their various sophisticated embellishments.

What clearly emerges to me is the recurrent positions taken that put modern attitudes in sharper focus, and that deprive some contemporary extreme formulations of their seductiveness. There has been little new offered to explicate the relationship we are considering; the investigation along scientific lines has merely begun, following a long period of speculative hypothesis-formation. Fervent announcements of the old positions unsupported by evidence are polemic exercises at this point, whether made by anthropologists or linguists. If we see much of the past theorizing as response to the intellectual climate of the then contemporary opinion, and recognize how much of what may be said today falls into the same category of reaction or even rebellion to the near past, a great deal of controversy current about language is deprived of its seeming novel significance. Actually, for such an important topic as language, the twentieth century has provided relatively few scholars who have worked *directly* with the *phenomena* concerned, and the major work of interest, certainly to nonlinguists, has been the respinning of older theories with the fashionable trappings of current formalism, as though formalism in itself were a guarantee of scientific insight.

I find myself attracted to what I am tempted to call the four questions or points raised for us this evening by Lounsbury's presentation. Those result from the intersection of the four variables of language and culture, and of the relativist and the universalist views (and their balance). These four intersections seem to me closely linked with the approaches we know generally as inductive and deductive, respectively, and further, the deductive-universalist mode, whether in language or culture, seems attached today to a formalism or strong model-orientation. The relatively more inductive methods with which the relativist view has been associated, and which stress ethnological (including linguistic) diversity and a strong data orientation, seem the very essence of the anthropological tradition, certainly at least as far back as Boas, during what would usually be referred to as the "scientific" period of this discipline.

In my own view the contribution anthropology or ethnology makes to explaining language and culture relations is its recognition of the certainty of cultural and linguistic diversity, its reluctance to agree to premature and excessively detailed specification of universals, and its stress on an inductive approach to the observable data. This certainly implies to me as well the now traditional anthropological view that counts as separate the observer and the observed, the avoidance of ethnocentric formulations including subjectivism and an excessively great dependence on intuition. This anthropological approach has been, I would guess, a strong reason for the different sense that cognition appears to have in anthropology, and other disciplines. I sense the gulf that separates those who see the study of language as a linguistic subbranch of cognitive psychology, or philosophy, rather than as a subfield of anthropology. In fact, I am extremely pessimistic that such a symposium can at this time be very productive, when quite different senses of language, cognition, and behavior are employed by linguists, philosophers of language, psychologists, and anthropologists. I sense fundamentally opposed views, even among those who call themselves linguists, that almost totally interfere with the exchange of ideas. A philosopher might very well ask an anthropologist: "Well, what position do you take on the Whorf hypothesis?" as the key question of language and culture and be quite disappointed to be told that the question is not interesting given that formulation. To suggest, as I would like, that relativist and universalist positions must be balanced in language and culture studies and that, as with induction and deduction, they are in practice inextricably mixed, is to say nothing of dramatic or very controversial interest, but to seem to "straddle the fence." Yet they certainly are mixed. One should, I feel, avoid a *uniquely* relativist or universalist approach. A model of either culture or language that fails to recognize this is impoverished. If this is granted, then it is only the quality or quantity of the mix that is interesting, and the awaited generalizations of importance depend on *empirical test* after the examination of much data. That is clearly not the most fashionable activity today. And a symposium is probably the last place to stress the ignorance of students of language and culture, especially with such distinguished colleagues present. Yet I know of no hyphenated field such as ethno-, socio-, or psycho-linguistics that, while investigating this relation, has any methodology of its own, and is not limited to the synthetic combination of the insights deriving from the two under-investigated hyphenated fields. What is required is substantive research of the sort that has only just begun to approach testing these questions already referred to by Lounsbury. The questions have certainly been around a very long time indeed;

the data examined are few. The time for generalizing lies, I would guess, off in the future.

One of the only kinds of domains in which remarkable success has been achieved by anthropological linguists is the lexical-semantic areas that are most highly discrete and internally systematic in their patterning. Par excellence among these has been kinship, and just as Lounsbury is most highly qualified to discuss language and culture relations, his work on kinship systems is the most outstanding, despite his great modesty. We have in this area the only occasion where the lexical data lend themselves so extremely well to such study, where extensive investigation (primarily field work) has been relatively sufficient to the analytic task, and where the balancing of the universalist and relativist approaches has so far been possible. But while the results are very rewarding in the field of kinship, they are less so in the lexical domains that are less able to be sharply delimited, and less so in most areas of lexicon where the semantic components are more obscure. Even more troublesome are the questions arising as to whether such studies are *merely* linguistic and can *have* much power to explain or relate to nonverbal social behavior. But even more disappointing is the seeming retreat to investigations of *lexical* areas, when it really was first suggested and appreciated that the *grammatical* structures were an index of world-view or cultural categorization, and surely it is clear that grammar is a very highly organized system with less transient and deeper relations to culture, despite linguistic lag.

The experience of diachronic linguistics has shown that while lexicon is relatively vulnerable to the effects of diffusion stemming from culture-contact and bilingualism, grammar is more invulnerable to such influences, and that where pidgins and creoles are observed, another aspect of the special status of grammar and the vulnerability of lexicon is found. Whorf, sharing this same view that the grammar is the preeminent key, as in the Whorfian "cryptotypes," also focuses less on lexicon in directing attention, as did Boas and Sapir, to the grammatical categories, as Lounsbury has pointed out.

I would expect that the grammatical categories, especially given their nonconscious quality, the "cryptotypes," the typology, the obligatory grammatical categories would be especially fruitful areas of research in language and culture relations, as for example in the work of Mathiot.

It should be entirely clear from Lounsbury's historical survey of language and culture investigations what difficulties are inherent in establishing agreement on the relativist and the universalist views of both language and culture, what in fact are the cultural or linguistic realities — what are the linguistic and semantic structures and how are they to be related to cultural and sociological realities. The presentation of the kinship material as exemplifying one type of study may however be a quite atypical sample of this relation. It may be the case that the grammatical rather than lexical parts of a language will eventually yield greater insights.

It may also prove to be the case that going from language to culture (as with componential analysis) is less productive than going from culture to language, and that, as Mathiot has pointed out, the linguist may be more in need of the anthropology and ethnographic data, and that these cultural data are more highly revealing of the semantic structure.

Extreme Relativism

SARA RUDDICK

New York University

PROFESSOR LOUNSBURY attacks an "extreme relativism" that, in his construction of the position, consists in the following argument:

1) language "defines" our experience;
2) there are no common factors in the concepts peculiar to different linguistic systems;
therefore; the experiences of speakers of languages so different as to constitute different linguistic systems cannot be compared.

The presupposition of Lounsbury's argument is that comparability depends upon "commensurability," that is, the existence of common factors in respect to which differing concepts can be "measured." "Noncomparability results from categorization of experience in terms of *unlike* prime categories."

Lounsbury tests this argument by reference to one "prime category," that of kinship terms, and finds it wanting. He claims that however unlike our uses of kinship terms and those of certain societies whose uses he describes, there is a common "conceptual component," namely, a biological basis for the concept of kinship. For the most part, he appears to accept, without clarification or defense, the first premise of the relativist's argument while attacking the second. Extreme relativists, according to Lounsbury, have looked for common factors by examining the "total category" under consideration and have failed to find factors common to all uses of the term. Louns-

bury finds common factors in the prime uses of prime categories. Commensurability is introduced by isolating a "primary
sense" of a kinship term ('father,' 'grandmother') so that the
terms designate "precisely the same genealogical relationships
as they do in English." By ingenious and plausible rules of
equivalence of relationships and by explanations of nongenea-
logical extensions of the primary uses, the remaining uses are
made intelligible. Lounsbury's method of investigating differences in prime categories is clearly more sophisticated and
productive than the total-category approach. However, it side-
steps the philosophical questions embodied in the relativist's
argument, a fact that Lounsbury himself seems to appreciate
when he doubts the philosophical interest of his discussion.

One issue that the relativist argument raises is whether the
comparability of prime concepts can be a matter of "empirical
investigation" as Lounsbury suggests. Doesn't the first premise
of the relativist's argument rule out the possibility of empirically testing the second premise? If "language 'defines' experience" we cannot look outside language to experience for factors common to languages. This point has been put by Peter
Winch:

> Our idea of what belongs to the realm of reality is given for
> us in the language that we use. The concepts we have settle
> for us the form of the experience we have of the world.[1]

> Reality is not what gives language sense. What is real and
> what is unreal shows itself *in* the sense that language has.[2]

Lounsbury by contrast implicitly appeals to "reality" in order to give sense to alien uses of kinship terms. His attack on
the relativist's argument presupposes its invalidity. The point
at issue is not supposed to be whether there are in fact star-
tling differences in the uses of kinship terms, which there
surely are if indeed the uses are all uses of kinship terms in
some shared sense of 'kinship.' The issue is whether there is
such a shared sense of 'kinship.' Lounsbury insures that there
is. The prime category of kinship is tailored to fit our prime

category when the senses isolated as prime are those that can be equated to our uses of the same term. What Lounsbury does, in effect, is to stake out an "area of vocabulary" in an alien language and then to translate that vocabulary into English in such a way that the aliens make sense to us. The sense they make moreover is a derived version of our sense. What he does not show is that what we call their kinship terms are for them kinship terms.

The issue of *their* understanding of their terms as opposed to *our* understanding of them does not seem to arise for Lounsbury. This is because he assumes that there are "real" facts of biological heredity and procreation that underlie our uses of kinship terms. Now, it is undeniable that the "facts" of biological procreation show themselves to be real within our language. These are among the "facts" that our concepts pick out as real, therefore among the facts that we find it conceptually difficult, if not impossible to deny. It would be a specious form of tolerance that pretended that each culture was entitled to its own "facts," its own reality. For we cannot *choose* to regard some things rather than other things as real or allow others to do so. Things are shown to be real in our languages. And when we first run across what appear to be bizarre uses of our concepts we will look for an understanding of the "reality" that those concepts express. That the real facts which give our concepts sense are both distorted and relatively unimportant in another's concept would be one criterion of the concept's belonging to a "different linguistic system." (Other criteria are needed of a concept's being sufficiently different to belong to a "different linguistic system." This is one of many questions about the relativist's argument that Lounsbury does not discuss.) But this does not imply Lounsbury's statement that "our question about whether a concept of 'kinship' is universal . . . reduce(s) to this empirical question: is it or is it not the case that people in all societies understand at least this much about the biology of procreation and heredity . . . that one's being is derived from one or more parents (of at most two kinds) and that through common derivation of such sort different individuals are 'kin' . . ." Lounsbury implies that sharing a concept of kinship involves understanding as much as we do. What the relativist claims is that we understand differently and that therefore questions of more or less understanding of an independent reality cannot be raised. There is no common measure of understanding, no extralinguistic reality making concepts "commensurable."

Lounsbury's paper does not discuss two issues usually at the heart of relativism, the relation between our "scientific" reality and other realities and the distinction between translation and understanding. There are scattered suggestions that Lounsbury accepts the equation of the real with the scientifically real (as, for example, in the quote above). As we have seen, he takes his success at translating alien terms into sensible English as showing a common understanding. Again, both of these issues are explicitly raised in Winch's statement of relativism, and both are related by him to a different conception of language. Here I can only sketchily suggest his formulation of these issues by quotation. Winch's work is certainly worth looking into in greater detail for several reasons.[3] It is said to be implicit in a good deal of anthropology and is intended to be especially applicable both to anthropology and sociology. Further, it embodies a way of understanding the behaviors of alien groups that I believe could be fruitful in dealing with problems of understanding other individuals, our own society, and even ourselves.

Winch's views are epitomized in the following:

> In the first place we should notice that the check of the independently real is not peculiar to science. The trouble is that the fascination science has for us makes it easy for us to adopt its scientific form as a paradigm against which to measure the intellectual respectability of other modes of discourse . . . God's reality (for example) is certainly independent of what any man may care to think, but what that reality amounts to can only be seen from the religious tradition in which the concept of God is used, and this is very unlike the use of scientific concepts . . . The point is that it is *within* the religious

use of language that the conception of God's reality has its place, though I repeat, this does not mean that it is at the mercy of what anyone cares to say; if this were so God would have no reality.[4]

Not anything can count as falling under a term Y, an apparent kinship term. Otherwise no reality would be shown in its use. In Winch's way of putting the matter (derived from Wittgenstein) there must be "rules," definite or open-ended, vague or precise, for the use of any expression that can be misused. And the possibility of misuse is a prerequisite for exhibiting any reality. But rules, according to the analogy, cannot be understood apart from the game in which they figure. Similarly, rules of language cannot be understood apart from the "traditions," practices, and cultures and other linguistic connections that make up a particular "mode of discourse." Some anthropologists to whom Lounsbury alludes may have had this in mind when they claimed that "all this business about biological connection utterly misses the point." It is not that these people don't "understand as much" as we do about biological connection. Rather, it may be that biological connection is not central to the "realities" that kinship terms exhibit and to the practices of which they are a part. Lounsbury himself alludes to the fact that 'kinship' terms play "an unusually large role" in primitive societies. Their very different role might suggest that they *weren't* kinship terms in our sense of the term in which biological connection is primary. We may not be dealing with unusual kinship practices but with practices and concepts only interestingly related to those we speak of as 'kinship.'

The problem in Lounsbury's approach to differences is how to decide the issue of commensurability. How different must concepts be before they are incommensurable? His answer seems to be that they are incommensurable where there is no common factor that, with the aid of equivalences and extensions, makes translation possible. In Winch's view the problem of commensurability in terms of common factors does not arise. Understanding rather than translation is in question and there can of course be degrees of understanding. The task for Winch is to propose tests of understanding that can indicate the kind and degree of understanding achieved. One such test, again derived from Wittgenstein, is that the "investigator" not only be able to follow the alien rules, i.e., to agree with the alien in their future application, but also be able to do so as a "matter of course," "blindly," from the inside as it were. He needn't be able to formulate rules as Lounsbury does, but he must understand their operations, the cases they don't cover, the vagueness they embody — all these and more being involved in the purposes they serve.

An example Winch takes from Wittgenstein is apt here, the alien practices being comparable to the bizarre uses of kinship terms. A society sells wood by piling it in heaps where the height of the piles seems to vary arbitrarily. It is then sold at a price proportionate to the *area* covered. They justify the practice by saying, "Of course, if you buy more timber, you must pay more." The relationship of that marketing practice to ours may well be like that of some alien uses of kinship terms to ours. In both cases we might be able to find common factors by which we could, with extensions, *translate* one into the other. We would have "made sense" of the alien. We might then be able to predict what they will do or say. But predicting and translating are not tantamount to understanding the sense they see in what they are doing. In Winch's scheme, where we try to do what they do with their understanding, making sense cannot turn on something as definite and secure as common factors. Rather, as we realize in trying to understand others' or our own societies, making sense is a prolonged attempt to see the realities "shown" in the concepts of others, i.e., to be able not only to say what they say, but to mean what they mean.

NOTES

1. *The Idea of a Social Science* (Humanities Press, 1958), p. 15.

2. "Understanding a Primitive Society," *American Philosophical Quarterly,* I, 4 (October 1964), 309.

3. There are a number of problems in Winch's position that I cannot deal with here. He has some difficulty accounting for deviant behavior and cultural change. He has not dealt with the problems of "false consciousness." The notion of "realm of discourse" or "language game" is left too vague. He works with an untenable distinction between cause and reason. Similar problems arise in the application of his concept of "rule-governed behaviour" to our understanding of the behavior of individuals. I believe, however, that these problems can be dealt with.

4. "Understanding a Primitive Society," p. 308. Winch himself does not fully accept the relativist consequences of his statement of relativism. However, I do not accept his argument on this point. See "Understanding a Primitive Society," pp. 322 ff. and "Nature and Convention" in the *Proceedings of the Aristotelian Society,* XX (1960), 231–52.

PART II

Linguistics and Philosophy

A

Linguistics and Philosophy

NOAM CHOMSKY

Massachusetts Institute of Technology

THE METHODS AND CONCERNS of linguists and philosophers are similar in so many respects that it would be folly, I believe, to insist on a sharp separation of these disciplines, or for either to maintain a parochial disregard for insights achieved in the other. A number of examples might be cited to illustrate the possibility of fruitful interchange between the two. Zeno Vendler, in his recent book *Linguistics and Philosophy*, goes so far as to maintain that "the science of structural linguistics" provides "a new technique" for analytic philosophy, one that "is nothing but the natural continuation of the line of development that goes through the philosophers of ordinary language to J. L. Austin." For reasons to which I will return in a moment, I am a bit skeptical about the contribution that linguistics might make to philosophy along the lines that he sketches, but I think that he has shown that certain concepts of linguistics can be used in a rewarding way in the investigation of problems that have arisen in analytic philosophy.

Conversely, as the attention of linguists begins to turn to problems of meaning and use, there is no question that they can learn much from the long tradition of philosophical investigation of such problems, although here too, I think, a note of skepticism is in order.

To facilitate the discussion of this and other topics, let me present a small illustration of a problem that is at the frontier of research today. In the descriptive study of any language a central problem is to formulate a set of rules that generate

what we may call the "surface structures" of utterances. By the
term "surface structure," I refer to the analysis of an utterance
into a hierarchy of phrases, each belonging to a specific category. This hierarchy can be represented as a labeled bracket-
ing of the utterance, in an obvious sense. For example, consider the two sentences:

(1) John is certain that Bill will leave
(2) John is certain to leave

The surface structures of these utterances can be represented, in a natural way, with the following labeled bracket-
ing:

(1') $[_S[_{NP}$ John] $[_{VP}$ is $[_{AP}$ certain
$[_S$ that $[_{NP}$ Bill] $_{VP}$ will leave]]]]]

(2') $[_S[_{NP}$ John] $[_{VP}$ is $[_{AP}$ certain] $[_{VP}$ to leave]]]

Paired brackets bound phrases; the label assigned to a pair of
brackets indicates the category of the bounded phrase. Thus in
(1), "certain that Bill will leave" is a phrase of the category,
Adjective Phrase; in both (1) and (2), "John" is a phrase of
the category, Noun Phrase; "will leave" is a Verb Phrase in
(1); and both (1) and (2) are phrases of the category, Sentence. One may question the details of these particular analyses, but there is little doubt that at some level of description,
these, or representations very much like them, constitute a significant aspect of the structure of the sentences (1) and (2),
and, more generally, that every sentence of the language has a
surface structure of roughly this sort. There is, for example,
strong evidence that the perceived phonetic form of the utterance is determined, by phonological rules of considerable generality, from representations of essentially this sort.

Granting this much, the linguist studying English will try
to formulate a set of rules that generate an infinite number of
surface structures, one for each sentence of English. Correspondingly, linguistic theory will be concerned with the prob-

lem of how such structures are generated in any human language, and will try to formulate general principles governing the systems of rules that express the facts of one or another such language.

Given the evidence available to us today, it seems to me reasonable to propose that in every human language surface structures are generated from structures of a more abstract sort, which I will refer to as "deep structures," by certain formal operations of a very special kind generally called "grammatical transformations." Each transformation is a mapping of labeled bracketings onto labeled bracketings. Deep structures are themselves labeled bracketings. The infinite class of deep structures is specified by a set of "base rules." Transformations applied in sequence to deep structures in accordance with certain fixed conventions and principles ultimately generate the surface structures of the sentences of the language. Thus a set of base rules defining an infinite class of deep structures and a set of grammatical transformations can serve to generate the surface structures.

To illustrate, consider sentences (1) and (2) again. The underlying deep structures might be represented roughly in the form (1″), (2″):

(1″) same as (1′)
(2″) $[_S[_{NP}[_S[_{NP}$ John] $[_{VP}$ to leave]]] $[_{VP}$ is $[_{AP}$ certain]]]$

We may think of these deep structures as expressing the fact that in (1), we predicate of John that he is certain that Bill will leave, whereas in (2), which is rather similar to (1) in surface structure, we predicate of the proposition that John leaves, that it is certain, in a very different sense of "certain." There is no difficulty in defining the concepts Subject and Predicate, in terms of configurations in deep structures, so that they express the intended interpretation. The operations that derive (2′) from (2″) include an operation of "extraposition," which from a structure very much like (2″) would yield the structure (3), and an operation of "it-replacement" which derives (2′) from a structure almost exactly like (3), but with "to" in place of "will" and "that" deleted:

(3) $[_S[_{NP}$ it] $[_{VP}$ is $[_{AP}$ certain]
    $[_S$ that $[_{NP}$ John] $[_{VP}$ will leave]]]]

Details aside, the theory of "transformational generative grammar" maintains that all surface structures are formed by application of such transformations — each of which maps labeled bracketings onto labeled bracketings — from deep structures that are often quite abstract. The sentences (1) and (2) are similar in surface structure, but very different in deep structure; the sentences (2) and (3) are very similar in deep structure, but quite different in surface structure. The deep structures of the language are quite restricted in their variety, and it appears that there are universal conditions that sharply restrict the class of possible rules.

Consider now the matter of semantic interpretation. It is clear from these quite typical examples that the surface structures give little indication of the semantic interpretation, whereas the deep structures are quite revealing, in this respect. Pursuing this line of reasoning, one might propose a further elaboration of the theory just outlined, in the following terms. Let us suppose that there is a system of "universal semantics" that specifies the class of possible semantic representations for a natural language much in the way that universal phonetics specifies the class of possible phonetic representations, by specifying a class of distinctive features and certain conditions on their combination. Observe that it would be perfectly reasonable to study universal semantics even without any clear idea as to what its constituent elements might be, just as one could draw fairly persuasive conclusions regarding universal phonetics from consideration of the slow growth of the number of distinct sentences with increasing length, the phenomena of rhyme and assonance, the lack of slow drift through the "space" of sentences under chains of repetition, etc., even without any conception of what the distinctive features of this system might be. In any event, still supposing this to be a reasonable approach, one might propose that a language contains rules associating deep structures with representations drawn from universal semantics, as it contains phonological rules relating surface structures to representations drawn from universal phonetics.

At this point in the development of such a theory, the linguist would do well to turn to work in analytic philosophy, particularly to the many studies of referential opacity. One essential empirical assumption in the preceding account is that surface structure cannot contribute to meaning; whatever contribution the expression P makes to the meaning of the sentence XPY must be determined by the deep structure underlying P. The investigation of referential opacity has turned up a great number of examples illustrating how replacement of one expression by another changes meaning, even when the semantic connection between the two is very close. The approach just outlined would have to guarantee that in each such case there is a corresponding difference in deep structure to which the difference in meaning can be attributed. Without pursuing the matter, I would simply note that the nature of these examples makes it appear very unlikely that such an approach can succeed; but, in any event, the study of this aspect of linguistic theory must certainly take into account a mass of evidence that has been accumulated in the course of philosophical investigation.

I have mentioned the possibility that insights developed in the course of philosophical analysis might be relevant to the study of a central part of linguistic theory, and that concepts of linguistics might be useful to the philosopher in his work. Nevertheless, it seems to me that one should not expect too much from an interchange of this sort, for a number of reasons. In the cases I have mentioned, what is proposed is that the incidental by-products of research in one field will be of use for the central concerns of another. Furthermore, it is a fact that neither field makes use of research techniques of a sophisticated or specialized nature. Thus one would expect that in each field, it would be quite possible to collect and analyze the information relevant to its specific concerns directly. It is, therefore, something of an accident when one field can build directly on results of the other.

For these reasons, I think that Vendler may be expecting too much of the method he suggests, namely, "an appeal to the facts of language already organized by the science of structural linguistics." I believe that modern linguistics has real achievements to its credit, and that some of these do have relevance to philosophical questions. But it must be kept in mind that these achievements owe little to modern science and less to modern technology. The gathering of data is informal; there has been very little use of experimental approaches (outside of phonetics) or of complex techniques of data collection and data analysis of a sort that can easily be devised, and that are widely used in the behavioral sciences. The arguments in favor of this informal procedure seem to me quite compelling; basically, they turn on the realization that for the theoretical problems that seem most critical today, it is not at all difficult to obtain a mass of crucial data without use of such techniques. Consequently, linguistic work, at what I believe to be its best, lacks many of the features of the behavioral sciences. Nor is it obvious that the development of explanatory theories in linguistics merits the honorific designation "scientific." I think that these intellectual constructions are nontrivial and often illuminating. However, apart from certain insights owed to modern logic and mathematics, there is no reason why they could not have been developed many years ago. In fact, were it not for the dominance of certain empiricist assumptions to which I will return directly, I suspect that they would have been developed long before now and that much of what is new and exciting in linguistics today would be taken for granted by any educated person.

There are many questions about language that a philosopher might ask to which linguistics provides no answer and no reasonable hope for an answer. For example, a philosopher concerned with problems of knowledge, or causality (to take an example of Vendler's), might well be interested in investigating in detail the properties of the words "know" and "cause." Since linguistics offers no privileged access to data of this sort, it would be merely a lucky accident if acquaintance with linguistics proved to be of substantial help in this inquiry. A linguistic form is not of importance to linguistics because of the intrinsic interest of the concept or proposition it expresses (if any), but because of the evidence it provides concerning some assumption about the nature of language. Thus the analysis of sentences (1), (2), and (3) has been of interest to linguistics because of the light it sheds on the nature of deep and surface structures and the grammatical transformations that link them. Such data are of importance to linguistics insofar as they can be explained on the basis of some interesting assumptions about the organization of grammar, and are inconsistent with other such assumptions. In themselves, these facts are of no more interest than the fact that certain marks appear on a photographic plate at the base of a South African mine shaft. The latter is critical for elementary particle theory for the same reason that the facts related to sentences (1)–(3) are important for the theory of language. Similar remarks can be made about the likelihood that the conclusions of philosophers or the data they accumulate will be important for linguistics.

To make the matter more concrete, consider again the examples (1)–(3). Conceivably, such sentences, and others like them, might be of some interest to a philosopher concerned with the various concepts of certainty. These examples are of interest to linguistics, at the moment, for entirely different reasons. Thus it is interesting that there is a nominalized expression corresponding to (1), but no nominalized expression corresponding to (2); (4) is a nominalized form of (1), but we cannot form (5), corresponding to (2):

(4) John's certainty that Bill would leave
(5) John's certainty to leave

The distinction is more general; thus consider (6) and (7):

(6) John is eager to leave
(7) John is easy to leave

Corresponding to (6), we have the nominal phrase (8); but
we cannot form (9) corresponding to (7):

(8) John's eagerness to leave
(9) John's easiness to leave

Notice that sentence (6) is like (1) in that the deep structure
is very close to the surface structure; whereas (7) is like (2) in
that the deep structure is very different from the surface structure. In fact, the surface structure of (7) would be formed by
operations much like those that form (2) from (2″) and (3),
by a derivation of roughly the form (10):

(10)(i) [$_S$ for one to leave John]$_S$ is easy (analogous to
         (2″))
    (ii) it is easy [$_S$ for one to leave John]$_S$ (analogous
         to (3))
   (iii) John is easy to leave (=(7), analogous to (2))

The generalization exemplified by (1), (2), (4)–(9) is
that a nominal phrase can be formed corresponding to a base
structure but not to a surface structure. Thus we have (4) corresponding to (1″) and (8) corresponding to (6) (more properly, to the deep structure underlying (6) as (1′) underlies
(1)), but no nominalized expression such as (5) and (9), corresponding to the surface structures (2) and (7). This general
observation can be illustrated by many other examples. It is interesting because of the support it lends to the assumption that
abstract deep structures of the sort illustrated play a role in the
mental representation of sentences. We find that when we
study English grammar on the basis of this and related assumptions, we are able to characterize quite readily the class
of sentences to which there correspond nominal phrases of the

sort under discussion. There is no natural way to characterize this class in terms of surface structure, since, as we have seen, sentences that are very similar in surface structure behave quite differently with respect to the formal processes involved in the construction of nominal expressions. We might go on to try to explain these facts at a deeper level by formulating a principle of universal grammar from which it would follow that the nominal phrases in question will correspond only to deep structures.

To summarize, the examples in question are important for the study of language because of the evidence that they provide in support of a particular theory of linguistic structure, not because of the fact that the various concepts of certainty are of interest in their own right. The philosopher concerned with certainty would learn very little from a collection of data that is of great interest for linguistic research.

Apart from accident or matters of personal history, linguistics will be of relevance to philosophy only insofar as its conclusions about the nature of language bear on questions that concern the philosopher. One cannot predict to what extent this will be true in the future; it might turn out, for example, that linguistic study of semantic and syntactic structure in the future will provide a firm basis for certain kinds of philosophical investigation — one thinks, for example, of the potential relevance of a systematic classification of verbs that would have cross-language validity. For the moment, this is more a hope for the future than a present reality, however. Still, I think that a case can be made that certain well-founded conclusions about the nature of language do bear on traditional philosophical questions, but in ways rather different from those just mentioned. Specifically, I think that these conclusions are relevant to the problem of how knowledge is acquired and how the character of human knowledge is determined by certain general properties of the mind. What I would like to do, for the remainder of this paper, is to restate certain proposals about this matter that have been developed elsewhere,[1] and then to consider a variety of problems and objections that have been raised by several philosophers with respect to these proposals.[2]

One might adopt the following research strategy for the study of cognitive processes in humans. A person is presented with a physical stimulus that he interprets in a certain way. Let us say that he constructs a certain "percept" that represents certain of his conclusions (unconscious, in general) about the source of stimulation. To the extent that we can characterize this percept, we can proceed to investigate the process of interpretation. We can, in other words, proceed to develop a model of perception that takes stimuli as inputs and assigns percepts as "outputs," a model that will meet certain given empirical conditions on the actual pairing of stimuli with interpretations of these stimuli. For example, the person who understands sentences (1) and (2) knows (whether he is aware of it or not) that in the case of (2) it is a proposition that is certain and in the case of (1) it is a person who is certain of something, in a very different sense of "certain." If we are interested in studying perception of language, specifically, the processes by which sentences are understood, we can begin by describing the percepts in such a way as to bring out this difference, as we did in proposing that (1″) and (2″), interpreted in the suggested manner, are essential components of the percept. We can then ask how these percepts are constructed by the hearer, given the input stimuli (1) and (2).

A perceptual model that relates stimulus and percept might incorporate a certain system of beliefs, certain strategies that are used in interpreting stimuli, and other factors — for example, organization of memory. In the case of language, the technical term for the underlying system of beliefs is "grammar," or "generative grammar." A grammar is a system of rules that generates an infinite class of "potential percepts," each with its phonetic, semantic, and syntactic aspects, the class of structures that constitutes the language in question. The percepts themselves are first-order constructs; we determine their properties by experiment and observation. The grammar that underlies the formation of percepts is a second-order construct. To study it, we must abstract away from the other factors that are involved in the use and understanding of language, and concentrate on the knowledge of language [3] that has been internalized in some manner by the language user.

Concentrating on this system, we can then inquire into the means by which it was acquired and the basis for its acquisition. We can, in other words, attempt to construct a second model, a learning model, which takes certain data as input and gives, as "output," the system of beliefs that is one part of the internal structure of the perceptual model. The "output," in this case, is represented in the "final state" of the organism that has acquired this system of beliefs; we are asking, then, how this final state was achieved, through the interplay of innate factors, maturational processes, and organism-environment interaction.

In short, we can begin by asking "what is perceived" and move from there to a study of perception. Focusing on the role of belief (in our case, knowledge of language) in perception, we can try to characterize "what is learned" and move from there to the study of learning. One might, of course, decide to study some other topic, or to proceed in some different manner. Thus much of modern psychology has decided, for reasons that do not impress me, to limit itself to the study of behavior and control of behavior. I do not want to pursue the matter here, but I will merely state my own opinion: that this approach has proven quite barren, and that it is irrational to limit one's objectives in this way. One cannot hope to study learning or perception in any useful way by adhering to methodological strictures that limit the conceptual apparatus so narrowly as to disallow the concept "what is perceived" and the concept "what is learned."

I think that interesting conclusions can be reached when one studies human language along the lines just outlined. In the areas of syntax and phonetics at least, a plausible general account can be given of the system of representation for percepts in any human language. Furthermore, there has been substantial progress in constructing generative grammars that express the knowledge of language that is the "output" of a learning model and a fundamental component of a perceptual model. There is, I believe, good evidence that a generative grammar for a human language contains a system of base rules of a highly restricted sort, a set of grammatical transformations that map the deep structures formed in accordance with base rules onto surface structures, and a set of phonological rules that assign phonetic interpretations, in a universal phonetic alphabet, to surface structures. Furthermore, there is also good evidence that certain highly restrictive principles determine the functioning of these rules, conditions of ordering and organization of a complex and intricate sort. There is a considerable literature dealing with these matters, and I will not try to review it here. I only wish to emphasize that there is no a priori necessity for a language to be organized in the highly specific manner proposed in these investigations. Hence if this theory of linguistic structure is correct, or near correct, some nontrivial problems arise for the theory of human learning. Specifically, we must ask how on the basis of the limited data available to him, the child is able to construct a grammar of the sort that we are led to ascribe to him, with its particular choice and arrangement of rules and with the restrictive principles of application of such rules. What, in other words, must be the internal structure of a learning model that can duplicate this achievement. Evidently, we must try to characterize innate structure in such a way as to meet two kinds of empirical conditions. First, we must attribute to the organism, as an innate property, a structure rich enough to account for the fact that the postulated grammar is acquired on the basis of the given conditions of access to data; second, we must not attribute to the organism a structure so rich as to be incompatible with the known diversity of languages. We cannot attribute knowledge of English to the child as an innate property, because we know that he can learn Japanese as well as English. We cannot attribute to him merely the ability to form associations, or to apply the analytic procedures of structural linguistics, because (as is easy to show when these proposals are made precise) the structures they yield are not those that we must postulate as generative grammars. Within the empirical bounds just stated, we are free to construct theories of innate structure and to test them in terms of their empirical consequences. To say this is merely to define the problem. Substantive questions arise only when a specific theory is proposed.

By investigating sentences and their structural descriptions, speech signals and the percepts to which they give rise, we can arrive at detailed conclusions regarding the generative grammar that is one fundamental element in linguistic performance, in speech and understanding of speech. Turning then to the next higher level of abstraction, we raise the question of how this generative grammar is acquired. From a formal point of view, the grammar that is internalized by every normal human can be described as a theory of his language, a theory of a highly intricate and abstract form that determines, ultimately, a connection between sound and meaning by generating structural descriptions of sentences ("potential percepts"), each with its phonetic, semantic, and syntactic aspects. From this point of view, one can describe the child's acquisition of knowledge of language as a kind of theory construction. Presented with highly restricted data, he constructs a theory of the language of which this data is a sample (and, in fact, a highly degenerate sample, in the sense that much of it must be excluded as irrelevant and incorrect — thus the child learns rules of grammar that identify much of what he has heard as ill-formed, inaccurate and inappropriate). The child's ultimate knowledge of language obviously extends far beyond the data presented to him. In other words, the theory he has in some way developed has a predictive scope of which the data on which it is based constitute a negligible part. The normal use of language characteristically involves new sentences, sentences that bear no point-by-point resemblance or analogy to those in the child's experience. Furthermore, the task of constructing this system is carried out in a remarkably similar way by all normal language learners, despite wide differences in experience and ability. The theory of human learning must face these facts.

I think that these facts suggest a theory of human intelligence that has a distinctly rationalist flavor. Using terms suggested by Peirce, in his lectures on "the logic of abduction," the problem of the theory of learning is to state the condition that "gives a rule to abduction and so puts a limit on admissible hypotheses." If "man's mind has a natural adaptation to imagining correct theories of some kinds," then acquisition of knowledge of a sort that we are considering is possible. The problem for the psychologist (or linguist) is to formulate the principles that set a limit to admissible hypotheses. I have made detailed suggestions in this regard elsewhere, and will not repeat them here. Roughly, I think it reasonable to postulate that the principles of general linguistics regarding the nature of rules, their organization, the principles by which they function, the kinds of representations to which they apply and which they form, all constitute part of the innate condition that "puts a limit on admissible hypotheses." If this suggestion is correct, then there is no more point asking how these principles are learned than there is in asking how a child learns to breathe, or, for that matter, to have two arms. Rather, the theory of learning should try to characterize the particular strategies that a child uses to determine that the language he is facing is one, rather than another, of the "admissible languages." When the principles just alluded to are made precise, they constitute an empirical assumption about the innate basis for the acquisition of knowledge, an assumption that can be tested in a variety of ways. In particular, we can ask whether it falls between the bounds described earlier: that is, does it ascribe a rich enough innate structure to account for the acquisition of knowledge, but a structure not so rich as to be falsified by the diversity of languages. We might also ask many other questions, for example, how the schema that is proposed as a basis for acquisition of knowledge of language relates to the principles that "give a rule to abduction" in other domains of human (or animal) intelligence.

What I am suggesting is that if we wish to determine the relevance of linguistics to philosophy, we must investigate the conclusions that can be established concerning the nature of language, the ways in which language is used and understood, the basis for its acquisition. I think that these conclusions have interesting consequences for psychological theory, in particular, that they strongly support an account of mental processes that is, in part, familiar, from rationalist speculation about these matters. They support the conclusion that the role of intrinsic organization is very great in perception, and that a highly restrictive initial schema determines what counts as "linguistic experience" and what knowledge arises on the basis of this experience. I also think, and have argued elsewhere, that the empiricist doctrines that have been prevalent in linguistics, philosophy, and psychology in recent years, if formulated in a fairly precise way, can be refuted by careful study of language. If philosophy is what philosophers do, then these conclusions are relevant to philosophy, both in its classical and modern varieties.

At this point, I would like to turn to some of the critical analysis of this point of view that has appeared in the recent philosophical literature, specifically, to the items referred to in note 2.

Goodman's treatment of these questions seems to me to suffer, first, from a historical misunderstanding; second, from a failure to formulate correctly the exact nature of the problem of acquisition of knowledge; and third, from a lack of familiarity with the work that has led to the conclusions that he criticizes, those that are outlined above.

His historical misunderstanding has to do with the issue between Locke and whoever it was that Locke thought he was criticizing in his discussion of innate ideas. Goodman believes that "Locke made . . . acutely clear" that the doctrine of innate ideas is "false or meaningless." I will not dwell on this matter, since it is a commonplace of historical scholarship that Locke's critique of the doctrine of innate ideas "assails it in its crudest form, in which it is countenanced by no eminent advocate." [4] Even Lord Herbert makes it clear that the common notions "remain latent" in the absence of appropriate stimulation, that they are the "principles without which we should have no experience at all" but that they will obviously not be constantly in consciousness, even to "normal men," and certainly not to those who are "headstrong, foolish, weak-minded and imprudent," to "madmen, drunkards, and infants," and so on. And as these ideas are elaborated by Descartes and others, it is repeatedly emphasized that while innate ideas and principles determine the nature of experience and the knowledge that can arise from it, they will ordinarily not be in consciousness. Since Locke's arguments fail to come to grips with the "dispositional" nature of innate structure that is insistently maintained by the leading proponents of rationalist doctrine, they also invariably miss the mark; it seems that he must have mistaken the actual views of Herbert, Descartes, the minor Cartesians, Cudworth, and others.

It is surprising that Goodman accuses those who "identify the innate ideas with capacities" of "sophistry." Goodman is free, if he wishes, to use the terms "idea" and "innate idea" in accordance with Locke's misunderstanding of rationalist doctrine, but hardly to accuse others of "sophistry" when they examine and develop this doctrine in the form in which it was actually presented. It is particularly surprising to hear Goodman speak of the necessity of applying the term "idea," in "its normal use." One would hardly expect Goodman to propose this sort of "ordinary language argument" against the use of a technical term. Furthermore, as Thomas Reid pointed out, if we use "idea" in the nontechnical way, then not only the position of Descartes, but also that of Locke and Hume reduces to absurdity — an observation that is correct, but that shows nothing more than the absurdity of insisting that a technical term must be understood in "the normal use" of the homonymous nontechnical term of ordinary discourse.

Let me turn, however, to the substantive problem of acquisition of knowledge, as Goodman formulates it in the specific case of language-acquisition. Quite properly, he distinguishes two cases: initial language, and second-language acquisition. But his analysis of the two cases leaves much to be desired.

Consider first the problem of second-language acquisition. In what I understand to be Goodman's view,[5] second-language acquisition poses no problem, since "once one language is available and can be used for giving explanation and instruction, the limitations [determined by an innate schematism] are transcended." This way of putting the matter misconstrues the situation in two basic respects. First, it is misleading to speak of the innate schematism that has been proposed as merely providing "limitations" for acquisition of language. Rather, what has been proposed is that this schematism *makes possible* the acquisition of a rich and highly specific system on the basis of limited data. To take one example, the problem is to explain how the data available to a language learner (first or second) suffices to establish that the phonological rules (the rules that assign phonetic representations to surface structures) apply cyclically, first to innermost phrases of the surface structure, then to larger phrases, etc., until the maximal domain of phonological processes — in simple cases, the full sentence — is reached. There is in fact good evidence that the rules do apply cyclically, but this evidence is not of a sort that can be used as the basis for induction from phonetic data to the principle of cyclic application, by any procedure of induction that has general validity. In particular, much of this evidence is derived from an analysis of percepts, that is, from investigation of the way in which someone who has already mastered the language interprets speech signals. It seems that this interpretation imposes a certain structure that is not indicated directly in the speech signal, for example, in the determination of stress contours.[6] Obviously the child cannot acquire the knowledge that phonological rules apply cyclically from data that are available to him only after he knows and makes use of this principle. This is an extreme example, but it nevertheless illustrates quite well the basic problem: to explain how a rich and highly specific grammar is developed on the basis of limited data that is consistent with a vast number of other conflicting grammars. An innate schematism is proposed, correctly or incorrectly, as an empirical hypothesis to explain the uniformity, specificity, and richness of detail and structure of the grammars that are, in fact, constructed and used by the person who has mastered the language. Therefore the word "limitation" in Goodman's formulation is quite inappropriate.

More serious, it must be recognized that one does not learn the grammatical structure of a second language through "explanation and instruction," beyond the most elementary rudiments, for the simple reason that no one has enough explicit knowledge about this structure to provide explanation and instruction. For example, consider the property of nominalization in English noted earlier, namely, that a certain class of nominal expressions correspond only to deep and not surface structures. The person who has learned English as a second language well enough to make the judgments illustrated by examples (1)–(10) has not acquired this knowledge through "explanation and instruction." Until quite recently, no one, to my knowledge, was aware of this phenomenon; the second-language learner, like the first-language learner, has somehow established the facts for himself, without explanation or instruction. Again, the example is quite typical. Only a trivial part of the knowledge that the second-language learner acquires is presented to him by direct instruction. Even the most cursory attention to the facts of second-language acquisition is sufficient to establish this. Hence, although second-language acquisition is, indeed, to be distinguished from first-language acquisition, the distinction is not of the sort that Goodman suggests. While it may be true that "once some language is available, acquisition of others is relatively easy," it nevertheless remains a very serious problem — not significantly different from the problem of explaining first-language acquisition — to account for this fact.

Consider now the more important matter of first-language acquisition, the problem to which the empirical hypotheses regarding innate schematism have been directed. Goodman ar-

gues that there is no problem in explaining first-language acquisition, because "acquisition of an initial language is acquisition of a secondary symbolic system": the fundamental step
has already been taken, and details can be elaborated within
an already existing framework. This argument might have
some force if it were possible to show that some of the specific
properties of grammar — say the distinction of deep and surface structure, the specific properties of grammatical transformations and phonological rules, the principles of rule ordering,
and so on — were present in these already acquired prelinguistic "symbolic systems." But there is not the slightest reason to
believe that this is so. Goodman's argument is based on a
metaphorical use of the term "symbolic system," and collapses
as soon as we try to give this term a precise meaning. If it were
possible to show that "prelinguistic symbolic systems" share
certain significant properties with natural language, we could
then argue that these properties of natural language are somehow acquired by "analogy," though we would now face the
problem of explaining how the "prelinguistic symbolic systems" developed these properties and how the analogies are
established. But the issue is academic, since, for the moment,
there is no reason to suppose the assumption to be true. Goodman's argument is a bit like a "demonstration" that there is no
problem in accounting for the development of complex organs,
because everyone knows that mitosis takes place. This seems to
me to be obscurantism, which can be maintained only so long
as one fails to come to grips with the actual facts.

There is, furthermore, a non sequitur in Goodman's discussion of first- and second-language acquisition. Recall that
he explains the presumed ease of second-language acquisition
on the grounds that it is possible to use the first language for explanation and instruction. He then goes on to argue that "acquisition of an initial language is acquisition of a secondary
symbolic system," and is hence quite on a par with second-
language acquisition. The primary symbolic systems he has in
mind are "rudimentary prelinguistic symbolic systems in which
gestures and sensory and perceptual occurrences of all sorts

function as signs." But evidently, these systems, whatever they may be, cannot "be used for giving explanation and instruction" *in the way in which a first language can be used in second-language acquisition.* Consequently, even on his own grounds, Goodman's argument is incoherent.

Goodman maintains that "the claim we are discussing cannot be experimentally tested even when we have an acknowledged example of a 'bad' language, and . . . that the claim has not even been formulated to the extent of citation of a single general property of 'bad' languages." The first of these conclusions is correct, in his sense of "experimental test," namely, a test in which we "take an infant at birth, isolate it from all the influences of our language-bound culture, and attempt to inculcate it with one of the 'bad' artificial languages." Obviously, this is not feasible, exactly as comparable experimental tests are not feasible in any other area of human psychology. But there is no reason for dismay at the impracticality of such direct tests as these. There are many other ways — those discussed earlier, and extensively in the literature — in which evidence can be obtained regarding the properties of grammars and in which hypotheses regarding the general properties of such grammars can be put to empirical test. Any such hypothesis immediately specifies, correctly or incorrectly, certain properties of 'bad' languages. It therefore makes an empirical claim that can be falsified by finding counterinstances in some human language, or by showing that under the actual conditions of language acquisition, the properties in question do not appear in the system that is developed by the language learner. In linguistics, as in any other field, it is only in such indirect ways as these that one can hope to find evidence bearing on nontrivial hypotheses. Direct experimental tests of the sort that Goodman, for some reason, regards as necessary, are rarely feasible, a fact that may be unfortunate but that is nevertheless characteristic of most research.

Goodman's further claim, that not "a single general property of 'bad' languages has been formulated," is quite unfair. There are dozens of books and papers concerned with formulating properties of universal grammar and examining their empirical consequences, and each such property specifies 'bad' languages, as just noted. One is free to argue that these attempts are misguided, inadequate, unconvincing, refuted by facts, etc., but not to deny blandly that they exist. I do not see how to avoid the conclusion that when Goodman speaks of "the unimpressive evidence adduced with respect to languages," he simply speaks out of ignorance, rather than from a considered analysis of the work that has been done in the field.

In discussing properties of "bad" languages, Goodman refers only to one case, namely, the case of the concocted language *Gruebleen,* which "differs from ordinary English only in that it contains the predicates 'grue' (for "examined before *t* and blue or not so examined and green") and 'bleen' (for "examined before *t* and blue or not so examined and green") in place of the predicates 'green' and 'blue.' " He argues that even in this case, one must be "painfully aware of the difficulties of answering" the question of what in general is "the difference between Gruebleen-like and English-like languages." I think that this is a rather marginal issue, since much more deep-seated properties of "English-like languages" have been formulated and investigated, but, since he brings up this example, it is well to point out that the difficulties to which he alludes are in large measure a consequence of the vagueness of the question he asks. Thus there is no difficulty in finding some property of Gruebleen that is not a property of "English-like languages," even a property of some generality. For example, consider the predicate "match" understood as in Goodman's *Structure of Appearance,* but applying now to objects rather than qualia. Thus two objects match "if and only if they are not noticeably different on direct comparison." [7] Gruebleen has the curious property that if an object A is examined before *t* and an object B is examined after *t,* and both are found to be grue (or both bleen), then we know that they will not match. But there is no *t* such that given two objects, one examined before *t* and one after *t,* and both found to be green (or blue), we can predict that they will not match. They may not match, but then they also may match, if both are green (or blue). In fact, it is undoubtedly a general property of natural languages that they are "English-like" rather than "Gruebleen-like," in this sense, in the domain of color terms. Thus there is no difficulty in establishing a fairly general distinction between Grue-bleen-like and English-like languages, in this specific respect. Of course, this would not satisfy Goodman's requirements, for his special purposes, because one can construct other problems of the grue-bleen type that are not taken account of by this property. As long as Goodman's vague notions "English-like" and "Gruebleen-like" are left unspecified, there is of course no way to meet his demand that a *general* property be stated distinguishing the two kinds of language, and any specific distinction that is proposed will always give rise to new riddles of induction. This is an interesting comment about the limitations of inductive methods, but has no more relevance to the problem of specifying the characteristics of universal grammar than to any other enterprise of science, say, the problem of specifying the genetic conditions that determine that a human embryo will develop legs rather than wings, under a given range of conditions.

I am not, incidentally, proposing that the property just cited serves to explain why every language-learner (in fact, every mouse, chimpanzee, etc.) uses green rather than grue as the basis for generalization. No doubt this is a simple consequence of certain properties of the sensory system, a conclusion that is quite uninteresting from Goodman's point of view, but not, for that reason, incorrect.

Returning to the main point, it is interesting that at one stage of his argument Goodman remarks, quite correctly, that even if "for certain remarkable facts I have no alternative explanation," "that alone does not dictate acceptance of . . . an intrinsically repugnant and incomprehensible theory." But now let us consider the theory of innate ideas that arouses Goodman's indignation, and ask whether it is "incomprehensible" and "repugnant."

Consider first the matter of comprehensibility. It does not

seem to me incomprehensible that some aspect of the "final state" of an organism or automation should also be an aspect of its "initial state," prior to any interaction with the environment, just as it is not incomprehensible that this aspect of the final state should have developed through internal processes, perhaps set in motion by organism-environment interaction of some sort. But consider the actual doctrines developed in the speculative psychology of rationalism, rather than Locke's caricature. Descartes, for example, argued that the idea of a triangle is innate in that "the idea of a true triangle . . . can be more easily conceived by our mind than the more complex figure of the triangle drawn on paper," so that when a child first sees the more complex figure, he will "apprehend not it itself, but rather the authentic triangle." As Cudworth elaborates this view, "every irregular and imperfect triangle [is] as perfectly that which it is, as the most perfect triangle," but we interpret sensory images in terms of a notion of "regular figure" that has its source in the "rule, pattern and exemplar" generated by the mind as an "anticipation," just as we interpret all sensory data in terms of certain concepts of object and relations among objects, certain notions of cause and effect, gestalt properties, functions in a "space" of possible human actions, and so on. Neither this view, nor its elaboration in modern psychology, is incomprehensible, though it may of course be misguided or incorrect. Similarly, there is no difficulty in comprehending the proposal that there are certain innate conditions on the form of grammar that determine what constitutes linguistic experience and what knowledge will arise on the basis of this experience. Again, one can easily design an automaton that will function in this manner, so that although the proposal may be wrong, it is not incomprehensible.

Whatever Goodman's attitudes might be to these formulations, it is interesting that he appears quite willing, at least in this paper, to accept the view that in some sense the mature mind contains ideas; it is obviously not incomprehensible, then, that some of these ideas are "implanted in the mind as original equipment," to use his terminology. His argument is directed not against the notion that "ideas are in the mind," but rather against the assumption that they are "in the mind" prior to experience, and surely if one assumption is comprehensible, then the other is as well (though neither, as noted, does justice to the classical rationalist view or to its modern variants). On the other hand, this approach to the problem of acquisition of knowledge will, no doubt, be "repugnant" to one who considers empiricist doctrine immune to doubt or challenge. But this is to treat empiricist doctrines as articles of religious faith. Surely it is not reasonable to be so bound to a tradition as to refuse to examine conflicting views about acquisition of knowledge on their merits.

Let me turn next to Hilary Putnam's contribution to the same symposium. Although his paper deals more directly with the points that are actually at issue, still it seems to me that his arguments are inconclusive, primarily, because of certain erroneous assumptions about the nature of the acquired grammars. Specifically, he enormously underestimates, and in part misdescribes, the richness of structure, the particular and detailed properties of grammatical form and organization that must be accounted for by a "language acquisition model," that are acquired by the normal speaker-hearer and that appear to be uniform among speakers and also across languages.

To begin with, Putnam assumes that at the level of sound structure, the only property that can be proposed in universal grammar is that a language has "a short list of phonemes." This uniformity among languages, he argues, requires no elaborate explanatory hypothesis. It can be explained simply in terms of "such parameters as memory span and memory capacity," and no "rank Behaviorists" would have denied that these are innate properties. In fact, however, very strong empirical hypotheses have been proposed regarding the choice of universal distinctive features, the form of phonological rules, the ordering and organization of these rules, the relation of syntactic structure to phonetic representation, none of which can conceivably be accounted for on grounds of memory limitations. Putnam bases his account largely on my "Explanatory Models in Linguistics" (see note 6), which examines in some detail the principle of cyclic application of phonological rules, a principle that, if correct, raises some rather serious problems. We must ask how the child acquires knowledge of this principle, a feat that is particularly remarkable since, as already noted, much of the evidence that leads the linguist to posit this principle is drawn from the study of percepts and is thus not even available to the child. Similar questions arise with respect to many other aspects of universal phonology. In any event, if the proposals that have been elaborated regarding sound structure are correct or near correct, then the similarities among languages at this level, and the richness of the knowledge acquired by the child, are indeed remarkable facts, and demand an explanation.

Above the level of sound structure, Putnam assumes that the only significant properties of language are that they have proper names, that the grammar contains a phrase-structure component, and that there are rules "abbreviating" sentences generated by the phrase-structure component. He argues that the specific character of the phrase-structure component is determined by the existence of proper names; that the existence of a phrase-structure component is explained by the fact that "all the natural measures of complexity of an algorithm . . . lead to the . . . result" that phrase-structure systems provide the "algorithms which are 'simplest' for virtually any computing system," hence also "for naturally evolved 'computing systems'"; that there is nothing surprising in the fact that languages contain rules of abbreviations. Hence, he concludes, the only innate conditions that must be postulated are those that apply to all reasonable "computing systems," and no Behaviorist should feel any surprise at this.

Each of the three conclusions, however, is vitiated by a false assumption. First, it is obvious that there are many different phrase-structure grammars consistent with the assumption that one of the categories is that of proper names. In fact, there is much dispute at the moment about the general properties of the underlying base system for natural languages; the dispute is not in the least resolved by the existence of proper names as a primitive category in many languages.[8]

As to the second point, it is simply untrue that all measures of complexity and speed of computation lead to phrase-structure rules as the "simplest possible algorithm." The only existing results that have even an indirect relevance to this matter are those dealing with context-free phrase-structure grammars and their automata-theoretic interpretation. Context-free grammars are a reasonable model for the rules generating deep structures, when we exclude the lexical items and the distributional conditions they meet. But even apart from this fundamental discrepancy, the only existing results relate context-free grammars to a class of automata called "nondeterministic pushdown storage automata," and these have no particularly striking properties insofar as speed or complexity of computation are concerned, and are certainly not "natural" from this point of view. In terms of time and space conditions on computation, the somewhat similar but not formally related concept of real-time deterministic automaton would seem to be far more natural. In short, there are no results demonstrating that phrase-structure grammars are optimal in any computational sense (nor, certainly, are there any results dealing with the much more complex notion of base structure with a context-free phrase-structure grammar and a lexicon, with much richer properties, as components).

But there is no point in pursuing this matter, since what is at stake, in any event, is not the "simplicity" of phrase-structure grammars but rather of transformational grammars that contain a phrase-structure component, the latter playing a role in the generation of deep structures. And there is absolutely no mathematical concept of "ease of computation" or "simplicity of algorithm" that even suggests that such systems have some advantage over the various kinds of automata that have been investigated from this point of view. In fact, these systems have never really been considered in a strictly mathematical context, though there are interesting initial attempts to study some of their formal properties.[9] The source of the confusion is a misconception on Putnam's part as to the nature of grammatical transformations. These are not, as he supposes, rules that "abbreviate" sentences generated by phrase-structure rules. Rather, they are operations that form surface structures from underlying deep structures, which are generated, in part, by phrase-structure rules. Although there has been considerable evolution of theory since the notions of transformational generative grammar were first proposed, one assumption that has remained constant is that the phrase-structure rules generate only abstract structures, which are then mapped onto surface structures by grammatical transformations — the latter being structure-dependent operations of a peculiar sort that have never been studied outside of linguistics, in particular, not in any branch of mathematics with which I am familiar. To show that transformational grammars are the "simplest possible" one would have to demonstrate that an optimal computing system would take a string of symbols as input and determine its surface structure, the underlying deep structure, and the sequence of transformational operations that relate these two labeled bracketings. Nothing known about ease or simplicity of computation gives any reason to suppose that this is true; in fact, the question has never been raised. One can think of certain kinds of organization of memory that might be well adapted to transformational grammars, but this is a different matter entirely.[10] I would, naturally, assume that there is some more general basis in human mental structure for the fact (if it is a fact) that languages have transformational grammars; one of the primary scientific reasons for studying language is that this study may provide some insight into general properties of mind. Given those specific properties, we may then be able to show that transformational grammars are "natural." This would constitute real progress, since it would now enable us to raise the problem of innate conditions on acquisition of knowledge and belief in a more general framework. But it must be emphasized that, contrary to what Putnam asserts, there is no basis for assuming that "reasonable computing systems" will naturally be organized in the specific manner suggested by transformational grammar.

I believe that this disposes of Putnam's main argument, namely, that there is "nothing surprising," even to a Behaviorist, in the linguistic universals that are now being proposed and investigated. Let me then turn to his second argument, that even if there were surprising linguistic universals, they could be accounted for on a simpler hypothesis than that of an innate universal grammar, namely, the hypothesis of common origin of languages. This proposal misrepresents the problem at issue. As noted earlier, the empirical problem we face is to devise a hypothesis about initial structure rich enough to account for the fact that a specific grammar is acquired, under given conditions of access to data. To this problem, the matter of common origin of language is quite irrelevant. The grammar has to be discovered by the child on the basis of the data available to him, through the use of the innate capacities with which he is endowed. To be concrete, consider again the two examples discussed above: the association of nominal phrases to base structures and the cyclic application of phonological rules. The child masters these principles (if we are correct in our conclusions about grammar) on the basis of certain linguistic data; he knows nothing about the origin of language and could not make use of such information if he had it. Questions of common origin are relevant to the empirical problems we are discussing only in that the existing languages might not be a "fair sample" of the "possible languages," in which case we might be led mistakenly to propose too narrow a schema for universal grammar. This possibility must be kept in mind, of course, but it seems to me a rather remote consideration, given the problem that is actually at hand, namely, the problem of finding a schema rich enough to account for the development of the grammars that seem empirically justified. The discovery of such a schema may provide an explanation for the empirically determined universal properties of language. The existence of these properties, however, does not explain how a specific grammar is acquired by the child.

Putnam's discussion of the ease of language-learning seems to me beside the point. The question whether there is a critical period for language-learning is interesting,[11] but it has little relevance to the problem under discussion. Suppose that Putnam were correct in believing that "certainly . . . 600 hours [of direct method instruction] will enable any adult to speak and read a foreign language with ease." We would then face the problem of explaining how, on the basis of this restricted data, the learner has succeeded in acquiring the specific and detailed knowledge that enables him to use the language with ease, and to produce and understand a range of structures of which the data presented to him constitute a minute sample.

Finally, consider the alternative approach that Putnam suggests to the problem of language-acquisition. He argues that instead of postulating an innate schematism one should attempt to account for this achievement in terms of "general multipurpose learning strategies." It is these that must be innate, not general conditions on the form of the knowledge that is acquired. Evidently, this is an empirical issue. It would be sheer dogmatism to assert of either of these proposals (or of some particular combination of them) that it *must* be correct. Putnam is convinced, on what grounds he does not say, that the innate basis for the acquisition of language must be identical with that for acquiring any other form of knowledge, that there is nothing "special" about the acquisition of language. A nondogmatic approach to this problem can be pursued, through the investigation of specific areas of human competence, such as language, followed by the attempt to devise a hypothesis that will account for the development of such competence. If we discover that the same "learning strategies" are involved in a variety of cases, and that these suffice to account for the acquired competence, then we will have good reason to believe that Putnam's empirical hypothesis is correct. If, on the other hand, we discover that different innate systems (whether involving schemata or heuristics) have to be postulated, then we will have good reason to believe that an adequate theory of mind will incorporate separate "faculties," each with unique or partially unique properties. I cannot see how one can resolutely insist on one or the other conclusion in the light of the evidence now available to us. But one thing is quite clear: Putnam has no justification for his final conclusion, that "invoking 'Innateness' only postpones the problem of learning; it does not solve it." [12] Invoking an innate representation of universal grammar does solve the problem of learning (at least partially), in this case, if in fact it is true that this is the basis (or part of the basis) for language-acquisition, as it well may be. If, on the other hand, there exist general learning strategies that account for the acquisition of grammatical knowledge, then postulation of an innate representation of universal grammar will not "postpone" the problem of learning, but will rather offer an incorrect solution to this problem. The issue is an empirical one of truth or falsity, not a methodological one of stages of investigation. At the moment, the only concrete proposal that is at all plausible, in my opinion, is the one sketched above. When some "general learning strategy" is suggested, we can look into the relative adequacy of these alternatives, on empirical grounds.

Henry Hiż's review article deals mainly with the distinction between competence and performance. One can attempt to explain technical concepts such as these in two different ways. At a presystematic level, one can try to indicate, necessarily in a loose and somewhat vague and only suggestive way, just what role the concept is intended to play in a more general framework, and why it seems to be a useful idea to try to develop. Discussion at this level is entirely legitimate, but there will generally be much room for misunderstanding. At a second level, one can develop the concept in as precise a way as the state of the field permits, with no consideration for motivation or general implications. At this level, the problem is to determine not what the concept in question is, but why there is any point in developing it.

At the presystematic level, I have tried to explain what I mean by "linguistic competence" in terms of models of use and acquisition of language, in the manner outlined earlier. At the systematic level, competence is expressed by a generative grammar that recursively enumerates structural descriptions of sentences, each with its phonetic, syntactic, and semantic aspects. It is hardly necessary to emphasize that any such grammar that we can actually present today is incomplete, not only because our knowledge of particular languages is deficient, but also because our understanding of phonetic and semantic representation and the kinds of structures and rules that mediate between them is limited and unsatisfactory in many respects.

Turning to Hiż's paper, there is, not surprisingly, a certain degree of misunderstanding between us at the presystematic level. Hiż suggests that my use of the notion "competence" "is to be understood as saying that introspection is a source of linguistic knowledge." I do agree that introspection is an excellent source of data for the study of language, but this conclusion does not follow from the decision to study linguistic competence. One might (irrationally, in my opinion) refuse to use such evidence, and still try to discover the generative grammar that represents "what is learned" and that plays a fundamental role in language use. This decision would be pointless, rather on a par with an astronomer's refusal, at one stage of the science, to use what he sees through a telescope as data, but the decision has nothing to do with the distinction between competence and performance. I have no doubt that it would be possible to devise operational and experimental procedures that could replace the reliance on introspection with little loss, but it seems to me that in the present state of the field, this would simply be a waste of time and energy. Obviously, any such procedure would first have to be tested against the introspective evidence. If one were to propose a test for, say, grammaticalness, that fails to make the distinctions noted earlier in the proper way, one would have little faith in the procedure as a test for grammaticalness. To me it seems that current research is not hampered significantly by lack of accurate data, but rather by our inability to explain in a satisfactory way data that are hardly in question. One who feels differently can support his point of view by demonstrating the gains in insight and understanding that can be achieved by refinements in techniques of data collection and analysis, say, by operational techniques for establishing grammaticalness, techniques that have been judged by the prior test of intuition and shown to be sufficiently sound so that one can rely on them in difficult or obscure cases. In any event, the whole matter has nothing to do with the decision to study linguistic competence.

Hiż regards it as "paradoxical" to assert, as I have, that linguistics "attempts to specify what the speaker actually knows, not what he may report about his knowledge." This he regards as "a peculiar sense of 'knowledge.'" To me it seems a rather ordinary sense, and a nonparadoxical usage. A person who knows English may give all sorts of incorrect reports about the knowledge that he actually possesses and makes use of constantly, without awareness. As noted earlier, when we study competence — the speaker-hearer's knowledge of his language — we may make use of his reports and his behavior as evidence, but we must be careful not to confuse "evidence" with the abstract constructs that we develop on the basis of evidence and try to justify in terms of evidence. Thus I would definitely reject three of the five conditions that, Hiż suggests, rules must satisfy if they are to constitute an account of competence in my sense, namely, that the native speaker feels that the sentences generated by the rules are in his language, that they have the assigned structures, and that what the speaker feels is true. Since performance — in particular, judgments about sentences — obviously involves many factors apart from competence, one cannot accept as an absolute principle that the speaker's judgments will give an accurate account of his knowledge. I am surprised that Hiż should offer this interpretation of my views immediately after having quoted my statement that the speaker's reports about his competence may be in error.

At least for the purposes of discussion, Hiż is willing to accept the view that a generative grammar, a system of rules assigning structures to sentences, can serve to characterize competence. He then points out, correctly, that the linguist is guided in his choice of a grammar by certain "general principles about language as such," and that this general theory — universal grammar — will have explanatory value if it selects particular grammars correctly. He then attributes to me, incorrectly, the view that universal grammar is to be identified with "a theory of language acquisition." My view, rather, is that universal grammar is one element of such a theory, much as competence is one element of a theory of performance. There are surely many other factors involved in language-acquisition beyond the schematism and weighting function that — if my suggestion is correct — play a part in determining the nature of the acquired competence. This misinterpretation of my proposal regarding the relation of universal grammar to language-acquisition parallels the misinterpretation of my proposal regarding the relation of competence to performance; in both cases, what is omitted is the reference to other factors that must be involved. In the case of language-acquisition, furthermore, it must be emphasized that the model I am suggesting can at best only be regarded as a first approximation to a theory of learning, since it is an instantaneous model and does not try to capture the interplay between tentative hypotheses that the child may construct, new data interpreted in terms of these hypotheses, new hypotheses based on these interpretations, and so on, until some relatively fixed system of competence is established. I think that an instantaneous model is a reasonable first approximation, but this, as any other aspect of research strategy, must ultimately be evaluated in terms of its success in providing explanations and insight.

Hiż regards the reference to classical formulations of problems of language and mind as "confusing and misleading historical baggage." I disagree with this judgment, but have nothing to add here beyond what I have written elsewhere.[13] My feeling is that the contributions of rationalist psychology and linguistics are interesting in themselves, and are quite relevant to present concerns, more so, in fact, than much of the work of the past century. One who finds these forays into intellectual history "confusing and misleading" can perfectly well disregard them. I see no issue here.

Before leaving this matter, I should mention that Hiż is inaccurate in stating that Herbert of Cherbury restricted himself to "religious knowledge." Nor can Thomas Reid be described as one of those concerned to develop a doctrine of innate universals. Furthermore, it is surely misleading to say that I "call upon" Descartes and others "to support" my "stand on innate universals." Their advocacy of a similar position does not constitute "support." Rather, I am suggesting that their contributions have been inadequately appreciated, and that we can still learn a good deal from a careful study of them.

Hiż objects to the fact that my proposals concerning universal grammar are based on detailed examination of a few languages rather than "examination of many cases." I certainly agree that one should study as many languages as possible. Still, a *caveat* should be entered. It would be quite easy to present enormous masses of data from varied languages that are compatible with all conceptions of universal grammar that have so far been formulated. There is no point in doing so. If one is concerned with the principles of universal grammar, he will try to discover those properties of particular grammars that bear on these principles, putting aside large amounts of material that, so far as he can determine, do not. It is only through intensive studies of particular languages that one can hope to find crucial evidence for the study of universal grammar. One study such as that of Matthews on Hidatsa (see note 8) is worth one thousand superficial studies of varied languages from this point of view. If someone feels that the base of data is too narrow, what he should do is show that some of the material omitted refutes the principles that have been formulated. Otherwise, his criticism has no more force than a crit-

icism of modern genetics for basing its theoretical formulations
on the detailed investigation of only a few organisms.

Hiż also argues that the principles of universal grammar,
even if true, may indicate only "the common historical origin
of languages." I have already pointed out why this hypothesis
is without explanatory force.

Hiż maintains that decisions about particular parts of
grammar (by the linguist) are "determined not by a general
theory but by internal usefulness within the particular grammar," and objects that I do not make this clear. Since I have no
idea what is meant by "internal usefulness," I have nothing to
say about this point. The issue is confused by his misinterpretation of my use of the notion "simplicity." When I speak of
"simplicity of grammar," I am referring to a "weighting function," empirically determined, that selects a grammar of the
form permitted by the universal schematism over others that
are also of the proper form and are compatible with the empirical data. I am not using the term "simplicity" to refer to
that poorly understood property of theories that leads the sci-
entist to select one rather than another. The evaluation measure that defines "simplicity of grammars" is part of linguistic
theory. We must try to discover this measure on empirical
grounds, by considering the actual relations between input
data and acquired grammars. Thus the notion "simplicity of
grammar" plays a role analogous to that of a physical constant;
we must establish it on empirical grounds, and there is no a
priori insight on which we can rely. The problems of defining
"simplicity of theories" in a general context of epistemology
and philosophy of science are entirely irrelevant to the issue of
determining, on empirical grounds, the properties of grammars
that lead to the selection of one rather than another in language acquisition. This point has been emphasized repeatedly.
See, for example, *Aspects*, chapter 1, section 7.

One final comment. Hiż suggests that "it should be easier
to explain why we assign such-and-such a structure to a sentence by pointing out how this sentence changes the readings
of neighboring sentences than by referring to innate universal

ideas and mental reality." Here he is confusing two entirely different kinds of explanation. If I want to explain why, yesterday afternoon at three o'clock, John Smith understood "the shooting of the hunters" as referring to the act of shooting the hunters, rather than the hunters' act of shooting, I will of course bring into consideration the situational context (not limiting myself to the "readings of neighboring sentences"). If I am interested in explaining why this phrase is suspectible to these two interpretations, but the phrase "the growth of corn" is susceptible to only one (namely, the corn's growing and not the act or process of growing corn), then I will appeal first to the particular grammar of English, and more deeply, to the linguistic universals that led to the construction of this grammar by a child exposed to certain data. Since entirely different things are being explained, it is senseless to claim that one manner of explanation is "easier" than the other.

Harman's critique is also concerned with the matter of competence and performance. He begins by ascribing to me a view that I have never held, and have explicitly rejected on numerous occasions, namely, that "competence [is] the knowledge that the language is described by the rules of the grammar," and that a grammar describes this "competence." Obviously, it is absurd to suppose that the speaker of the language knows the rules in the sense of being able to state them. Having attributed to me this absurd view, Harman goes on to struggle with all sorts of purported confusions and difficulties of interpretation. But he cites nothing that could possibly be regarded as a basis for attributing to me this view, though he does quote remarks in which I explicitly reject it. Therefore, I will not discuss this part of his argument at all.

In Harman's framework, there are two kinds of knowledge: knowing that and knowing how. Obviously knowledge of a language is not a matter of "knowing that." Therefore, for him, it must be a matter of "knowing how." A typical speaker "knows how to understand other speakers"; his competence is his ability "to speak and understand the language described by [the] grammar" that describes the language. I do not know what Harman means by the locution "knows how to understand," but clearly he is using the term "competence" in a different way from what I proposed in the work he is reviewing. In my sense of "competence," the ability to speak and understand the language involves not only "competence" (that is, mastery of the generative grammar of the language, tacit knowledge of the language), but also many other factors. In my usage, the grammar is a formal representation of what I have called "competence." I have no objection to Harman's using the term in a different way, but when he insists on supposing that his usage is mine, naturally, only confusion will result. Again, I see no point in tracing in detail the various difficulties into which this misinterpretation leads him.

According to Harman, the "competence to speak and understand the language" is a skill, analogous to the skill of a bicycle rider. Given his insistence that knowledge of language is a matter of "knowing how" (since it is obviously not "knowing that"), this is not an unexpected conclusion. But he suggests no respect in which ability to use a language (let alone the competence, in my sense, that constitutes an element of this ability) is like the ability to ride a bicycle, nor do I see any. The proper conclusion, then, would be that there is no reason to suppose that knowledge of language can be characterized in terms of "knowing how." I therefore see no point in the analogy that he suggests. Knowledge of language is not a skill, a set of habits, or anything of the sort. I see nothing surprising in the conclusion that knowledge of language cannot be discussed in any useful or informative way in this impoverished framework. In general, it does not seem to me true that the concepts "knowing how" and "knowing that" constitute exhaustive categories for the analysis of knowledge. Nor is it surprising that Harman finds it difficult to understand my remarks, or those of anyone else who is concerned with knowledge of language, given that he insists on restricting himself to this framework.

Harman tries to show that there is a fundamental incoherence in my proposal that in acquiring or using knowledge of a

language (in developing "an internal representation of a generative system" or making use of it in speaking or understanding speech), the child makes use of an innate schematism that
restricts the choice of grammars (in the case of acquisition) or
an internalized grammar (in the case of language use). His argument seems to me unclear. As I understand it, it seems to
proceed as follows. He argues that this internalized system
must be presented in "another more basic language," which the
child must come to understand before he can make use of this
schematism to learn this language, or before he can make use
of the grammar to understand speech. But this, he argues,
leads to a vicious circle or an infinite regress. Thus if we were
to say that the child knows the "more basic language" directly,
without learning, then why not say also that he knows "directly
the language he speaks," without learning; a vicious circle. Or,
if we say that he must learn the more basic language, then this
raises the question how the more basic language is learned,
and leads to an infinite regress. This argument is totally in-
valid. Consider the case of acquisition of language. Even if we
assume that the innate schematism must be represented in an
"innate language," neither conclusion follows. The child must
know this "innate language," in Harman's terms, but it does
not follow that he must "speak and understand it" (whatever
this might mean) or that he must learn it. All that we need assume is that he can make use of this schematism when he approaches the task of language-learning. So much for the infinite regress. As to the vicious circle, there is a very simple
reason why we cannot assume that the child knows the language he speaks directly, without learning, namely, that the
assumption is false. We cannot claim that every child is born
with a perfect knowledge of English. On the other hand, there
is no reason why we should not suppose that the child is born
with a perfect knowledge of universal grammar, that is, with a
fixed schematism that he uses, in the ways described earlier, in
acquiring language. This assumption may be false, but it is
quite intelligible. If one insists on describing this knowledge as
"direct knowledge of a more basic language," I see no reason

to object, so long as we are clear about what we mean, but would merely point out that there is no reason at all to doubt that the child has this direct knowledge. Hence there is no vicious circle, and no infinite regress. Similarly, if we consider the case of language use, there is neither incoherence nor implausibility. There is surely no infinite regress and no vicious circle in the assumption that in language use (speaking or understanding) the user employs an internally represented grammar. We can easily construct a model (say, a computer program) that functions in this way. I therefore fail to see any basis for Harman's belief that there is an infinite regress or vicious circle inherent in, or even suggested by this formulation.

In the second part of his paper, Harman turns to my argument that current work in linguistics supports a view of language and mind that has a distinctly rationalist flavor, and is in conflict with the empiricist views that have dominated the study of language and mind in recent years. He asserts that to infer a grammar from data, a model of language-learning must already have detailed information about the theory of performance. This is an interesting proposal, and it deserves to be developed. But I cannot go along with his rather dogmatic claim, hardly argued in the paper, that this approach must necessarily be correct, and that any other approach must fail to provide any insight into the problem of acquisition of knowledge. I think that the work of the past few years on universal grammar does, in fact, suggest and in part support an interesting, rather classical approach to the problem of how knowledge is acquired. In the absence of any argument as to why this approach must fail to be illuminating, I see no reason not to continue with the investigation of how principles of universal grammar might select a particular grammar on the basis of the data available.

Let us turn now to the issue of rationalist and empiricist approaches to problems of language and mind. As Harman points out, if we describe an innate schematism biased toward (or restricted to) a specific form of grammar as part of the "principles of induction used," and define "resourceful empiricism" as a doctrine that makes use of such "principles of induction" as this, then surely "resourceful empiricism" cannot be refuted, "no matter what the facts about language [or anything else] turned out to be." Of course, this new doctrine of "resourceful empiricism" would now incorporate "principles of induction" that are, so it seems, quite specific to the task of language-acquisition and of no general validity.

The concept "resourceful empiricism" so defined seems to me of little interest. The issue that concerns me is whether there are "ideas and principles of various kinds that determine the form of the acquired knowledge in what may be a rather restricted and highly organized way," or alternatively, whether "the structure of the acquisition device is limited to certain elementary peripheral processing mechanisms . . . and certain analytical data-processing mechanisms or inductive principles." (*Aspects,* pp. 47f.) I have argued that "it is historically accurate as well as heuristically valuable to distinguish these two very different approaches to the problem of acquisition of knowledge," even though they of course "cannot always be sharply distinguished" in the work of a particular person. (*Ibid.,* p. 52.) In particular, I have tried to show that it is possible to formulate these approaches so that the former incorporates the leading ideas of classical rationalism as well as the modern variant I have been describing, and that the latter includes classical empiricist doctrine as well as the theories of acquisition of knowledge (or belief, or habit) developed in a wide range of modern work (Quine's notions of quality space and formation of knowledge by association and conditioning; Hull's approach in terms of primitive unconditioned reflexes, conditioning, and habit structures; taxonomic linguistics, with its analytic procedures of segmentation and classification and its conception of language as a "habit system," and so on).[14] Needless to say, there is no necessity to view the various attempts to study language-acquisition within this framework; I can only say that I think it is both useful and accurate. These alternatives can be made fairly precise and investigated in terms of their empirical consequences. Harman's proposal to define "resourceful empiricism" in such a way as to include both approaches, and to be, as he notes, immune to any factual discovery, is merely a pointless terminological suggestion and cannot obscure the difference between the approaches mentioned or the importance of pursuing and evaluating them.[15]

To summarize, I doubt that linguistics can provide "a new technique" for analytic philosophy that will be of much significance, at least in its present state of development. Nevertheless, it seems to me that the study of language can clarify and in part substantiate certain conclusions about human knowledge that relate directly to classical issues in the philosophy of mind. It is in this domain, I suspect, that one can look forward to a really fruitful collaboration between linguistics and philosophy in coming years.[15]

NOTES

1. See, for example, my contribution to the symposium on innate ideas published in *Synthese*, XVII, 1 (March 1967), 2–11, and the references cited there on p. 11.

2. Specifically, the contributions by Nelson Goodman and Hilary Putnam to the symposium cited in note 1, pp. 12–28, and the review articles by Henry Hiż and Gilbert Harman in the issue of the *Journal of Philosophy* devoted to "Some Recent Issues in Linguistics," LXIV, 2 (February 2, 1967), 67–87. The latter two are largely devoted to critical analysis of Chapter I of my *Aspects of the Theory of Syntax*, MIT Press, 1965.

3. Since the language has no objective existence apart from its mental representation, we need not distinguish between "system of beliefs" and "knowledge," in this case.

4. A. C. Fraser (ed.), in his edition of Locke's *Essay Concerning Human Understanding*, 1894, republished by Dover, 1959, p. 38 of the Dover edition.

5. Cf. p. 24. Given the dialogue form of his article, it is difficult to be certain that one is not misrepresenting his position. However, I see no other way to interpret these remarks.

6. For some discussion, see my paper "Explanatory Models in Linguistics," in E. Nagel, P. Suppes, A. Tarski (eds.), *Logic,*

Methodology, and Philosophy of Science, Stanford University Press, 1962. For some recent and much more extensive discussion, see N. Chomsky and M. Halle, *Sound Patterns of English,* Harper and Row, New York, 1968, and the references cited there, and my paper "Some General Properties of Phonological Rules," *Language,* XLIII (March 1967), 102–28.

7. N. Goodman, *Structure of Appearance,* 2nd edition, Bobbs-Merrill, p. 272. The distinction between Gruebleen and English that I am now discussing is not to be confused with a pseudodistinction, correctly rejected by J. Ullian on the basis of a different usage of the notion "match." See *Phil. Rev.,* July 1961.

8. Not, incidentally, in all. Although this is hardly important here, it seems that many languages do not have proper names as a primitive category, but rather form proper names by recursive processes of an elaborate sort. See, for example, G. H. Matthews, *Hidatsa Syntax,* Mouton, The Hague, 1965, pp. 191f.

9. See, for example, S. Peters and R. Ritchie, "On the Generative Capacity of Transformational Grammars," *Information and Control,* forthcoming, and J. P. Kimball, "Predicates Definable over Transformational Derivations by Intersection with Regular Languages," *Information and Control,* II (1967), pp. 177–95.

10. For some speculations on this matter, see G. A. Miller and N. Chomsky, "Finitary Models of Language Users," part II, in R. D. Luce, R. Bush, and E. Galanter (eds.), *Handbook of Mathematical Psychology,* Vol. II, Wiley, 1963.

11. See E. H. Lenneberg, *Biological Foundations of Language,* Wiley, 1967, for evidence bearing on this issue.

12. Or for his assumption that the "weighting functions" proposed in universal grammar constitute the "sort of fact . . . [that] . . . learning theory tries to account for; *not* the explanation being sought." No one would say that the genetic basis for the development of arms rather than wings in a human embryo is "the kind of fact that learning theory tries to account for," rather than the basis for explanation of other facts about human behavior. The question whether the weighting function is learned, or whether it is the basis for learning, is an empirical one. There is not the slightest reason to assume, a priori, that it is to be accounted for by learning rather than genetic endowment, or some combination of the two.

There are other minor points in Putnam's discussion that call for some comment. For example, he asserts that since certain ambiguities "require coaching to detect," it follows that "the claim that grammar 'explains the ability to recognize ambiguities' . . . lacks the impressiveness that Chomsky believes it to have." But he misconstrues the claim, which relates to competence, not performance. What the grammar explains is why "the shooting of the hunters" (the example he cites) can be understood with hunters as subject or object but that in "the growth of corn" we can understand "corn" only as subject (the explanation, in this case, turns on the relation of nominalizations to deep structures, noted earlier). The matter of coaching is beside the point. What is at issue is the inherent sound-meaning correlation that is involved in performance, but only as one of many factors. Putnam also misstates the argument for assuming the active-passive relation to be transformational. It is not merely that the speaker knows them to be related. Obviously that would be absurd; the speaker also knows that "John will leave tomorrow" and "John will leave three days after the day before yesterday" are related, but this does not imply that there is a transformational relation between the two. Syntactic arguments are given in many places in the literature. See, for example, my *Syntactic Structures*, Mouton, 1957; *Aspects of the Theory of Syntax*.

13. In my *Current Issues in Linguistic Theory*, Mouton, 1964, §1; *Aspects of the Theory of Syntax*, Chapter 1, §8; *Cartesian Linguistics*, Harper and Row, 1966.

14. Harman observes correctly that I ignore the "enormous philosophical literature on induction," and limit myself solely to an investigation of the procedures of taxonomic linguistics as "the only proposals that are explicit enough to support serious study." He does not, however, show how anything in the literature on induction bears on the problems I am considering. The reason is that there is nothing. The literature on induction is quite interesting, but it happens to deal with entirely different questions. It does not even hint at procedures of analysis or acquisition of belief or confirmation that would overcome the problems that I have been discussing. There is, for example, nothing in the literature on induction that gives any insight into how the principles cited above as examples (the cycle of phonological rules or the rule of nominaliza-

tion) might be reached "by induction" from the data available. But it is such questions as these that must be faced in the study of language-acquisition.

15. Two minor points in this connection. Harman sees only a "tenuous historical connection" between procedures of segmentation and classification and phrase structure grammar. The connection is actually much closer. Zelig Harris, in his *Methods of Structural Linguistics,* tried to show how a systematic use of such procedures, amplified by a simple inductive step, would lead to a set of rules that might be regarded as generating an infinite set of sentences. A set of Harris' "morpheme to utterance" formulas, though not quite the same as phrase structure grammar, is quite similar. The concept of "phrase structure grammar" was explicitly designed to express the richest system that could reasonably be expected to result from the application of Harris-type procedures to a corpus. Harris, and other methodologists of the 1940's, were developing an approach to linguistic analysis that one can trace at least to Saussure.

Secondly, Harman is quite correct in pointing out that in my reference to "the only [empiricist] proposals that are explicit enough to support serious study," I omitted mention of Harris' and Hiż's method of studying co-occurrence relationships. He feels that this method is "similar in spirit to the taxonomic procedures." I don't see the point in arguing this, one way or another. In any event, I know of no reason to suppose that such procedures can lead to or can even provide evidence for or against the postulation of a generative grammar.

B

Linguistics and Philosophy

W. V. QUINE

Harvard University

CHOMSKY HAS EXPRESSED general doubts as to how much philosophy stands to gain from linguistics or linguistics from philosophy. But he did express the belief that linguistics contributes to philosophy in one quarter, by supporting rationalism as against empiricism.

With the following claim of Chomsky's, at least, we are all bound to agree:

> We must try to characterize innate structure in such a way as to meet two kinds of empirical conditions. First we must attribute to the organism, as an innate property, a structure rich enough to account for the fact that the postulated grammar is acquired on the basis of the given conditions of access to data; second, we must not attribute to the organism a structure so rich as to be incompatible with the data.

All this I find indisputable. If this is rationalism, and incompatible with Locke's empiricism, then so much the better for rationalism and so much the worse for Locke. The connection between this indisputable point about language, on the one hand, and the disagreements of seventeenth-century philosophers on the other, is a scholarly matter on which I have no interesting opinion. But what does require to be made clear is that this indisputable point about language is in no conflict with latter-day attitudes that are associated with the name of empiricism, or behaviorism.

For, whatever we may make of Locke, the behaviorist is

knowingly and cheerfully up to his neck in innate mechanisms of learning-readiness. The very reinforcement and extinction of responses, so central to behaviorism, depends on prior inequalities in the subject's qualitative spacing, so to speak, of stimulations. If the subject is rewarded for responding in a certain way to one stimulation, and punished for thus responding to another stimulation, then his responding in the same way to a third stimulation reflects an inequality in his qualitative spacing of the three stimulations; the third must resemble the first more than the second. Since each learned response presupposes some such prior inequalities, some such inequalities must be unlearned; hence innate. Innate biases and dispositions are the cornerstone of behaviorism, and have been studied by behaviorists. Chomsky mentioned some of that work himself, but still I feel I should stress the point.

This qualitative spacing of stimulations must therefore be recognized as an innate structure needed in accounting for any learning, and hence, in particular, language-learning. Unquestionably much additional innate structure is needed, too, to account for language-learning. The qualitative spacing of stimulations is as readily verifiable in other animals, after all, as in man; so the language-readiness of the human infant must depend on further endowments. It will be interesting to find out more and more, if we can, about what this additional innate structure is like and how it works. Such discoveries would illuminate not only language but learning processes generally.

It may well turn out that processes are involved that are very unlike the classical process of reinforcement and extinction of responses. This would be no refutation of behaviorism, in a philosophically significant sense of the term; for I see no interest in restricting the term "behaviorism" to a specific psychological schematism of conditioned response.

Conditioned response does retain a key role in language-learning. It is the entering wedge to any particular lexicon, for it is how we learn observation terms (or, better, simple observation sentences) by ostension. Learning by ostension is learning by simple induction, and the mechanism of such learning is

conditioning. But this method is notoriously incapable of carrying us far in language. This is why, on the translational side,
we are soon driven to what I have called analytical hypotheses.
The as yet unknown innate structures, additional to mere quality space, that are needed in language-learning, are needed
specifically to get the child over this great hump that lies beyond ostension, or induction. If Chomsky's antiempiricism or
antibehaviorism says merely that conditioning is insufficient to
explain language-learning, then the doctrine is of a piece with
my doctrine of the indeterminacy of translation.

When I dismiss a definition of behaviorism that limits it to
conditioned response, am I simply extending the term to cover
everyone? Well, I do think of it as covering all reasonable men.
What matters, as I see it, is just the insistence upon couching
all criteria in observation terms. By observation terms I mean
terms that are or can be taught by ostension, and whose application in each particular case can therefore be checked inter-
subjectively. Not to cavil over the word "behaviorism," perhaps
current usage would be best suited by referring to this orientation to observation simply as empiricism; but it is empiricism
in a distinctly modern sense, for it rejects the naïve mentalism
that typified the old empiricism. It does still condone the recourse to introspection that Chomsky has spoken in favor of,
but it condones it as a means of arriving at conjectures or conclusions only insofar as these can eventually be made sense of
in terms of external observation.

Empiricism of this modern sort, or behaviorism broadly so
called, comes of the old empiricism by a drastic externaliza-
tion. The old empiricist looked inward upon his ideas; the new
empiricist looks outward upon the social institution of language. Ideas dwindle to meanings, seen as adjuncts of words.
The old inner-directed empiricists — Hobbes, Gassendi, Locke,
and their followers — had perforce to formulate their empiricist
standard by reference to ideas; and they did so by exalting
sense impressions and scouting innate ideas. When empiricism
is externalized, on the other hand, the idea itself passes under a
cloud; talk of ideas comes to count as unsatisfactory except

insofar as it can be paraphrased into terms of dispositions to observable behavior. Externalized empiricism or behaviorism sees nothing uncongenial in the appeal to innate dispositions to overt behavior, innate readiness for language-learning. What would be interesting and valuable to find out, rather, is just what these endowments are in fact like in detail.

C

Innate Knowledge

RULON WELLS

Yale University

1. OF THE SEVERAL ISSUES, not very closely interrelated, that Professor Chomsky raises in his paper, I will concentrate on one: the question to what extent the understanding of language is innate. The fundamental point that I shall try to make is that Chomsky has not taken the requisite steps to set this question up in such a way that innateness can be a scientific, testable hypothesis. The main reason is that he doesn't sufficiently explore alternative hypotheses; and, in particular, doesn't sufficiently distinguish between those alternatives that differ in framework but that do not differ in observable consequences, and those alternatives between which a "crucial test" is possible.

To substantiate my claim I shall undertake to sketch a hypothesis alternative to Chomsky's innatism. Let me at once forestall a reply. Someone may say that precisely what Chomsky has done is to set up two alternative hypotheses — innatism (or rationalism) and empiricism; to signalize a crucial test between them; and to show that when this test is made, innatism emerges confirmed and empiricism emerges refuted. I agree that he has done this, understanding his terms in his way (I shall shortly find fault with his history); but I shall sketch a range (spectrum, family) of hypotheses that differ quite substantially from the two to which he confines his attention and between which he locates his issue. Some of these hypotheses will differ in conceptual framework from Chomsky's, but the difference will *not* be such as to admit of crucial test. In particular I want to consider hypotheses, not testably different from Chomsky's innatism, which give much less prominence to language. The general trust of Chomsky's position is to make language seem the fundamental human ability. I have criticized this position in my article "Distinctively Human Semiotic,"[1] and will continue the criticism here. The gist of my criticism is that we are not compelled to take his position; there are alternative positions, equally compatible with the facts, in which the role of language is much less prominent. Chomsky's argument for *his* position commits the fallacy of affirming the consequent in its most blatant form.

2. Perhaps surprisingly, it happens that history will be a helpful way to work into our problem. Chomsky has chosen to align himself with a series of thinkers from Descartes to Steinthal. (Reference to Steinthal is implicit in the reference to Whitney in *Current Issues*, Katz and Postal, p. 59. The passage quoted from Whitney — very objectionably distorted by disregard of context — occurs in an article of 1872 entitled "Steinthal on the Origin of Language"; in this article, Whitney criticizes Steinthal's "Humboldtian" claim that language is not *learned*, either by the individual child or by the human race.) As will duly become clear, I can best make my points by focusing on Locke for the empiricist side and, for the innatist side, those whom he criticizes and those who criticize him. I choose Locke as the spokesman for empiricism because he, above all others, takes innatism as his chief target. (The tradition of opposing empiricism to rationalism suggests an issue that I do not intend to go into: rationalism holds that not only are there innate truths, but these truths lead us to fundamental metaphysical insights that go beyond anything we can learn from experience. Rationalism may be thought of as innatism plus an added thesis, and the added thesis is of no concern here.)

3. There is throughout Locke's *Essay* a double object: ideas and cognitions. (Locke does not himself use the term 'cognitions.' As it is not standard English to speak of 'knowledges' and as I need a convenient plural to match 'ideas,' I will foist 'cognitions' on him.) We are to inquire into the origin

both of our ideas and of our cognitions. Propositions are made up of ideas, and are about the agreement or disagreement of ideas; cognitions are those propositions that we know, with certainty or with probability, to be true. There is a general principle relating ideas and cognitions: our cognitions reach no further than our ideas. A corollary, which figures prominently in Locke's critique of innatism, is that a cognition cannot be innate unless all the ideas in it are innate.

The *Essay* is, after all, an *Essay Concerning Human Understanding*. The two objects of the understanding are ideas and cognitions. Locke is only concerned to refute innatism *as regards the objects of the understanding*. Three consequences of this limitation are particularly important. (1) In his private reply of 1697 to Thomas Burnet (quoted by Fraser on p. 1.xliv of his edition, and see also 1.72n *ad* 1.2.8), he says, ". . . I never denied such a *power* to be innate, but that which I denied was that any *idea* or *connection of ideas* was innate." (2) Hume (*Inquiry Concerning Human Understanding*, §2, end, fn.) asks, "What can be meant by asserting that self-love, or resentment of injuries, or the passion between the sexes is not innate?" However, it isn't clear that these feelings, which are treated by Hume himself as passions, not as objects of the understanding, would for Locke fall under the understanding. And if they do not, the questions what it would mean to call them innate, and whether they are innate, lie outside the scope of Locke's *Essay*. (3) Some of the things considered by Chomsky to be innate are habits, patterns of response, etc. But there is a serious question whether to treat these as cognitions. The question cannot be dismissed as verbal, because if patterns of response, behavior patterns, etc. can be considered as cognitions, then automata and brutes as well as human beings have cognitions; and some of these — perhaps, for automata, all — will be innate, rather than acquired. But in that case, language as pattern of response will no longer be distinctively human, contrary to Chomsky's intention. There is also a historical consequence. Such an innateness will not be what Descartes, Humboldt, etc. were talking about; Descartes is concerned

with innate ideas, which for him are ideas innate *to the soul*.
To return to Locke: since Locke is only concerned to deny innate ideas and innate cognitions, a Lockean is not bound to
deny all innate habits. For Locke the criterion of knowledge is
consciousness (awareness). Now (to take Chomsky's example), a child might in some sense 'know' the Principle of Cyclic
Application without being aware of it, in which case it would
not fall under Locke's purview. We may say that eventually
our purview must be widened, but in making interpretative
historical remarks about Locke we should be aware of his intended scope. Moreover, when we do widen our purview we
shall be confronted with the task of relating language as pattern of response, as habit, as skill, etc. with language as object
of conscious knowledge.

Another point about Locke's scope: the understanding is
not the same as the mind, but is a part of it (2.1.5, 2.9.4).

The tradition has done a great disservice to Locke and to
accuracy by accepting the slogan that he is concerned with
ideas. He is concerned with cognitions even more than with
ideas, from the first book of the *Essay* to the last, and does not
regard them as a species of ideas — Cognition is for him a category coordinate with Idea, not subordinate to it; and this point
is particularly important because Locke is superior in this regard to Berkeley, Hume, and perhaps to most empiricists until
Russell and the logical positivists; Berkeley *plays* down the distinction, and Hume, in his account of predication and of belief,
deliberately tries to *break* it down. (Behaviorists, S-R learning
theorists, etc. have unwisely followed Hume in this matter
rather than Locke.)

4. Locke's "historical, plain method" (Intr. §2) takes as
its first inquiry (§8) how ideas come into the mind. As to why
the origins of our ideas should concern him, the immediate answer is that innatism is expressly a doctrine about the origins
of (some of) our ideas and cognitions, and Locke means to
offer an alternative to innatism. A profounder answer is that to
show the origin of something is to show whether it is genuine
or spurious. This genetic conception — that a proof of authen-

ticity is a *pedigree* — is as old as Plato; and even though Kant
(A84/B116) rejects the 'physiological' (Aix), 'noongonic'
(A271/B327) approach of the celebrated Locke by distinguishing the question *quid juris* from the question *quid facti*, still he
too demands a *Geburtsbrief,* and merely says (Aix; A86/B119)
that the one furnished by Locke was not proper.

    5. It is a "commonplace of scholarship," to use Chomsky's
phrase, that Locke in attacking innate ideas is attacking a man
of straw. As early as 1702, Henry Lee (quoted by Fraser 1.117
ad 1.3.26; cf. 92 *ad* 1.3.1) says that "in the strict sense he puts
upon the word *innate* . . . surely he has no adversary." Ham-
ilton (1846), quoted by Fraser 1.68 *ad* 1.2.4, speaks of Locke's
"pursuit of an *ignis fatuus* — . . . his refutation of the Cartesian theory of Innate Ideas, which certainly as impugned by
him neither Descartes nor the representatives of his school ever
dreamt of holding." Fraser himself (1.37 *ad* 1.1.1) says of innatism that "Locke assails it in its crudest form, in which it is
countenanced by no eminent advocate."

    All of these observers fail to observe some relevant con-
siderations.

    (1) Supposing that no one at all had ever held the doc-
trines that Locke assails, it might still have been worth while to
assail them. Often, in *Auseinandersetzung,* it proves better to
deal with an Ideal Type than with the particular doctrines of
particular people, especially where the intended ultimate targets are two or more people who differ appreciably from each
other.

    (2) Moreover, in this particular case, I suggest that
Locke meant to say that innatists *ought* to hold the crudest
form of their 'ism,' even if they don't. That is, the basic appeal
of innatism is most fully satisfied by the crudest form, which
suffers only from the difficulty of being patently false. Advocates then modify the view — patch it up, rather — to save it
from easy refutation, but at the cost of making the doctrine
pointless. No doubt this is what Locke would reply to the
modified innatism that makes various cognitions innate *as po-
tentialities.*

(3) In point of fact, some people did hold the view that Locke assailed. Whether or not we cast aspersions on these people by denying their 'eminence,' Locke had his critics; and we can see that some of these critics, at least, criticized Locke because they felt that (in effect) it was *their* views that he had criticized.

The fact that most of Locke's critics were theologians proves to be significant. We get a clue if we ponder the significance of the examples that Locke gives of alleged innate cognitions (and ideas). One gathers from these that the innatists with whom Locke was concerned derived heavy support from teleological considerations: God imprinted innate ideas and innate cognitions upon men's understandings in order to make them sufficiently provided for their moral governance. (Locke's reply is that this device ascribed to God is neither sufficient nor necessary.) If any idea is innate, surely that of God is (1.3.7, 8, 18); if there were any cognition that God deemed it wise to imprint innately, surely it would be the cognition that he is to be worshiped, and his commands obeyed. (In Herbert of Cherbury, innatism is motivated by deism: innate cognitions make revelations and churches unnecessary.) For examples drawn from the theoretical sphere, Locke cites the laws of identity and of noncontradiction (not of excluded middle, for whatever reason), which were the stock-in-trade of scholastics more than of Cartesians. It looks to me as if Locke's intended target is not eminent Cartesians, much less Descartes himself (*vide infra*), but an eclectic view with a good deal of Oxonian scholasticism in it ("perplexed with obscure terms and useless questions," Fraser 1.xix), some themes from Cambridge Platonism, and some rather generalized influence from the Cartesians. This eclectic view might lack eminent advocates, but would be widespread in England among academics and ecclesiastics.

6. Locke and Descartes. Chomsky gives the impression, especially in *Cartesian Linguistics*, that Locke's arguments against innatism were forestalled and answered by Descartes

himself. There are several reasons why such a claim cannot be admitted.

(1) In his "Notes against a program," articles 12–14 (Haldane and Ross 1.442–43), Descartes explains his purpose in classifying ideas into innate, adventitious, and 'made' (*factus*, rendered 'fictitious' by Haldane and Ross on 1.160 and 'factitious' on 1.442). Regius, against whose Program Descartes' "Notes" are directed, holds a view superficially like Locke's, and Descartes says (442; cf. 448) of this view that Regius "appears to dissent from me only in words . . . he makes an affirmation in effect identical with mine, but denies it in words." But Descartes in that very passage gives ample indication that his analysis of Regius' view, and of whether he himself differs from it, is shallow. For he states in article 13 (p. 443) that *all* ideas are innate. In the Third Meditation, where he had introduced his classification (p. 160), he had considered the possibility that all ideas are innate, and the possibility that none are; and in article 13, citing his *Dioptrics*, he reminds Regius of his doctrine that, although "nothing reaches our mind from external objects through the organs of sense beyond certain corporeal movements," the ideas of those movements do not reach the mind from external objects, but "are themselves innate in us." Innate in us, then, means innate in souls; Descartes' view of innateness is embedded in the context of his view about soul and body and their interaction. Descartes expressly states, in the context of his interactionism, something that Locke said no one would be so extravagant as to state, namely that "so much the more must the ideas of pain, color, sound and the like be innate" — those ideas which Boyle called secondary qualities, and which Locke regarded as among the simple ideas that are first furnished by the senses.

I may say parenthetically that the doctrine of article 13 that all ideas are innate differs appreciably from his doctrine of 1641. Then, especially in his reply (Haldane and Ross 2.204–33) to Gassendi's Objections, he viewed some ideas as innate but others as adventitious. "Mind can act independently of the brain; for certainly the brain can be of no use in pure thought; its only use is for imagining and perceiving" (2.212). And (213) Gassendi is wrong in thinking that to see one must use one's eyes; ". . . I did not then deal with the sight and touch which are effected by means of organs, but solely with the thought of seeing and touching; and that this does not imply the use of these organs is testified to us every recurring night in dreams." I am unable to tell whether the discrepancy between his replies to Gassendi and to Regius is the result of a sweeping, inadvertent exaggeration in the latter reply, or of a genuine change of view; but a change of view would not be surprising, since the question of exactly describing the action of body on mind is involved, a question about which Descartes never did reach a satisfactory and settled doctrine.

The view expressed to Regius is a step away from his 1641 view and toward the view of Leibniz that the monads have no windows. (Locke, 2.11.17, allows two windows: sensation and reflection.) Still, it is not the same as Leibniz's view, because although it does not allow any *ideas* to reach our mind from external objects, still it does allow something to reach it, namely, "certain corporeal movements." In other words, Descartes does still teach interaction. But the phrasing of the end of article 13 shows that his reason for denying that ideas reach our mind is the same as Leibniz's for denying windows, namely the heterogeneity of body and mind. As Leibniz puts it, influx of an accident from one substance to another is unintelligible.

(2) There is a second matter on which Descartes might be thought to have forestalled Locke. Leibniz, controverting Locke's view that the senses are the ultimate source of all our ideas, offers (*New Essays*, 38, 42, 70; cf. 79) as an alternative account that the senses give occasion to the soul to draw ideas from its own depths. But Leibniz doesn't tell us what difference he sees between the senses' being the source of ideas and being the occasion of them. But though Leibniz doesn't tell us, Descartes does. In the fourteenth article of his reply to Regius, he distinguishes occasion from cause. In this article he also

very lucidly shows how ideas may be in the soul potentially (and so might be thought to have given a less crude form of innatism than what Locke assails), but it goes beyond the doctrine of potential presence when he introduces this distinction between, as he puts it, "remote and accidental causes" and "proximate and primary causes." A would-be reviver of Descartes' innatism needs to reckon with this distinction, and consider whether it can be adapted into something that would be found acceptable today. Locke, like Descartes, saw the possibility of there being hypotheses that differed only verbally from his own, and considered that innatism which makes innate ideas present in the soul potentially to be such a hypothesis; if, however, with Descartes, we add to innatism the distinction of occasion from cause, and hold that the senses (or the sense organs?) are occasions, but never causes, we get a doctrine whose difference from Locke's is not merely verbal. It doesn't follow, though, that now the difference has become testable, for the distinction between occasion and cause may not be one that empirical science can handle. Descartes illustrates it with a commonsense example, and operating at the commonsense level we can make use of it in saying that, for instance, a friend's visit to my city is only the occasion, not the cause, of my going to the museum. I may have intended to go to the museum sooner or later, and was merely waiting for a convenient time, or an appropriate occasion; and it *was* only an occasion if (a) other incidents would, equally well, have served as occasions, and (b) furthermore, none of these possible occasions, taken singly or taken collectively, was necessary. I could have gone to the museum without any occasion.

But empirical science is interested not in *could have* but in *would have;* in Wilfrid Sellars' terms ("Aristotelian Philosophies of Mind," in *Philosophy for the Future,* ed. R. W. Sellars et al., 1949, p. 545), it is interested not in capacities but in dispositional properties. Now Descartes' treatment of interaction is not on a par with his treatment of causation between bodies; in body-body causation, he deals with dispositions, but in body-mind causation he merely deals with capacities. A distinction between causes and occasions can be fundamental, within a capacity-framework, but it can only be a minor difference of detail within a disposition-framework. Common sense retains it because common sense works with capacities more than with dispositions.

The general conclusion to be drawn about Descartes' innatism is this: it is thoroughly entwined with his interactionism; it is a strand that has to be unraveled and unsnarled, and cannot be simply lifted out of the body of his philosophy, and does not furnish any ammunition against empiricists.

7. To speak of "innatism" and of "empiricism" could foster the impression that each of these is a monolithic doctrine. In an effort to foster the opposite impression, I shall speak of the innatism-family and the empiricism-family, or of innatisms and of empiricisms in the plural. Locke himself does not do this, and it is a task of some magnitude to formulate various innatisms that Locke takes account of and to organize them into a family.

I find it illuminating to make a distinction between the meaning of an innatism and the arguments for it. The meaning or sense is given by the metaphor that God stamped, imprinted, engraved characters on the understanding at its inception; whatever we make of this meaning, the arguments that Locke considers may be put into two main classes: teleological and evidential. The teleological argument is that God did this as part of his way of equipping human beings for their purpose in life. The evidential arguments in effect treat innatism (in whatever sense) as a hypothesis with various observable consequences; each consequence that is observed to be a fact is then regarded as an argument for innatism.

Locke's counterarguments can be classified in the same way. His teleological argument agrees about the purpose of human life, but argues that God would have achieved this purpose otherwise than by innate ideas and cognitions. His evidential arguments may be subdivided. (a) In some cases, he argues against innatism that it has observed consequences that are contrary to observed fact. It is chiefly 'crude' innatism against which he presses this argument. (b) In some cases, he argues against an innatism whose consequences agree with observed fact that there is an alternative hypothesis — his own empiricism — which agrees equally well with observed fact. Here the question arises whether there is any other than a verbal difference between this innatism and his empiricism. Descartes, Locke, and Leibniz all consider the possibility of merely verbal differences, but none of them does more than merely toss out this suggestion offhand, without any serious effort to develop it. Actually, careful scrutiny will show that in none of the three cited instances where this suggestion is made could it be sustained. I have already discussed the instance from Descartes. When Locke makes the suggestion (1.1.5), he makes it about a version of innatism (". . . Truths may be imprinted on the mind which it never did, nor ever shall know . . . All the truths a man ever comes to know will, by this account, be every one of them innate") that is conceivable, but so implausible that no one holds it; what actual innatists hold is that *some* truths are innate but not all. But these actual innatists are neither able to give a rationale for distinguishing the innate truths from the others, nor to give a sense to 'innate in the understanding' that is free from self-contradiction. We may conclude that Locke does not suggest that any actually held innatism differs only verbally from his empiricism. As for Leibniz, to turn to the third case, he suggests (p. 45; cf. p. 47) that "perhaps our clever author will not wholly differ from my view. For . . . he admits that ideas which do not originate in sensation come from reflection," and (p. 111, *ad* 2.1.2), proposing to modify the scholastic *Nihil est in intellectu, quod non fuerit in sensu* by adding *nisi ipse intellectus,* he comments: "This view sufficiently agrees with your author of the Essay." But the reason given is that Locke "seeks the source of a good part of ideas in the spirit's reflection upon its own nature." In point of fact this is an inaccurate representation of Locke's views; elsewhere (pp. 23–24) we find Leibniz recognizing that his conception of reflection differs from Locke's on just this point: "Reflection is not limited to the operations alone of the mind, as is stated (1.1.4 [and many other places]); it reaches even to the mind itself . . ." So, the merely verbal difference between Locke and Leibniz comes to this, that if Locke's doctrines be modified in the direction of Leibniz's, he somewhat resembles Leibniz. Elsewhere (p. 71), Leibniz, citing his disagreement with Locke about the distinction between necessary truths and truths of fact (cf. p. 38) says "the sequel will show which of us is right," which could not happen if their difference were only verbal; and a number of times (pp. 15, 38, 42) he says, aptly, that the difference between his account and Locke's is rather like the difference between Plato's and Aristotle's. Further on, a genuine crucial test is found. In response to Molyneux's query, could the bornblind, his sight restored, distinguish by sight a cube from a sphere? Locke (2.9.8) answers No; Leibniz (p. 139) answers Yes. Thus we see that there are a number of substantive differences between Locke and Leibniz, in addition to differences in their frameworks (to which Leibniz doesn't do justice, owing to his chosen point-by-point order of discussion). The suggestion, therefore, that Locke's view is only verbally different from Leibniz's must be modified first by weakening the alleged real identity to a mere real resemblance, and second by restricting it not to their total views, but only to their views on reflection.

8. Locke is clear, though brief, on the point that innatism is unnecessary, but he doesn't say as much as he could have about why his alternative is preferable. But hovering in the background, though never in focus, there seems to be an appeal to some sort of simplicity. I believe it is relevant here to cite two considerations that Locke several times urges. One is that either all ideas and cognitions are innate or none are, since no rationale can be found for dividing those that are from those that are not. The other is his purport to describe his own experience, coupled with an appeal to his readers to observe theirs and compare it with his. The first consideration though not an argument from simplicity would, in conjunction with the simplicity-ideal, yield the argument that it is simpler if all ideas and cognitions are innate, or none are, than if some are

and some are not. The second consideration is an appeal to a *vera causa*. Locke neither uses the phrase "true cause" nor cites Newton, whom we think of as the originator of the concept of the true cause (in his Rule I of Reasoning, where he also says that "Nature affects not the pomp of superfluous causes"); but when Locke says, in his second consideration, that some at least of our ideas and cognitions have their origin in experience, this is not significantly different from saying that for some at least of our ideas and cognitions, experience is a true cause.

These two considerations, as restated by me, now join to yield an argument that is in the background though not the focus of Locke's view. This argument is that empiricism is doubly simpler than any innatism: it employs only one cause, not two causes, of all our ideas and cognitions; and the one cause that it employs is a 'true' cause, i.e., an observable one. One may counterattack this argument; but all I wish to do here is to show how close it is to Locke's explicit argumentation. This is part of my effort to show that Locke has much more cogency — much more of a 'case,' in a quasi-legal sense, than he is commonly given credit for.

9. The immediate purpose of my excursion into history is to become clear about what the issues were. With this question answered, and not until then, we can face the question whether those issues are sufficiently like issues before us today so that, by the comparison, and with a knowledge of how those issues were resolved in the seventeenth and eighteenth centuries, we can save ourselves the trouble of reliving the whole episode. I have been laboring the point that the doctrines of Descartes, of Locke, of Leibniz, etc., are not neat bundles of easily detachable strands, but snarls, or perhaps woven fabrics, in which no one strand can be detached without simultaneous attention to the other strands. It follows that we cannot significantly consider an issue between, say, Locke and Leibniz in abstraction from other issues and from points of agreement between them. Yet this is just what Chomsky has done in his search for historical antecedents, siding for example with Des-

cartes while paying no attention to the ensnarlment of his innatism with his dualism, and thus prepared to relieve Descartes of doctrines that he (Chomsky) considers outmoded, while not prepared to extend the same kind of selective treatment to Locke.

10. I would like to call attention to the important contributions of Thomas Henry Huxley. In two papers of 1870 and 1874 (reprinted as chapters 4 and 5 of his *Collected Essays,* Vol. I.: *Method and Results*) and in his book *Hume* (1878; reprinted as *C. E.*, Vol. VI) he discusses Descartes' views on innatism, the mind-body dualism, the conception of brutes (and of human beings?) as conscious automata, etc. In particular, his discussion (*C. E.* 6.98ff.) of Descartes' reply to Regius is notable; he (p. 100) poses the question, "if all the contents of the mind are innate, what is meant by experience?," and goes on to answer; even when he falls into the vulgar error of judging Locke's critique of innatism to be misdirected, his wording is circumspect (101–02): ". . . *Viewed in relation to the passages just cited* [my italics — RW], the arguments adduced in his famous polemic against innate ideas are totally irrelevant." The question is, whether, in historical fact, Locke's arguments are to be viewed in that relation, i.e., as directed against Descartes.

11. I have been at pains to bring out how close Locke is to presenting us with a consistent, coherent (though complex) hypothesis. I am not able here to give details, but as I interpret his hypothesis its main testable difference from the hypothesis of Leibniz — so far as Leibniz's account of 'occasions' is given a testable formulation — concerns the order in which various ideas and cognitions are acquired. For instance, Locke's doctrine of reflection is not simply different in words from Leibniz's innatism; not only for the reason already mentioned, that Locke postulates reflection only upon the operations of the mind, but also for another reason that is a consequence of the first: reflection must begin in an individual human mind chronologically later than sensation begins, because the operations that are reflected upon are operations upon sensations.

Locke's hypothesis postulates (a) a number of powers of the human mind (to call them innate powers would be harmless, except that it is redundant), each power operating under specified conditions; and (b) various laws relating these various powers. It is because the conditions under which each power operates are specified that these powers count as the stronger dispositions, rather than as the weaker capacities, distinguished by Wilfrid Sellars; and it is because of the laws relating the powers that it is not trivial or tautological to postulate these powers. Here lies the chief difference between Locke and not only Leibniz but also Descartes. Where Descartes tends to stress the generic resemblance between all the operations of the human mind that he recognizes, and in dealing with innate ideas is content to say that (potentially, at least) the soul thinks them, Locke's tendency is to stress the specific differences, and, with each idea or cognition, to specify the kind of thought by which it is thought.

Leibniz finds an opportunity (*New Essays*, end of Preface, pp. 54–63) to twit Locke with his change of mind about action at a distance, and his admission of Newtonian gravitation even though he cannot conceive it. Gravitation, says Leibniz, is an occult, not a proper power, and bodies' attracting each other by it is "as if watches marked the hours by a certain horodictic faculty without needing wheels, or as if mills ground the grain by a fractive faculty without needing anything resembling millstones." If this was a reasonable demand in physics, it would seem a reasonable demand in psychics too, and Locke with his detailed mechanism of ideation and cognition did a much better job than Leibniz at supplying wheels to supplement the horodictic faculty.

Locke's hypothesis is very vague by present-day standards, but the laws that he postulates, though vague, are clear in outline. They are laws of chronological succession. One such law, already mentioned, is that reflection comes after sensation. Another law is gradualism: again and again Locke stresses that this or that operation gets exercised, and the corresponding power cultivated, little by little. Two more laws are that the power of forming general (*alias* abstract) ideas comes after the power of forming particular (concrete) ones, and that the power of forming abstract ideas comes after the power of reasoning. (As a sort of analogue or parallel to this last law, Locke holds that what distinguishes man from all brutes is not the power of reasoning but the power of abstraction.)

Laws relating powers can be distinguished, at least in a rough and ready way, from conditions under which powers operate. For instance, in addition to various chronological laws, abstraction is subject to the conditions that attention and effort are required. It is not clear whether in Locke's hypothesis there is any compensatory relation between conditions and laws; whether, in the present instance, extra attention and effort can ever make up for lack of experience; but it seems clear that in his view compensation, if there is any, has its limits; a certain minimum of experience is a sine qua non for whose deficit no attention and effort can compensate. It is one of the vaguenesses of Locke's hypothesis that nothing is said about this.

Many other ways in which the hypothesis is insufficient can be cited, but I have said enough to be ready to turn to a main point. Locke is willing to make various mental powers innate, but not any objects (ideas or cognitions), whereas Cartesianism, Leibnizianism, and the eclectic innatism that Locke considers are more than willing to ascribe innateness to various objects. Now what sort of difference is this? Shall we consider it a merely verbal difference? Or shall we consider it a difference in frameworks, meaning thereby something different from a merely verbal difference? In part we cannot answer these questions until the hypotheses we are discussing — especially the innatist ones — be made more precise by being revamped from a framework of capacities to a framework of dispositions. In part, crucial tests can be thought of (as conceivabilities, even if they are not feasible). In allusion to the earliest recorded instance of such tests (Herodotus 2.2), I will call these Psammetichus-experiments.

12. Let us now turn to some modern hypotheses about the

origin of ideas and cognitions, and let us with Professor Chomsky limit our attention and discussion to language. What are the problems about language-learning?

I propose to use 'learn' in the broad sense of 'come to know.' The Greeks had two words for 'learn' where we have one, the differentia being *mathein* 'being taught' required a teacher, whereas *heurein* 'finding out' did not. The issue between Steinthal and Whitney, alluded to in Section 2, is verbal to the extent that for Steinthal learning requires a teacher, in other words he construes 'learning' in the narrow sense of 'being taught.' It is then not too implausible to say that ordinarily human beings do not *learn* their mother tongue. But it would involve equivocation if we argued from 'not learned' in the narrow sense of 'learn' to 'innate'; it is only from 'not learned' in the broad sense that the argument holds.

It is unfortunate that ordinary usage permits us to speak of knowing a language, and to say that a hearer understands a language. Russell has pointed out the advantage of considering that fundamentally all knowledge is knowledge of propositions; if we want to put that insight at the service of our discussion of language we must show how to construe knowing a language as knowing that such and such propositions about the language are true.

But as soon as we speak of 'knowing that,' we are reminded of Ryle's distinction between knowing-that and knowing-how. Let us, at least for a while, assume that this is a proper and profound distinction, and consider its bearing on language.

Knowledge of a language may be a complex in which some ingredients are aptly described as knowings-that, others as knowings-how. A great deal would naturally be placed in the latter category, for instance S's (i.e., the speaker's) knowledge of how to make the several sounds. But also a great deal would be placed in the former, for instance H's (the hearer's) knowledge that U (the heard utterance), considered as sound, has such and such a meaning.

Chomsky has stressed the conception of a language as a

set of rules. How may this conception be integrated with the distinction between knowing-how and knowing-that?

I will quote a passage from his paper in this volume, and a passage from his Appendix to Eric Lenneberg's *Biological Foundations of Language* (1967). In the present volume he says, "The grammar that underlies the formation of percepts is a second-order construct. To study it, we must abstract away from the other factors that are involved in the use and understanding of language, and concentrate on the knowledge of language that has been internalized in some manner by the language user." In his Appendix to Lenneberg, he says (p. 415): "How does a person learn the principle of cyclic application? . . . Why assume that the principle is learned at all? . . . The most reasonable conclusion seems to be that the principle is not learned at all, but rather that it is simply part of the conceptual equipment that the learner brings to the task of language acquisition . . . There should be nothing surprising in such a conclusion. There would be no difficulty, in principle, in designing an automaton which incorporates the principles of universal grammar and puts them to use to determine which of the possible languages is the one to which it is exposed."

By juxtaposing these two passages and making certain tentative but reasonable assumptions I seem to be able to extract some notable consequences. Internalization (in the first passage) I assume to be the same as incorporation (in the second). The second passage treats innateness as the contradictory or complementary property of being learned. Moreover, it makes a certain innate power of human beings unsurprising by showing how a certain analogous (or intensionally stronger) property might be incorporated in an automaton. This prompts me to supply the tacit premiss (which I intend to treat as terminological and unobjectionable) that a power or other property incorporated in an automaton may be said to be incorporated in it, i.e., internalized in it. The juxtaposition of the two passages suggests that in human beings what is internalized is innate, and vice versa; and putting all these conclusions together I gather that Chomsky does not intend to make any significant distinction, either in human beings or in automata, between 'internalized,' 'incorporated,' and 'innate.' I presume that it would be the same with brute (i.e., nonhuman) animals.

But this is a notable consequence, because elsewhere (in the present volume and many other places) Chomsky has made it clear that the only kind of learning he recognizes is learning *by induction*. Perhaps this is to be explained historically by his involvement with behaviorists and S-R psychologists, some (most? all?) of whom treat induction as the main mode of learning and furthermore assimilate induction to trial-and-error learning. In any case, it follows that what Chomsky deems innate would not all be deemed innate by Locke, who, by characterizing learning simply as coming to know, is prepared to admit other modes of learning besides induction. So, contrary to what Chomsky seems to think, a factual issue has not yet developed between himself and such a representative empiricist as Locke.

Further notable consequences follow. We gain light on what internalization or incorporation means from the knowledge that universal grammar can be incorporated in an automaton. The automaton is finite (whether or not it is of the special sort called a finite-state automaton), but the grammar is infinite in that it generates an infinite corpus. The way in which this finitude and this infinity are reconciled is a limitation imposed *ab extra* on the grammar; e.g., a maximum length to its terminal strings. According to this canonical form, the description of the rule-set followed by the automaton has two parts: (1) the abstract description of the rule-set proper, which, in the mathematical sense, generates an infinite corpus; and (2) the additional rule that limits the maximum length, or that in some other way cuts back the infinite corpus to a finite corpus that the automaton can produce.

Here we encounter an ambiguity in the word "can" (or "could") that is of the greatest moment. If we say that the automaton *can* produce an infinite corpus, we mean — that is, the only ground that we are entitled to urge — that the first part of its rule-set generates an infinite corpus. If we say that the automaton *cannot* produce an infinite corpus, we mean that its entire rule-set — parts one and two taken together — generates only a finite corpus. Thus when the two senses of "can," or, if one prefers, the two grounds for predicating "can produce an infinite corpus" of the automaton, are distinguished, it is seen that there is no contradiction between saying that the automaton can produce an infinite corpus and that it cannot.

Now, if we say that the entire rule-set is incorporated in, internalized in, innate to the automaton, it is natural to say also that every part of the rule-set is incorporated; and, in particular, to say that part one is incorporated. And from there it is a small and seemingly unobjectionable step to saying that the automaton has within it an infinite power. This is alright, *so long as* we are not misled; which is to say, so long as we don't forget that part two is also incorporated in the automaton.

As far as I know, Chomsky has never said that an automaton has within it an infinite power. On the contrary, he has — in *Current Issues,* in *Cartesian Linguistics,* and elsewhere — given the impression that the difference between automaton and brute, on the one hand, and man on the other, is just the difference between finite and infinite power. And what I have undertaken to do is to refute him out of his own mouth; to show how, according to his own account of internalization, an automaton (and presumably a brute) can be regarded as incorporating an infinite power, and how, to finish the picture, a human being, equally with an automaton and a brute, will have a 'part two' that imposes a finitude limitation. The capacity of man may be ever so much greater than the capacity of automaton or of brute; but the difference will be the difference between one finite magnitude and another, which is the kind of difference that we call a difference of degree, and not a difference of kind. Descartes may have been a good guide when he proposed to find in the power of speech one of the criteria for distinguishing man from automaton and from brute; but he was a poor guide when he alleged as his reason the "infinite variety" of speech.

NOTES

1. Rulon Wells, "Distinctively Human Semiotic," *Social Science Information* (*Information sur les Sciences Sociales*), VI, 6 (December 1967), 103–24.

1

On the Alleged Uniqueness of Language

REUBEN ABEL

The New School

THE CRUX of Professor Chomsky's position is that man's linguistic competence is *sui generis;* it thus presents a problem for scientific explanation. An infant apparently does not learn, and an adult can seldom state, the deep structural principles of the universal "generative grammar" that must be postulated in order to account for our ability to use language as we do. Human speech is creative and diverse, unlike animal communication, in which there is a rigorous functional relation between specific stimuli and specific responses. Knowledge of the "generative grammar" must therefore be innate in human beings. Chomsky has written approvingly (*Cartesian Linguistics,* pp. 20, 29) that

> the fundamental property of a language must be its capacity to use its finitely specifiable mechanisms for an unbounded and unpredictable set of contingencies . . .

> human language, in its normal use, is free from the control of independently identifiable external stimuli or internal states and is not restricted to any practical communicative function, in contrast, for example, to the pseudo-language of animals . . . This virtual identification of linguistic and mental processes . . .

And in this symposium he asserts that

> there is no reason why we should not suppose that the child is born with a perfect knowledge of universal grammar, that

is, with a fixed schematism that he uses . . . in acquiring language.

A seductive thesis, this! Do we dare to succumb to it? It boldly answers the great question, what is man?; and it simultaneously solves a host of satellite problems. But some of us will be wary: we have already been burned by phlogiston, put to sleep by the ether, overheated by caloric, submerged in the collective unconscious, and transported by an *élan locomotif*.

For Chomsky's "explanation" is suspiciously *ad hoc*. Language is not in fact unique in the spectrum of human capacities. Consider, for example, the enormous gamut of nonverbal social intercourse. This ranges from religious ritual, and etiquette at a formal banquet, to how you behave in a subway crowd, and in a museum, and when ignoring strangers on the street. The thousands of persons with whom you interact (few of them ever seen by you before, few to be encountered again); the diverse interpersonal situations (potentially infinite in number, seldom if ever reexperienced) — is not this intricate state of affairs isomorphic with that of linguistic behavior? The contingencies are novel, unbounded, and unpredictable; the "rules" are (presumably) finite and recursive; your unreflective awareness of appropriate conduct in new social contexts is formally identical with your intuitive sense of grammatical usage. Or consider what is involved in driving a car through traffic. The rules may be learned in an hour, and they suffice to guide us through a potentially infinite number of different situations. Or consider the playing of a game such as football. Shall we postulate an array of "innate schematisms" to "explain" these abilities?

No; Chomsky's solution is too facile. Linguistic competence is not unique, but is continuous with other human capacities. Let us not so readily abandon Occam's razor.

2

Semantical Vehicles, Understanding, and Innate Ideas

ARTHUR DANTO

Columbia University

ALTHOUGH mastery of the formation and comprehension of sentences is the touchstone of linguistic competence, I shall consider sentences as but one type of *semantical vehicle*. Philosophically prominent types of semantical vehicles have been, in addition to sentences (or propositions), terms, concepts, pictures, names, and, as I propose to show, *ideas*. A semantical vehicle is any entity that bears a *descriptive meaning*. The descriptive meaning of a sentence s is given by a rule that specifies those conditions under which s is true; but again, I am concerned here with semantical vehicles in the most general way, and I shall regard "true" as but one of a class of *positive semantical values*. A concept has a positive semantical value when it is instantiated, a name when it has a bearer, a picture when it has an original that it 'truly' depicts, etc. In general, we may schematize the rule of descriptive meaning for semantical vehicles with the following, in which v is any semantical vehicle, $(+)$ the semantical value appropriate to vehicles of the type that v exemplifies, and where $/k/$ is the set of conditions under which v in fact bears $(+)$:

R: $v(+)$ if and only if $/k/$.

Here R is a *rule of descriptive meaning* for v, giving truth conditions for v when v is a sentence, existence (or instantiation) conditions for v when v is a concept (or term), and so forth.[1]

Obviously, v bears the *negative* semantical value ($-$) when /k/ fails.

It is important that we note that R does not *require* v to bear ($+$) in an absolute way, but only on condition that /k/ holds, so a sentence (for example) has the same descriptive meaning whether true or false. For the typical sentence s, since descriptive meaning is invariant as regards any difference in semantical value borne by s, a man may normally *understand s* without *knowing* that s. I assume the standard epistemological truism that the truth of s is entailed by its being the case that someone *knows* that s. Accordingly, understanding does not entail knowledge, as meaning does not entail truth. I note parenthetically that the tradition in epistemology has been forged by the apparently unslaked hope that some semantical vehicles may be found, the understanding of which *does* entail knowledge, so that, if one is master of the Rule of descriptive meaning for such a semantical vehicle v, one cannot pretend at once to understand v and to doubt that, or whether, v bears the ($+$) semantical value. The stock example of such a quest for certainty (as I term these) is the Ontological Argument of Anselm, but God is not the only concept understanding of which is to bring knowledge and banish doubt: there is also the analytical judgment, the adequate idea of Spinoza, the logically proper name of Russell, the Paradigm Case, etc. In each of these candidates for a successful quest for certainty, we are dealing with a semantical vehicle whose positive semantical value is allegedly enforced by its own rule of descriptive meaning.

It may be seen, against the background of these preambular remarks, that *ideas,* in the philosophical tradition of the seventeenth and eighteenth century, have a great deal more in common with such conspicuously linguistic entities as names, sentences, and terms than would be suggested by the dominantly psychological terms in which they have been discussed. Briefly, we may induce upon ideas a structure of descriptive meaning under which they exhibit their status as semantical vehicles, bearing positive or negative semantical values depending upon whether their "truth conditions" hold or not. And indeed, this gives rise directly to the Problem of the External World, which we largely owe to Descartes, who in effect observed that in the typical case, he could understand his ideas readily, all the while in complete ignorance of whether they bore, any of them, the appropriate positive semantical value through successful satisfaction of a relation with correspondentia. Descartes' — and Locke's — notorious Representationalism describes a structure that we all more or less cheerfully accept in connection with sentences, or with *bona fide* linguistic units: we are all disposed to *linguistic* representationalism, which holds that whether or not a sentence (with fixed meaning) is true depends upon factors external to the sentence, viz., upon the *world* when the sentence is about the world. Typically, no amount of examination of the sentence as such will tell you whether it is true or false: you cannot, by mere internal criteria, separate sentences into two heaps, the true ones and the false ones, the way, by internal criteria, you could separate the three-word sentences from the rest. Well, Descartes held nothing different regarding ideas: no mere examination of their structured surfaces enabled one, by internal marks, to identify the true ones: as he said, ideas, just as such, are neither true nor false. No mere inference will carry me from a structural examination of the idea i to i ($+$) unless — and the move is inevitable — there is to be recourse to ontological argumentation.

That ideas have descriptive meaning may be seen from their intentionality: we speak of ideas *of x,* just as we speak of pictures *of,* descriptions *of,* or sentences *about x.* It is to be appreciated that "of x" — like "about x" — is an absolute property of an idea, *not* an external relation between an idea and its correspondant — for then we should have no ideas of unicorns, inasmuch as the relation in that case would collapse for want of a term. Understanding an idea is understanding what it is an idea *of,* which is given by the rule of descriptive meaning for that idea. But when it is according to such a rule, an idea-of-x, it does not follow that it must bear the ($+$) semantical

value appropriate to ideas. That is not up to understanding to
say. One has to know whether the (+) conditions for the idea-
of-x are satisfied: and this presents quandaries when, as with
Descartes, and certainly with Locke, what we know are our
ideas alone. It then becomes agonizing how we can pretend to
more than understanding, and skepticism takes its dismal rise.
But my concern here is less with the quandaries our masters
were led into with their theories of ideas than I am with the
fact that whatever else they may have been, ideas were, in
their systems, semantical vehicles, with positive semantical values (so they hoped at least in some cases), and so units of understanding that were also, hopefully, units of knowledge. It
does not immediately matter that those writers were not clear
as to which sorts of semantical vehicles ideas most resembled.
Descartes seems to have regarded them as protosentences, inasmuch as they could be true or false when asserted, and inasmuch as they appeared to be subject to what we today think of
as propositional attitudes: *"comme, lorsque je veux, que je
crains, que j'affirme ou que je nie, je conçois bien alors quelque
chose comme le sujet de l'action de mon esprit, mais j'ajoute
aussi quelque autre chose par cette action à l'idée que j'ai de
cette chose la."* [2] I cannot affirm or deny a *term.* Locke, on the
other hand, seems largely to have taken *terms* as the semantical model for his ideas. But in fact, in most of the writers in
this tradition, ideas fell into various semantical groupings.

I am stressing that in this tradition, ideas *have* descriptive
meaning, and that they *are* not meanings. Locke is often
charged with holding a theory of meaning that, in my terms, is
such that, if *v* in R is a *term,* then /k/ has reference to ideas,
these allegedly being 'the meaning' of *v.* Philosophical reputa-
tions have grown fat upon criticism of the seemingly preposterous theory of meaning set out in Book III of Locke's *Essay,*
where Locke famously proposes that words stand for ideas in
the mind of him that uses them. This sounds as though it
madly suggests that "Fido" stands not for the faithful dog
Fido, but for the fond idea-of-Fido in Fido's master's mind.
Locke of course did think of words as means for communicat-

ing ideas, and hence as 'signs' for them; and this has been taken to guarantee the public unintelligibility of words, inasmuch as their meanings (=ideas) are inaccessible to all save their unique owners. Words ought then to collapse into mere noises, but as they do not, and as ideas remain private, Locke's theory is demolished. But in fact it is possible to salvage Locke's theory by a natural and, so far as I can tell, intended interpretation of the operative word "stands for." The word "dog" does not stand for, does not "signify" the *idea*-of-dog, in the way in which the latter signifies, or stands for, actual dogs, as it must, on the Representationalist theory, in case the idea of dogs has some correspondant in the external world. Rather, it stands for or signifies the latter in exactly the way the *written* word *dog* stands for or signifies the *spoken* word *dog*. But the spoken word, and the written word, and, finally, the *idea* stand for actual dogs when the standard referential conditions hold. In other words, the written, the spoken, and the ideative vehicle indifferently refer to the same thing: the *Sinn* and the *Bedeutung* here are the same, indifferently as to the medium we are concerned with, viz., indifferent as to whether the medium is written, or spoken, or ideative. In this regard, then, Locke's expression "stands for" concerns the connection between semantical vehicles in different media — spoken, graphic, or ideative — *which have the same descriptive meaning.* Just as, questions of *Farbung* to one side, we may write whatever we can say, and vice versa, so may we *think* whatever we either may say or may write. It happens that we have three (at least) media in which to operate. Such a view is already in Aristotle, who writes: "Spoken words are the symbols of mental experience, and written words are the symbols of spoken words." [3] Had we only the first conjunct, we would have an anticipation not of Locke, but of the vulgarization of Locke his critics have foisted on us: but as the second "are the symbols of" hold between written and spoken words, the connection is inter-medial in both cases, and so I suggest it to be in Locke when one reads him sympathetically. Ideas, so far as concerns their meaning, are intelligible in conformity with just the same rules of descriptive meaning as the counterparts in other media, and the mere fact that they should occur in a private medium entails nothing whatever so far as concerns privacy of meaning. The meaning is public, even if the vehicle should be private. Its privacy no more affects its meaning than its ephemerality affects the meaning of a spoken rather than a written word. Indeed, with the slightest extension of ingenuity, we can get a likely theory of thinking from these notions. Just as we do not have to speak when we write — we do not have at once to *say* the words we *inscribe* — so we do not need to *say* the words that we think. Thinking is mental saying, as saying is auditory writing. We thus are able to answer both yes and no to the ancient question whether we must think in words. In one sense, yes, for ideas are but the translations into the mental medium of words in the graphic or spoken media. But then no, if this be thought to mean that thinking is just silent speaking of words, when words are appreciated as graphic or verbal events. For just as the *spoken* "dog" *in no way* resembles the written "dog," neither does the ideative "dog" have to resemble either of these in order to satisfy the same rule of descriptive meaning that renders them counterparts having the *same* meaning, albeit in different media. The laws of thinking then are but the laws of speaking, viz., grammar; and psychology and linguistics differ solely as to the media of their objects, so far at least as the latter concerns semantics, and the former concerns thinking.

I shall not here endeavor to defend the theory of ideas, although I believe some such theory is defensible,[4] but to point out that in the tradition in which they figure centrally, ideas are not mental accompaniments of language, but *are* language, standing to the world in just the relationships in which language does when it is used descriptively. Accordingly, if some special mental accompaniment *is* required in order to explain linguistic capacities, this mental accompaniment would have equally to be invoked in accounting for our competence with ideas. Whatever is psychologically necessary for explaining our competence with written or spoken language is indifferently required in connection with ideative language. I make a special point of this because a good many philosophers are uncomfortable with references to the inner states of men, and have thought that our understanding of linguistic processes has waxed as we have moved from covert mental to overt linguistic performances. But this progress, if that is what it is, is misdescribed insofar as it is regarded a move from ideas to language: for once again, ideas *are* semantical vehicles, subject to all the same rules and restrictions, and so it is a move from language in one medium to language in another. Remembering that ideas are not invoked to explain linguistic competence, since the same mechanisms would have now to be invoked in order to explain ideative competence, we may perhaps begin to achieve some purchase on the contest over innate ideas, which has recently been resuscitated through the speculations of Noam Chomsky.[5]

.   .   .

Roughly speaking, Chomsky's view is this. The known facts regarding linguistic competence are such that we cannot account for it in its entirety as due to learning. He does not deny that some portion of this skill is learned, but he does suppose that if we subtract this portion from the entire phenomenon of linguistic performance, we are left with a considerable residue which is *innate* at least in the sense that it is *unlearned*. Obviously, the move from *unlearned* to *innate* is abrupt, inasmuch as learning is but one avenue of acquisition, viz., if we could take Spanish pills and thereafter converse as *hidalgos*, we should have been caused (adventitiously) to be masters of Spanish without having learned the language. Whatever the case, Chomsky has in mind what one might regard as an inductive learning theory, viz., we acquire fragments of language in specific learning situations, and produce these fragments as responses to stimuli — a procedure radically discrepant, as he sees it, with the endless linguistic creativity we all manifest, producing apt sentences under situations never before faced, and understanding sentences we never learned at all. Language cannot be learned a sentence at a time, and un-less learning theory is radically modified in such a way that the production and comprehension of novel sentences *can* be re-garded as learned, we have no recourse but to what Chomsky refers to as innateness.

Defenders of inductive learning theory, such as Quine,[6] have been at pains to tender irenic gestures on the topic of in-nateness, holding that they, too, after all hold to some such no-tion. Learners are not mere passive respondents to stimuli: they come to the task with certain antecedent predispositions. Operant behavior, in Skinner's theory, is by no means learned: we come into the learning situation *with* operant behavior, and learning consists chiefly in the latter's modification: and so learning theory itself is committed to a doctrine of innateness, in case we equate being innate with being unlearned. We do not learn what Quine speaks of as "language-readiness"; and in this conciliatory vein, Quine hopes to capture what he is will-ing to grant as innateness without having to grant what he re-gards as philosophically reprehensible, namely, mentalism. It is not *innateness* so much as *ideas* that he would disallow.

The difficulty with this view is that by its criterion, even that archfoe of innate ideas, John Locke, would have to have been regarded an exponent of the theory he is famous for hav-ing attacked. Locke distinguishes "impressions" — which he denies that the "souls of men receive in their first beings" — from our "inherent faculties" — which he does not deny are in-nate. Locke variously, and largely metaphorically, describes the *sorts* of things whose alleged innateness he rejects, e.g., "characters as it were stamped upon the mind of man [which it] brings into the world with it"; "natural characters engraved in the mind"; [7] etc. Throughout his discussion, however, he re-fers to our natural faculties, which enable us to achieve all that we require by way of understanding and knowledge "without the help of any innate impressions." Since, in Locke's structure, the natural faculties correspond to operant dispositions, or to "language-readiness" in Quine's structure, we might speak of the former as "idea-readiness," inasmuch as ideas are seman-

tical vehicles, and conclude that whatever Locke regarded as
in issue with innate ideas is beyond the range of this philosophically innocuous sort of innateness. *My* query is whether
what Chomsky has chosen to think of as innate ideas corresponds in any measure to what Locke rejected. In fact, I believe the query merits a negative answer, and that structurally
speaking there is considerable parity between Locke's thought
and Chomsky's. The point is worth making, in part because
Chomsky has sought to locate his theories in a rather different
historical tradition from that of Locke's, and in part because
seeing Locke as a precursor of Chomsky enables us to read
him in a rather different light than the traditional commentary
affords. It goes without saying that this view of Locke is only
possible in the light of what Chomsky has worked out. It
would be historical *lunacy* to seek to diminish his achievement
by suggesting it all lay in Locke. Rather, Chomsky's achievement permits us to look to Book II of the *Essay* rather than to
Book III ("Of Words") for Locke's theory of language. My
contribution to this is the suggestion that ideas are semantical
vehicles, bits of language coincidentally mental.

•   •   •

Chomsky employs an input-output model in his discussion
of language acquisition. The input is circumscribed and degenerate. The output — linguistic competence — simply cannot be
accounted for by reference to input solely, differing in quantity
and quality over what has been received. Accordingly, the discrepancy must be accounted for by means of the intermediat-
ing mechanism that Chomsky postulated, namely, the *language acquisition device* (LA). "An engineer faced with the
problem of designing a device meeting given input-output
conditions would naturally conclude that the basic properties
of the output are a consequence of the design of the device." [8]
Chomsky's task has been to describe this design, but my main
concern here is to emphasize the fact that *innateness* has reference to the design of the LA mechanism. This is a very generous sense of innateness. It has, for example, a ready extension

to sausage-making machines. It would be a futile debate were men to contest the question of innate sausages when one of them meant, in insisting that there were, that the design of the machine must be invoked in order to explain the discrepancy between sausage meat and those regular, cylindrical products; and the other man, in insisting that there were not, was saying that no meat went into those sausages that did not first enter the machine. Yet Chomsky's quarrel with Locke is just of this sort. Briefly, Locke's point is that there is no innate *input*. It is only relative to *this* that the mind is a *tabula rasa* at birth. It is so in the sense that the sausage machine is a *tabula rasa* when it issues from the factory, viz., it contains none of the stuff it is destined to process up into *wurst*. It is consistent with this that it may have as complex an 'innate' structure as may be needed; and we shall see directly that in this respect, Locke's *tabula rasa* has likewise an exceedingly complex innate structure.

Let us recall that Locke offers a theory of understanding. The mechanisms of understanding, that is, the machinery that must be invoked in order to explain how understanding occurs, cannot *itself* be understood by the means it is called into account for: either it has to be understood in some quite different way or else not understood at all. For otherwise we should have an infinite regression on our hands. If we had to acquire the LA device, if the LA device were itself the output of some input-output situation and discrepant with the input, some other innate device would be needed. The point is that if the machinery of the mind is required in order to explain how ideas are understood, *it* could not consist in ideas, for then either these are understood without it (and perhaps the machinery is then dispensable) or a similar mechanism is needed all over again. And so, one would think, LA could not consist of language if it was to explain how language is understood. The point is a delicate one for Chomsky, who tends to speak of LA as comprising certain *theories*: a phonetic *theory,* a grammatical *schema,* a *method* of interpretation, and the like. Are these theories somehow formulated? And if so, in what language? Perhaps the LA device *is* constituted of language, perforce unacquired and necessarily universal, i.e., omniglottal. But linguistic competence regarding this language *must* be radically different from the linguistic competence it is brought in to account for, or nothing will have been explained. And *mutatis mutandum,* reverting to Locke, if the mechanism for the understanding of ideas is to be regarded as ideative in turn, it can only be so in a way radically different from that in connection with which it was invoked to explain. When Locke speaks of no innate ideas, he means something like that. I shall now seek to justify this.

Let us first advert to creativity, inasmuch as this appears to be one of the crucial features of linguistic competence for Chomsky's theory. In the tradition of Locke, creativity has commonly been regarded the office of the *imagination.* It is indeed *exactly* the question of creativity that motivates the most celebrated discussion in Locke's *Essay:* "Whence comes it [= the mind] by that vast store which the busy and *boundless* fancy of man has painted on it with an *almost endless* variety?" [9] Locke's theory is that this vast and almost endless stock of ideas derives from singularly impoverished sources. Quite *plainly,* our ideas cannot have been learned one at a time and inductively. Indeed, the bulk of them cannot have been learned *at all.* It is only that the *materials,* out of which this is all processed up, are caused by experience in a way strikingly like that described as *imprinting* by recent theorists of instinctive behavior. These materials answer, in the engineering model, to input. Locke's problem, accordingly, is almost exactly analogous to Chomsky's. His animus against innate ideas is only that none of the *materials* of knowledge — or understanding — are innate. Simple ideas are those that are in the mind only in case they are *put* in the mind. The imagination is impotent to produce out of its own resources a simple idea. Hence the celebrated discussion of the blind man who does not know what red is, however otherwise powerful his imagination may be. Complex ideas may be amongst the input, and in fact typically are in many instances; but it is consistent with

Locke's theory that all of these may be fabricated through the compounding activities of human fancy.

It is worth stressing that the input here may be quite as degenerate as the linguistic input, although Locke, to my knowledge, makes very little of this. He does of course note the rather meager set of ideas out of which our final stock of ideas is framed, but he does not especially remark upon the degenerate nature of our stimuli. Chomsky notes the degree to which a learner's actual sentential input "deviate[s] in form from the idealized structures defined by the grammar he develops." [10] Yet surely the same may be said for our sense experience generally. Our concepts are exactly idealizations of vagrant, fragmentary, suboptimal experiences we rectify into something perhaps correspondent with no one of the relevant experiences at all. I mention this because the compensating mechanism that enables us, say, to form a concept of a penny out of discrepant penny-experiences may be just the mechanism cited by Chomsky in achieving an idealized sentential paradigm. This, if true, would suggest that much the same mechanisms are involved in the processing of input as in the processing of perceptions generally, whereby we generate idealized types out of shabby tokens. But I cannot press the question any further here, except to remark that we might have in the light of this to consider whether perception is not already more linguistic an operation than one might have believed. Locke evidently believed it was, for ideas, after all, are *at once* objects of perception *and* semantical vehicles, so that the contents of experience have an automatically semantical character. The fusion is a dangerous one, of course, for it can lead directly to Representationalism.

• • •

Locke quite correctly regarded us as passive so far as concerns the acquisition of simple ideas. A great deal of clownish criticism of this notion of passiveness has been made by drawing special attention to the selectiveness and focus of rational experience. But Locke hardly was denying this when he spoke of us as passive. He meant, rather, that a given *type* of simple idea has no way of being acquired *except* through being received: the modalities through which simple ideas are furnished the mind are by way of *gifts* (viz., 'the gift of sight'): we cannot *fabricate* simple ideas. They are beyond the limit of the will. In the topic of action, a comparable point might be made that the basic actions we perform are given us to perform, they are our congenital stock of operations, and we simply are impotent to perform an action outside our repertoires, e.g., to close our ears in the way in which we close our eyes, namely by *just* closing them. In this respect we are passive so far as concerns the acquisition of our repertoires, and it is no argument against this that, once given us, we can focus and direct our actions.

Now, once equipped with some of the basic materials, "the mind . . . exerts several acts of its own, whereby out of its simple ideas . . . the others are framed." [11] And it is here that Locke undertakes to describe the mechanisms of the idea-compositing device that processes the passively received matter out of which the entire fabric of human comprehension arises. These complex ideas "though their number be infinite and the variety endless," fall, Locke felt, into a few main groups. To each main group corresponded a distinct set of mental acts. Locke distinguished *synthesizing*, where ideas are fused into ideas; *relating*, wherein ideas are compared but not allowed to fuse; and *abstraction*. The products of these actions were modes, substances, and relations. With Locke's taxonomy and his budget of mental operations I am very little concerned. Rather I want just to emphasize the extraordinary amount of innate apparatus presupposed in the activity of compositing. Whence do we derive our metaideas of modes, substances, and relations? And no less important, if there is any chance at all that this is innate, is the fact that we carry in our minds a ready-made metaphysics of substances and modes? Perhaps Locke's theory is not to be credited at all. But how amazingly like Chomsky's it all sounds, inasmuch as the rules we internalize enable us, if Chomsky is right — and here it could be Locke himself writing — "to assign semantical interpretations to signals quite independently of whether [we have] been exposed to them or their parts, so long as they consist of elementary units that [we] know and are composed by the rules [we have] internalized." [12]

.   .   .

In historical fairness, it must be said that Locke was more concerned with the economy of means that with the prodigality of the product. The most impressive pages of the *Essay* are those analytical exercises in which he attempts to show how concepts seemingly removed from experience nevertheless are recursively built out of simple ideas, and are intelligible finally only through experience. Understanding flows through the entire system from these sparse sources, much as truth flows through a system from its primitive sentences, along the logical routes. The rules of idea-formation are the conduits of intelligibility as the rules of inference are the conduits of truth. Locke's inveighing against innate ideas is in effect a claim that there is no innate understanding: understanding enters from without. But once it has entered the mind, it activates an elaborate mechanism that pumps it, so to speak, to quite fantastic heights, producing ideas we understand perfectly though we have had no experiences correspondent with them.

It would be misspent virtuosity to protract any further the striking parallels between Locke's views and Chomsky's. I would like, nevertheless, to pose a question that each of them raises for us, which indeed was raised already by Aristotle in the passage that I cited. He writes:

> Just as all men have not the same writing, so all men have not the same speech sounds, but the mental experiences, which these directly symbolize, are the same for all, as also are those things of which our experiences are the images.[13]

So with Locke, whose essay was on *human* understanding. And so with Chomsky, whose point has been that just the same mechanisms, just the same language-acquisition devices must be invoked to explain how we learn languages *invariantly as to the languages,* since anyone could learn a different language than his own. The question I raise is this: To what extent is this view inconsistent with that promise of total conceptual permissiveness which Nietzsche proposed,[14] and, less dramatically, with the linguistic relativisms of Whorf and, to some degree, of Quine (albeit Quine's relativism pertains more to the theory of reference than to the theory of meaning)? And secondly, to what extent does the innate structure of language formation sink into the world, giving it linguistic form, or the form of our language(s)? So far as LA is universal, we live perforce in the same world if the structure of our world reflects the structure of language. Obviously, something produced by means of a different LA would not be recognizably a language, nor would the world correlative with this, if there *is* this cor-relativity, be recognizably the world. A *wholly* different language or a *wholly* different world would be unintelligible, but is the *very idea* unintelligible? [15]

NOTES

1. I develop these matters in my *Analytical Philosophy of Knowledge* (Cambridge University Press, 1968), esp. ch. 7.

2. René Descartes, *Méditation Troisième.*

3. Aristotle, *De Interpretatione,* 16ᵇ22–25.

4. See my paper "Beliefs as Sentential States of Persons," in the forthcoming proceedings of the Brockport philosophical conference. Also *Analytical Philosophy of Knowledge,* Ch. 4.

5. Noam Chomsky, "Recent Contributions to the Theory of Innate Ideas," *Synthèse,* XVII, 1 (March 1967), 2–12.

6. I refer to Quine's oral remarks at the conference, presumably printed in the present volume.

7. Locke, John, *Essay Concerning Human Understanding,* Bk. I, ch. 1, sec. 2.

8. Chomsky, *loc. cit.,* p. 7.

9. Locke, *op. cit.,* Bk. II, ch. 1, sec. 2. Italics added.

10. Chomsky, *loc. cit.*, p. 7.

11. Locke, *op. cit.*, Book II, ch. 12, sec. 1.

12. Chomsky, *loc. cit.*, p. 5.

13. Aristotle, *op. cit.*

14. I here refer to Nietzsche's *Nihilism.* See my *Nietzsche as Philosopher* (New York: Macmillan, 1965).

15. I am grateful to the Columbia University Council in the Humanities for summer grants enabling me to work on matters reflected in the present essay.

3

The Emperor's New Ideas

NELSON GOODMAN

Harvard University

IN BRIEF REPLY to some of Chomsky's arguments:

1. I plead not guilty to the charge of ignoring the standard critical evaluation of Locke's argument against innate ideas. What has always shocked me is how badly the commentators miss the central point of Locke's powerful case. Locke had, as I have, a good deal of trouble understanding the so-called theory. He therefore formulated every clear version he could think of and showed each to be either trivially true or obviously false. The remaining versions were too subtle for either him or me to grasp. He did indeed refute the theory only in its cruder — i.e., more intelligible — forms; the rest are forever immune to refutation.

2. On the other hand, I plead guilty to the charge of ignorance of most of current linguistic theory. Linguists are probably justified in taking toward me an attitude like that of Candide's companion toward the playwright ". . . who does not know a word of Arabic and yet the scene is in Arabia; moreover . . . is a man who does not believe in innate ideas; tomorrow I shall bring you twenty articles against him." [1] Such ignorance probably explains why I can never follow the argument that starts from interesting differences in behavior between parallel phrases such as "eager to please" and "easy to please"; that characterizes these differences as matters of "deep" rather than "surface" structure; and that moves on to innate ideas.

The extent of my obtuseness will be underlined if I remark that also "cat" and "rat," like "eager" and "easy," are similar in many ways, and that certain parallel longer expressions in which they are embedded behave quite disparately. "Cattle" is plural, "rattle" is singular. There is such a thing as a rattling but not such a thing as a cattling. And while rattles rattle, cattle do not cattle; that is, just as we can 'nominalize' "eager to please" but not "easy to please," so we can 'verbalize' "rattle" but not "cattle." Are all these peculiarities 'deep' as contrasted with the difference between "cat" and "sat"? I am not denying that the case of "eager" and "easy" may have important features not shared by the case of "cat" and "rat." I am asking for the grounds for the inference from such features, or from any other peculiarities in the behavior of words, to innate ideas.

Use of the term "deep" in these contexts seems to me ill grounded and prejudicial. Mathematicians do indeed use the term "deep," but only — as they use "elegant" — to make quite unofficial and extrasystematic comment. No mathematical argument rests on a distinction between what is deep and what is shallow.

One might argue that the shapes and colors in paintings are in some sense surface (or obvious) features, while the features that identify a picture as by a certain artist or of a certain school or period are in some sense deep (or obscure). Yet we learn with rather few examples to make some of the latter rather subtle distinctions. Must the mind therefore have been endowed at birth with a 'schematism' of artistic styles?

3. The linguist may be forgiven for a vocational myopia that blinds him to all symbol systems other than languages. Anyone else recognizes that gestures, nods of approval and disapproval, pointings, facial expressions, bodily demonstrations, sketches, diagrams, models, play an important role in the acquisition and inculcation of skills of all sorts; and that mastery of symbols of many of these kinds occurs before, and aids enormously, in the acquisition of language.

Chomsky argues that if the symbol systems we acquire

prior to the acquisition of a full-fledged language have the characteristics he finds to be essential for a language, then acquisition of the prior systems would be equally remarkable and in need of explanation, while if the prior systems do not have these features, they can be of little help in acquiring a language. The latter part of this argument seems to me quite specious. If a man has made a clock by hand, that is a remarkable accomplishment. I understand it better if he tells me how he first fashioned crude tools, used these to make more refined ones, and eventually made the clock. I do not protest that he could not have made the clock without first having made a timekeeping instrument. The tools used in making the clock are not timekeepers, and from the clock alone we cannot infer back to any specific characterization of the tools made and used at any stage along the way.

4. After arguing that the matter of "grue" and "bleen" is rather irrelevant to the point at issue, Chomsky writes ". . . every language learner (in fact, every mouse, chimpanzee, etc.) uses green rather than grue as a basis for generalization." I am sure that speakers accustomed to projecting "grue" rather than "green" would be equally confident that animals use grue rather than green as a basis for generalization.

5. Chomsky argues that if I am willing to speak of ideas in the mind, I should not find incomprehensible the notion of an idea being in the mind from the start. But from the fact that I know what an embodied idea is — an idea couched in words or other symbols — it does not follow that I know what a disembodied idea is. I know what a horse with spirit is, but not what the spirit is without the horse.

As I use the term "idea" we can reasonably ask whether or not the mind has an idea of one or another characteristic of its behavior. For Chomsky, apparently, such a question is meaningless; for he seems to take such characteristics as themselves ideas. My objection to this is not the violence it does to past or present practice, but the way it encourages an equivocation that gives plausibility to an otherwise preposterous thesis. The innocuous truism that the mind tends to behave in certain ways rather than others is implicitly taken as evidence for the obviously false hypothesis that embodied ideas are in the mind at the start or for the incomprehensible hypothesis that disembodied ideas are.

But just what Chomsky means by "idea" is hard to determine. He rejects most profferred explanations without providing any clear statement of his own. If ideas are not applied symbols, features of structure, dispositions, ways of behaving, mechanisms, what are they? To be told that "idea" is a theoretical term helps very little. He speaks of 'schematisms,' but what are these other than systems of linguistic or other symbols used for organizing experience? Perhaps they are *principles* according to which the mind organizes experience, though the mind need not be aware of these principles; they are in the mind only in the sense that they can be inferred from what the mind does. But are these principles anything more than descriptions, by an observer, of the resultant organization? Chomsky's answer may be that what is in question is much more than one among alternative sets of descriptions; it is a theory that by its explanatory and predictive power may vanquish competitors and shine forth as the one and only truth about the mind. Yet even so, the theory need no more be in the minds in question than the theory of gravitation need be in bodies. And since a theory may be embodied in one language or in many languages, but can hardly exist apart from languages, how could it be in the mind prior to language?

Here we may be told that of course the theory is not said to be in the mind described, but rather that the theory ascribes innate ideas to the mind. But what are these ideas? Not applied symbols, dispositions, etc. Are they principles, then? This leads us again around a circuit that is devious enough to make us forget that we are going nowhere.

The theory of innate ideas is by no means crude. It is of exquisite subtlety, like the gossamer golden cloth made for that ancient emperor. But the emperor needs to be told that his wise men, like his tailors, deceive him; that just as the body covered with the miraculous cloth has nothing on it, the mind packed with innate ideas has nothing in it.[2]

NOTES

1. Voltaire, *Candide*, ch. 23.
2. I am indebted to Robert Schwartz for comments that have led to some revisions of an earlier draft of this paper.

4

Linguistic Competence and Empiricism

GILBERT HARMAN

Princeton University

IN "Psychological Aspects of the Theory of Syntax" (*Journal of Philosophy*, LXIV [1967], 75–87), I argued for the following two things: (1) "Chomsky's use of the phrase 'linguistic competence' embodies at least two confusions" (p. 80). (2) "He has . . . not shown that the facts of transformational linguistics defeat an empiricist theory of language learning" (p. 87). Professor Chomsky's present comments on that paper misrepresent it at almost every point; but when his misrepresentations are cleared away, his remarks can be seen to confirm my two conclusions.

1. We would not ordinarily say that a typical speaker of a language has knowledge of the rules of a transformational grammar. We would ordinarily attribute such knowledge to a grammarian if to anyone. For various reasons — mainly to provide a background for his argument against what he calls "empiricism" — Professor Chomsky attributes such knowledge to every speaker of the language. It is true that he denies that the typical speaker has conscious knowledge of all or even any of the grammatical rules; but he does attribute to the typical speaker unconscious, "intuitive," or "tacit" knowledge of these rules. Since Professor Chomsky uses the phrase "linguistic competence" to refer to a speaker's unconscious knowledge of the rules of grammar, his use of this phrase inherits whatever confusions are involved in the latter notion. So I argued.

In his comments, Professor Chomsky calls the view that a

speaker has knowledge of the rules of grammar "an absurd view." I agree. We disagree about whether Professor Chomsky holds this "absurd view." He says:

> [Harman] begins by ascribing to me a view that I have never held, and have explicitly rejected on numerous occasions, namely that "competence [is] the knowledge that the language is described by the rules of the grammar." Obviously it is absurd to suppose that the speaker of the language knows the rules in the sense of being able to state them.

The last sentence contains a misrepresentation, since no one has suggested that Professor Chomsky says a speaker has *conscious* knowledge of the rules of grammar. In the sentence immediately following the one Professor Chomsky quotes I wrote:

> Since a speaker can rarely, if ever, say what the rules of his language are, Chomsky introduces a theory of unconscious knowledge about the language. (pp. 75–76)

I do not know why Professor Chomsky now wishes to deny he holds that view. Although he claims I offer no evidence in support of my interpretation, I cite fifteen different places in *Aspects of the Theory of Syntax* in which the view is stated. It is also stated in Professor Chomsky's present paper. He says:

> For example, the person who understands sentences (1) and (2) knows (whether he is aware of it or not) that in the case of (2) it is a proposition that is certain and in the case of (1) it is a person who is certain of something, in a very different sense of "certain."

In the paragraph following that, a speaker's possession of a generative grammar is equated with his possession of a "system of beliefs" (unconscious ones of course). Two paragraphs later these beliefs are equated with "knowledge of language," i.e., what he elsewhere calls "linguistic competence." In several places acquisition of knowledge of a language is construed as "theory construction." Many other passages could also be cited.[1] Therefore there can be no question but that Professor Chomsky accepts the "absurd view" that a speaker has (unconscious) knowledge of the rules of grammar and, furthermore, that he uses the phrase "linguistic competence" to refer to a speaker's unconscious knowledge of these rules.

2. Professor Chomsky imagines that I can argue in this way only because I have a "framework" in which there are only two kinds of knowledge: knowing that and knowing how. He supposes that this leads me to the mistaken view that knowledge of a language, i.e., linguistic competence, is a form of knowing how. However I fail to see how this issue has any bearing on whether Professor Chomsky uses the phrase "linguistic competence" to stand for a speaker's unconscious knowledge of the rules of grammar. I have just argued the latter point without any reference to knowing how.

It is true that in my article I took knowledge of a language to be a form of knowing how, which I contrasted with a grammarian's knowledge that the rules of grammar are such-and-such. Therefore I said that Professor Chomsky's use of the phrase "linguistic competence" rests in part on a confusion between knowing how and knowing that. I am willing to concede that knowledge of a language is not a form of knowing how in any ordinary sense of this phrase. Therefore it would be more accurate (if less epigrammatic) to say that Professor Chomsky's use of the phrase "linguistic competence" rests in part on a confusion between a speaker's knowledge of a language and a grammarian's knowledge of that language.

3. Professor Chomsky also attributes to me the view that linguistic competence is a "skill, analogous to the skill of a bicycle rider." This is a bad analogy in many respects, as he points out. But it is not mine. I refer to a bicycle rider in order to make a logical point. "The cyclist must keep balanced on the bicycle. Exactly what he needs to do will be dictated by cer-

tain principles of mechanics that he is unaware of." (p. 81)
We would not say for this reason that the cyclist has an unconscious knowledge of the principles of mechanics. From Professor Chomsky's comments I gather that he agrees. But what
further reason is there to say, as he does, that a speaker of a
language has an unconscious knowledge of the rules of grammar?

Professor Chomsky ignores this argument (which appears
in a context of greater detail than I have just offered). Instead
he uses the passage in order to attribute to me the view that
linguistic competence is analogous to the skill of a bicycle
rider. That is simple misrepresentation.

4. In my original paper I cited several of Professor Chomsky's remarks about a speaker's unconscious knowledge of the
rules of grammar, his development of "an internal representation" of these rules, etc. I claimed and claim that those remarks
are implausible if interpreted literally, although following Professor Chomsky I also pointed out that there is a way to interpret them as remarks about psychological models. I made a
similar claim about his view that a child learning a language
must construct a "theory" of the language on the basis of certain "primary linguistic data."

Professor Chomsky seriously misrepresents this section of
my paper. He purports to discuss what I say about his views of
language-learning. He says, "Harman tries to show that there
is a fundamental incoherence in my proposal . . ." In fact I
tried to show only that his proposal is *implausible* if taken literally. And so it is. It entails that before he learned his first
natural language a person already knew another language in
which he formulates a theory about the natural language. Professor Chomsky does not dispute the entailment. He argues
however that its consequent is not incoherent. I agree of
course; but I did not claim that it is incoherent, only that if
taken literally it is implausible.

Nor is it unimportant for the assessment of Professor
Chomsky's views whether they are to be taken literally. On the

one hand they must be taken literally if they are to serve as background for his reinterpretation of the rationalist-empiricist debate. On the other hand, they cannot be taken so literally if they are to remain at all plausible as accounts of a typical speaker's knowledge of a language and of language-learning.

Professor Chomsky makes it appear that I say his view is, when taken literally, incoherent. He does this by completely misrepresenting my argument. He attributes to me the claim that his proposal about language-learning "leads to a vicious circle or an infinite regress." In fact, my argument about language-learning mentions neither vicious circles nor infinite regresses. These are mentioned on the previous page in connection with my discussion of knowledge of a language. There I argued as follows: If Chomsky's account of what it is to know a language is taken literally, a person Smith knows a natural language only because he knows another language (or system of representations) in which he has represented the rules of his natural language. This view is implausible.

> How, for example, would Smith understand the more basic language? In order to avoid either an infinite regress or a vicious circle, one would have to suppose that Smith can understand at least one language directly, without unconsciously knowing the rules for that language. But if this is admitted, there is no reason why Smith cannot know directly the language he speaks. (p. 76)

Whatever the merits of this argument, it does not claim (as Professor Chomsky says it does) that his proposal leads either to a vicious circle or an infinite regress.

Professor Chomsky's misrepresentation of this argument has several curious aspects to it. For example, this is the way he restates the conclusion of the argument:

> Thus, if we were to say that the child knows the "more basic language" directly, without learning, then why not say he knows "directly the language he speaks," without learning; a vicious circle.

Notice first that that is a pretty peculiar use of the phrase "vicious circle." Second, Professor Chomsky writes as if one can know a language directly, i.e., without unconsciously (or otherwise) knowing the rules of the language, only if one has not learned the language. But he offers no reason at all for this strange view.

5. As I noted in my original article:

> For philosophers, Chomsky's most interesting claim is that facts about language learning support what he calls a "rationalist" theory of language learning as against an "empiricist" theory. (p. 82)

I offered several arguments against Professor Chomsky's claim. For the most part he simply ignores those arguments. When he does refer to them, he misrepresents them. Yet I do think the arguments raise serious obstacles to his rationalist program.

He reinterprets the rationalist-empiricist dispute as an argument about what principles would be needed by a "linguistic acquisition device" in order for this device to be able to infer the grammar of the language from "primary linguistic data." My first argument against that proposal concerned the implausibility of treating such a device as if it infers something from data. I pointed out that, given the sort of "data" the mechanism would get, if we are to treat it as making any sort of inference we must assume it infers (or already "knows") a theory of performance. I noted some difficulties this raises. I also argued that, instead of taking the device to make inferences, it would be more accurate to think of it as a feedback mechanism of a certain sort. If we think of a linguistic acquisition device as that sort of feedback mechanism, then we cannot formulate the issue between rationalism and empiricism as Professor Chomsky does. So this is a serious objection. Professor Chomsky ignores the objection except to say this:

> [Harman] asserts that to infer a grammar from data, a model of language-learning must already have detailed information

about the theory of performance. This is an interesting proposal and it deserves to be developed. But I cannot go along with his rather dogmatic claim, hardly argued in the paper, that this approach must necessarily be correct . . .

That suggests I agree with Professor Chomsky's general view and was making a proposal internal to that view. In fact I was engaged in bringing out difficulties in his general view. I do not propose that models of language-learning should incorporate a theory of performance. I propose rather that such models should not be conceived as making inferences at all but should be conceived as feedback mechanisms of a certain sort. Furthermore, my claim (that a model of language-learning that infers a grammar from data must incorporate detailed information about the theory of performance) is not dogmatically made but is supported by argument. Professor Chomsky does not say what if anything is wrong with that argument.

6. But let us waive that objection. Let us suppose that the linguistic acquisition device makes inferences from primary linguistic data. Then the dispute between rationalism and empiricism becomes (on Professor Chomsky's reinterpretation) a dispute over whether the device needs further information or principles built into it over and above the primary linguistic data and principles of inductive inference. The empiricist holds that the device can arrive at correct grammatical rules by inductive inference from primary linguistic data alone. The rationalist denies it.

As I pointed out in my original article, "Whether or not empiricism, so defined, is defensible depends upon what is to count as inductive inference" (p. 84). I also pointed out that "There is an enormous philosophical literature on induction. Chomsky ignores this literature" (p. 86). Professor Chomsky addresses himself to this complaint in a note (n. 14) when he says, "[Harman] does not, however, show how anything in [the] literature on induction bears on the problems I am considering. The reason is that there is nothing." He is just wrong about this. For example, Nelson Goodman's "New Riddle of Induction" in *Fact, Fiction, and Forecast* (Cambridge, Mass.: Harvard, 1955) is relevant; and in my article I said why: "We know from Goodman's 'New Riddle of Induction' that any consistent set of inductive procedures must favor certain generalizations over others" (pp. 85–86). Another way to put the point in terms of subjective probability theory is this: we can explain what rational inductive procedures are up to some arbitrary choice of initial probability distribution. But if we are to learn from experience at all, then our initial assignment of probabilities must from a certain point of view arbitrarily favor certain hypotheses over others.

How are we to discover a person's initial probability distribution, i.e., the initial probability distribution of his linguistic acquisition device? Equivalently, how are we to discover what constitutes his (its) inductive procedures? The only way that we have is to see what the person (or his device) does. And that is what makes it difficult to see that there is any real difference between empiricism and rationalism. The rationalist will take information from linguistics to point to innate noninductive principles that must be used by the linguistic acquisition device. But as I said in my original article,

> A resourceful empiricist, knowing some inductive logic, will deny that information from linguistics refutes his theory; instead he will take the information to reveal something about the correct set of inductive procedures. (p. 85)

There is no real difference between these positions. That is, there is no real way to distinguish rationalism from empiricism along the lines Professor Chomsky suggests. A similar argument shows, I think, that there is no real difference between Professor Chomsky's "rationalist" view and Professor Putnam's suggestion [2] that we should attempt to account for language-acquisition in terms of general multipurpose learning strategies, since any account of "general strategy" must arbitrarily favor certain strategies over others of the same logical form.

As far as I can see, Professor Chomsky does not appreciate the force of this argument. He takes it to rest on a special definition of "resourceful empiricism" (his phrase, not mine) so that I have shown only that a peculiar kind of empiricism coincides with rationalism. Therefore it is important to see that the argument is perfectly general. Goodman's argument shows that *any* inductive methods that work at all must favor what are from a certain point of view arbitrary hypotheses over others of the same logical form. *Any* initial subjective probability assignment that permits learning from experience must do the same.

The resourceful empiricist is any empiricist who knows a little inductive logic and is therefore able to defend his view resourcefully. Professor Chomsky's barbarism "resourceful empiricism" refers not to a very special view that is empiricism in name only but to empiricism as it would be defended by a resourceful empiricist. It is no wonder that Chomsky finds such empiricism "of little interest": it coincides with rationalism resourcefully defended. Chomsky apparently prefers unresourceful empiricism, i.e., empiricism defended by an empiricist who isn't very resourceful. No doubt he is right in thinking that rationalism — or at least resourceful rationalism — is to be preferred to unresourceful empiricism. However I find *that* "of little interest."

NOTES

1. Notice that Chomsky does not distinguish knowledge *of* the rules from knowledge *that* the rules are so-and-so. See also, e.g., his remarks in the symposium on innate ideas: "The problem is, precisely, to determine how the child *determines that* the structure of the language has the specific characteristics that empirical investigation of language leads us to postulate, given the meagre evidence available to him." *Boston Studies in the Philosophy of Science,* Vol. III, p. 86, my emphasis.

2. In the innate Ideas symposium.

5

Comments on Harman's Reply

NOAM CHOMSKY

Massachusetts Institute of Technology

LET ME TRY to reconstruct the discussion between Harman and me, as it now stands. In *Aspects of the Theory of Syntax* and other publications I proposed a certain way of approaching the problems of knowledge, acquisition, and use of language. In his "Psychological Aspects of the Theory of Syntax," Harman presented a critique. In my paper for this symposium, I argued that he had misrepresented my position. In his comments, he maintains that I had misrepresented his critique. It will come as no surprise to the reader to learn that I think he has misrepresented my critique of his critique. In the hope that we are not entering an infinite regress, I will try to restate what appear to me to be the central issues.

Consider the matter of "knowledge of language." My proposal, which Harman quotes, was that "every speaker of a language has mastered and internalized a generative grammar that expresses his knowledge of the language. This is not to say that he is aware of the rules of the grammar . . ." As Harman now states in his Reply, I propose the technical term *linguistic competence* "to refer to a speaker's unconscious knowledge of the rules of grammar." I do not, however, use the term "competence" in either of the two ways defined in Harman's article "Psychological Aspects." In this article he maintains, incorrectly, that my use of "competence" embodies a confusion between two types of knowledge, namely: "competence is knowledge in the sense of knowing how to do something; it is ability"; or it may be "tacit knowledge," "knowledge that something is the case" (p. 81). Similarly on p. 75, he defines two

152

senses of "competence," which he incorrectly attributes to me, namely: (1) "competence is knowing how to speak and understand a language"; (2) Chomsky "takes a grammar to describe competence as the knowledge that the language is described by the rules of the grammar." In his Reply, he now cites my actual proposal, namely, that "competence" is a technical term "to refer to the speaker's unconscious knowledge of the rules of grammar." When Harman in his Reply states "so I argued," he is clearly in error, as can be seen by comparing the characterization of "competence" in his Reply with the characterizations of "competence" that I have just quoted from his article. In the article, he struggles with various problems that result from incorrectly attributing to me two interpretations of "competence," neither of which I have used, both of which I explicitly rejected in the citations he quotes. The source of these misinterpretations, I presume, is Harman's insistence on interpreting "knowledge of language" in terms of his concepts of "knowing how" and "knowing that," which seem to me quite inadequate to the task.

What I described as "an absurd view" is the view that Harman mistakenly attributes to me in his "Psychological Aspects," namely, the view that competence, in my sense, is "the knowledge that the language is described by the rules of the grammar." This would be to attribute to the speaker the knowledge that is possessed, if at all, by the linguist: namely, the knowledge *that* the rules of the grammar are so-and-so.

According to Harman's "Psychological Aspects":

> . . . there are two senses in which a person may be said to have knowledge of a language. A typical speaker, call him "Smith," knows how to understand other speakers of his language and to communicate with them, although he cannot describe the language very well. Smith has knowledge of the language in one sense. A linguist, Jones, knows about the language, knows that it is described by certain rules, etc. Jones has knowledge of the language in a second sense. Is competence supposed to be what Smith has or what Jones has?

He then goes on, in the quotation which I cited, to attribute to me the absurd view that the speaker has the knowledge that Jones has, the linguist's knowledge, "the knowledge that the language is described by the rules of the grammar," although all of the quotes that he cites show that I explicitly reject this view. I do not see how to make any more clear than this that in his "Psychological Aspects" he has totally misrepresented my views, and that his denial of this fact in his Reply is in explicit contradiction to what is clearly stated in his original article.

Given this misinterpretation, I saw no reason in my contribution to this symposium, and I see no reason now, to try to trace the various confusions that Harman develops, none of which have any relation to the views I actually hold and that Harman quotes at length.

In §3 of his Reply, Harman states that I misrepresented him as proposing that linguistic competence (in his sense of "competence" — that is, the ability to use the language) is analogous to the skill of a bicycle rider. In his article he says that "it is useful to compare a linguistic-performance model with a model of a bicycle rider" and goes on to develop an argument based on a presumed analogy between the two cases. I took this to mean that in his view, "the 'competence to speak and understand the language' is a skill, analogous to the skill of a bicycle rider." I am glad to learn, from his Reply, that he does not hold this view. Therefore we apparently agree that there is no useful analogy between the ability to use a language and the ability to ride a bicycle. I would suggest, therefore, that this comparison is not, as he states in his article, "useful," but is rather entirely beside the point. As to the question asked in his Reply, why one should say "that a speaker of a language has an unconscious knowledge of the rules of his grammar" when we do not make an analogous statement about the "unconscious knowledge of the principles of mechanics" by the bicycle rider, I think the answer is simple, once the lack of significant analogy between the two cases is accepted: we do not attribute knowledge of mechanics to the bicycle rider if in fact this assumption does not help explain his ability to ride a bicycle; we do attribute knowledge of the rules of grammar to the speaker-hearer if this assumption does contribute to an explanation of his ability to use a language. Or, to eliminate the irrelevant reference to the skill of the bicycle rider, the answer is, simply: we postulate that a speaker of a language has an unconscious knowledge of the rules of grammar if this postulate is empirically justified by the role it plays in explaining the facts of use and understanding and acquisition of language.

Harman argues in §4 of his Reply that I misrepresented his argument relating to the infinite regress or vicious circle that, he seems to believe, is implicit in my views. He may be right. I do not see that he presented any argument, and therefore I tried to construct one. What he states in his article is that

> to avoid either an infinite regress or vicious circle, one would have to suppose that Smith [the speaker of a language] can understand at least one language directly, without unconsciously knowing the rules for that language. But if this is admitted, there is no reason why Smith cannot know directly the language he speaks. Thus, literally interpreted, Chomsky's theory would almost certainly be false.

He goes on to assert that a literal interpretation of my views regarding acquisition involves "the absurd assumption that before he learned his first natural language Smith already knew another language." He presents no argument that is intelligible to me either in his article or his Reply to justify these conclusions. Let me merely restate my views, and explain why I do not think that there is an infinite regress or a vicious circle or an almost certain falsehood or an absurdity (the only possibilities that Harman allows).

My suggestion is that the principles of universal grammar are an innate property of the human mind; among other things, these principles define the set of "attainable grammars" and provide a "weighting function" that selects one attainable grammar over others that are compatible with the primary linguistic data available to the language learner. I see no objection to saying that "knowledge of these principles" (obviously, unconscious knowledge) is innate, though I do not want to insist on this (in my view, perfectly appropriate and understandable) terminology. It would be easy to program a computer to operate in this fashion; surely there is no vicious circle or infinite regress. If Harman believes that this suggestion is "almost certainly false" or "absurd" he must have access to information about mental processes or about the nervous system that is unavailable to me.

Consider now language use. I proposed that the mature speaker has internalized a grammar with specific properties that I and others have discussed in many places, and that in understanding speech he makes use of this grammar to assign a percept to a signal. Again, it is possible to design a computer program that operates in this manner (and, in fact, there has been a fair amount of experimentation with such programs). There are many possible ways in which such a program might make use of the rules of the stored grammar; it is a central problem of psycholinguistics to explore these possibilities. Again, there is obviously no infinite regress or vicious circle in this perfectly realizable proposal, and if Harman knows it to be "almost certainly false" or "absurd," it can only be on the basis of information not available to me. I see nothing further to say on this topic.

In §5 of his Reply, Harman turns to the question of rationalism and empiricism. He is correct in saying that I ignored most of his arguments, because, as I stated, they did not bear on the questions that I was considering or the position that I have been trying to develop. He is also correct in stating that I misstated his proposal about the theory of performance. I restated it within my framework, as he correctly remarks. His proposal is that there is some sort of "feedback mechanism that adjusts the rules represented in the attached potential performance model so as to maximize the way in which the resulting model gets along in conversation," etc. In his Reply, he states that this proposal is "supported by argument." I leave it to the reader to judge the accuracy of this. In any event, my own view is that although it might be interesting to try to develop the idea that Harman sketches, I see no reason to accept his dogmatic claim that the very different approach I have outlined is "absurd" or "almost certainly false" and so on. I detect no argument to support these claims.

The final point has to do with the literature on induction, which, as Harman correctly states, I ignore. My reason for ignoring this literature is that it has no bearing on the problem that interests me, namely, the problem of how an acquisition model can make use of the primary linguistic data to construct a grammar of the sort that it seems we must postulate. Specifically, consider the two examples mentioned in my paper: the principle that phonological rules apply in a cycle, determining (partially) perceived phonetic form from surface structure, and the rule that associates certain types of nominal expressions with deep rather than surface structures. There is nothing in the literature on induction to suggest how these properties of grammar can be derived from the data of speech. The same is true of innumerable other examples that might be mentioned, and that are discussed in the literature.

Here Harman and I are just talking past each other. He argues that the literature on induction is relevant, and cites two examples: Goodman's observations on the "new riddle of induction," and Jeffrey's remark that initial probability distributions will arbitrarily favor certain hypotheses over others. I agree that these are interesting remarks, which illustrate some of the limitations of the logic of induction. Choice of predicates and choice of initial probability distributions fall outside of the domain of inductive logic, but clearly will have an effect on what inductive procedures will yield. But these observations on the limitations of inductive logic give us no assistance at all in dealing with the problem of language-acquisition that I formulated, and restated above. Inductive logic does not tell us — here we are in perfect agreement — how the initial predicates or the initial probability distribution should be chosen. This is one reason why there is no point in turning to the

"enormous philosophical literature on induction" for some substantive assistance in dealing with the problems of acquisition
of knowledge. Furthermore, there is not the slightest reason to
suppose that a proper choice of predicates or of initial probability distributions will, in itself, make possible the application
of inductive logic to the problem of language-acquisition.
Rather, my suggestion is that one should proceed along entirely different lines — those sketched above and in the cited
literature — to deal with this problem.

Harman and I are in total agreement that what I called
"resourceful empiricism" incorporates, as a special case, the
"rationalist" approach that I have been trying to develop. For
example, this "resourceful empiricism" can incorporate the
schematism of universal grammar and the weighting function
proposed, and can extend the term "induction" to refer to the
use of these principles in language acquisition. As noted in my
contribution to this symposium, I agree fully with Harman that
this "resourceful empiricism" will be compatible with anything
that is discovered about language or anything else, which is
why I suggest that it be disregarded, as a vacuous position.
The empiricist and rationalist views sketched in my article are,
I believe, genuine alternatives in the sense that each expresses
an interesting empirical hypothesis, and each accommodates
specific proposals that have been developed. "Resourceful empiricism" accommodates anything that has been or will be developed, and is therefore of no interest at all. I fail to see any
issue here.

To restate my position: there are three general approaches
that can be distinguished, what I called "empiricism," "rationalism," and "resourceful empiricism." The third, by definition, includes any specific empirical proposal that anyone can
formulate. It can accommodate the view that knowledge of
English is innate, that knowledge of universal grammar is innate, that language-learning is based on absolutely unique "inductive" principles that apply nowhere else, that there are
more general "learning strategies" of which the strategies for
language-acquisition are a special case, etc. Having no content,

the approach is of no interest. One does not need to "know a little inductive logic" to be a resourceful empiricist; rather, knowledge of inductive logic contributes nothing to this position. The empiricist and rationalist alternatives that I outlined in *Aspects* and elsewhere do seem to me genuine alternatives. I think an interesting empirical issue can be raised by sharpening them, and I think that there is much to be learned by confronting them with evidence. The empiricist view, as I outlined it, seems to me to incorporate a great deal of speculation and theory in philosophy, psychology, and linguistics — practically all of the modern work, in fact. I have tried to show that there are empirical reasons for believing that this approach is misguided, and have suggested that the suggested alternative, which incorporates some of the leading ideas of classical rationalism, seems much more promising. To the "resourceful empiricist," this debate is internal to his general approach, which, being vacuous, is compatible with whatever will be discovered. As to the "enormous philosophical literature on induction," the interest of which I do not in the least question, it simply adds nothing to the resolution of any of the substantive questions that arise when we face the problem of accounting for language-acquisition in a serious way.

My own view about the matter of induction is essentially that of Peirce, in the lectures quoted in my contribution to this symposium, that while induction may be used for "corrective action," it is the innate principle that "gives a rule to abduction and so puts a limit upon admissible hypotheses" that plays the central role in the acquisition of knowledge. This view can, I believe, be rather sharply distinguished from classical empiricism and those modern approaches to acquisition of knowledge that have developed from it (insofar as they have empirical substance). One thing is certain: pointless terminological proposals — such as the proposal to define "empiricism" so as to accommodate all possible views — will not help in resolving the very interesting and serious questions that remain, no matter what terminologies people may devise.

6

Empiricism, Rationalism, and Innate Ideas

SIDNEY HOOK

New York University

IF I UNDERSTAND the philosophical relevance of Chomsky's claims, he is contending (1) that a study of linguistic phenomena justifies the conclusion that "a child is born with perfect knowledge of universal grammar, that is, with a fixed schematism that he uses . . . in acquiring languages"; (2) that empiricism is unable to do justice to the well-attested facts of language-learning and use, especially the creative aspects apparent in the normal mastery of any language; and (3) that traditional rationalism finds some support, if not strong confirmation, in the results of current linguistic theory as interpreted by Chomsky.

I have difficulty with all three of these contentions.

1. To say that a child is "born with knowledge" raises the question in what sense the word "knowledge" is being used. We rarely speak this way of children except in the way we sometimes speak of animals. When someone says that an animal is born with a knowledge of how or where to suckle, what is meant is that it is born with certain innate powers — we used to refer to them as "instincts," and later as "tendencies" or "predispositions," — of discriminatory response. What one is born with is not acquired. Yet we also know that many powers remain latent or dormant, and do not flower into performance without some environmental stimulus. As soon as the child is born he is subjected to some experience. His behavior may be the result of his experience and culture (history); e.g., the specific language he speaks, his courtship practices, or it may be

the result of his innate powers. But whatever is attributed to nurture or nature is always an *inference* from observed behavior patterns.

When we ask of a child: "Does he know how to sing?" before we have observed or tested him, we normally assume that he has the power to sing. If the answer is "no," we normally assume that he has not learned or been taught how to sing. But the negative answer may be due to the fact that the child lacks the power to sing because he is tone-deaf. When the child learns how to sing there is practically an "infinite" variety of songs he can identify, differentiate, and repeat, practically an "infinite" variety of tunes he can modify or vary in some way or another. Even so, I do not believe that we would ever be tempted to say that the child is born with a "perfect" knowledge of song, still less of harmony or other musical principles. Were it not for the use of the word "perfect," I would interpret Chomsky's conclusion as a stupendous truism, somewhat akin to the realization that dawns upon a child that one doesn't have to be especially bright to speak Chinese, and that had he been born Chinese, he, too, would have learned to speak Chinese, with the fluency and ease of the Chinese children whose proficiency he has envied.

The linguistic capacity of man is a much more complicated kind of capacity than the capacities involved in acquiring other habits and skills. One does not have to agree with Bertrand Russell that the type of skill involved in the acquisition of speech is "throughout exactly similar to that involved in learning how to play a game or ride a bicycle," to recognize that they are analogous or commensurable. It differs from the latter in that the skill is not so much a bodily skill as a social one, and that it therefore is a type of action that cannot occur outside a social context, whereas the former can. I see nothing rash in granting the likelihood that a Caspar Hauser or any other human being brought up and fed by "invisible hands" could master the art of riding a bicycle; but I cannot grant any likelihood to the supposition that he would learn how to speak in such circumstances or how to use a typewriter, aside from thumping the keys. Language as an art should be compared to social arts like learning how to bake a cake or make an omelette — which once learned makes possible an indefinite number of similar actions — rather than to purely physical arts like jumping or swimming. As a social art it may reflect what all societies have in common. It is in social behavior, the conjoint behavior in fulfilling or frustrating purposes, in role-playing and taking-the-place-and-part-of-another, along lines indicated by Peirce, James, Mead, and Dewey, that the structure of language develops. It is not the existence of language that makes society possible but the existence of society that makes language possible. Of course by *defining* human society as a society in which speech exists, it becomes bootless to make any distinction. But if we believe that human society has developed out of animal societies, it is in the way that society is organized that we must look for the emergence of speech patterns, and not in the antecedent structure of the human mind.

When Chomsky talks about a child being born with a "perfect knowledge of universal grammar" he is, of course, not referring to those elements of speech that depend upon specific and local experiences, upon geography or history, or even on whatever is common or universal in experience, but on something that cannot be acquired or learned in any way. It is not a skill or habit or even a capacity, for whatever we have "perfect" knowledge of cannot be perfected or improved in any way. If universal grammar cannot be learned or discovered in the way we learn or discover other things, and if they cannot be intelligibly assimilated to biological processes inherited with the germ plasm, then what remains for Chomsky to say other than that they are remembered? And what is this but a revival of the Platonic doctrine of knowledge as a form of reminiscence? This highly speculative hypothesis, which involves an extreme kind of dualism even if it does not entail an acceptance of reincarnation, raises more difficulties than it settles.

2. Chomsky seems to equate empiricism with conven-

tional interpretations of Locke, Hume, and Mill, and with modern forms of behaviorism in psychology. But surely, when we speak of empiricism, some recognition should be given to the work of Peirce, James, and Dewey, who considered themselves empiricists despite their criticism of the simple associationist psychology of the nineteenth century and the reductive behaviorism of the twentieth. For Dewey, we do not learn merely by experience in the traditional sense. Without the *capacity* to learn not all the experience in the world, understood simply as what happens to an organism, results in knowledge. Knowledge is an *achievement* in which the learner not only suffers or undergoes but is active and reactive. From the point of view of an interactional or transactional view of experience, organizing principles can be introduced to order and reorder events to realize human purposes more adequately. These principles are natural, social, and historical. There is no need for a transcendental mythology.

From this perspective, it follows that sensations are not known but "had." They acquire cognitive relevance in the context of some hypothesis or idea that guides activity when we seek to resolve some problem. As Dewey puts it: "The senses lose their place as gateways of knowing to take their rightful place as stimuli to action." The opposition between traditional empiricism and rationalism is thereby outflanked. The results of experience are taken as an inescapable check on any assertion that claims to give knowledge about the world, while the indispensable significance and role of ideas, of "reason" as a directing and organizing principle of activity, is fully recognized. "Reason" is not a fixed schematism of mind that controls behavior separate from it, but a pattern of ideas suggested by past, and corrected by present, experience. Its source — to repeat — is history and culture broadly conceived, not a transcendental psychology or ontology. The prolonged infancy, with its notorious and lengthy physical and biological dependence of the human child, in contradistinction to the offspring of all other animal species, reinforces the strength of the mediating role of the family and community in acculturating the child to the world. "Things come to him," writes Dewey, "clothed in language, not in physical nakedness, and this garb of communication makes him a sharer in the beliefs of those about him." Buttressing Dewey's experimental naturalism are his critique of the Stimulus-Response bond, and his attempt to explain the presence of knowledge and ordered symbol-oriented behavior by an elaborate mosaic of associations. Actually, we cannot tell what constitutes a stimulus in a field of indefinitely large numbers of stimuli until a selective response of the organism takes place. The readiness of the organism, not only the triggering physiological mechanisms but its cultural and social dispositions, are engaged.

Once we recognize the active role of the learner in learning, the sociocultural matrix of the meanings of expressions, and the presence of conjoint behavior as a criterion of understanding one another, there seems to be no reason why the organism cannot acquire the neural patterns and powers that account for its ability "to form and understand previously unheard sentences." It seems both more plausible and fruitful to assimilate this ability to the ability to form and understand *heard* sentences — once the Lockean notion of experience is abandoned, the activity of the organism in its experience recognized, and the ability to form and understand heard sentences not reduced to the operation of a mimetic machine—than to postulate innate ideas to account for the phenomenon.

3. Rationalism is a philosophy of many varieties. In the sense in which it is contrasted with empiricism, it stresses the capacity of man to discover truth about the world independently of experience. This does not necessarily entail a belief in innate ideas. Experience may *suggest* ideas that are not innate but that once suggested and entertained may serve as premises that entail conclusions true about the world, and in some forms, true about any world. The *validity* of the ideas and their conclusion does not depend upon the specific experiences that suggest or give rise to them but their discovery or coming into awareness does.

It would seem that a more plausible candidate for the status of innate ideas would be not the principles of a universal grammar but the principles of a universal logic. No matter what principles of a universal grammar are alleged to hold, it is possible to conceive of alternatives to them. Not so, however, for the logical laws of identity and contradiction. Since they define the limits of sense, they cannot be defied or denied without lapsing into nonsense. They are conditions of intelligible discourse, and because they hold for anything that can be said to make sense, some philosophers have held, although such belief is not necessary, that they are ontological principles, too.

As far as Locke was concerned, his denial of innate ideas extends to principles of logic, too. Although he does not contest their validity, he does contest the view that they are innate, not only because children and "all that have souls" do not necessarily have them in their understanding but because in actual fact human thinking often violates the principles of logic. Men are often unaware of the fact that propositions they firmly believe are true are mutually incompatible. The laws of logic cannot be innate in Locke's sense, because they are standards to which discourse must conform if we are properly to identify things and communicate with each other.

Locke writes: "For if these words 'to be in the understanding' have any propriety, they signify to be understood. If therefore these two propositions: 'Whatsoever is, is' and 'It is impossible for the same thing to be and not to be,' are by nature imprinted, children cannot be ignorant of them." One might retort to Locke that in a sense children are not ignorant of them, since they make use of these principles as standards of discourse as they mature. But all this shows is a capacity to learn the laws of logic: it is not itself knowledge. At any rate, it cannot be a "perfect" knowledge comparable to Chomsky's "perfect" knowledge of universal grammar. Locke is surely right in distinguishing at this point between the capacity, whether innate or acquired, for knowing, and the achievement of knowledge. Otherwise "all the truths a man ever comes to know will, by this account, be everyone of them innate, and this great point will amount to no more but only to a very high improper way of speaking."

Locke is not altogether consistent in recognizing the distinction between the capacity for knowledge and the achievement of knowledge, and his epistemology would have been quite different had he applied it to sensory knowledge and considered ideas as claims to knowledge of objects rather than as objects of knowledge, in other words, as hypotheses rather than as sense data. He also believed that our moral and mathematical beliefs, although not innate, are a priori known with certainty, and demonstrable in the strict sense. But these beliefs at best can give only formal truths. Locke's empiricism did not prevent him from embracing metaphysical and theological propositions of a character that render both his empiricism and rationalism infirm.

If knowledge is an achievement rather than a tacit or implicit possession, then we can never properly be said to have knowledge except on the basis of some evidence. The child who cannot read a clock but who guesses the right time does not really know what time it is. From this point of view we cannot claim to have knowledge of the laws of logic in the way we have knowledge of other things, because the claim itself and the reading of the evidence for it presupposes the laws. The fact that we can apply the laws of logic to anything and everything, that they function as standards of all inquiry and intelligible discourse, can be interpreted in various ways. Peirce and James fall back on the evolutionary hypothesis to explain, in the case of the latter, the psychogenetic structure of the human mind, and in the case of the former, the "uncanny" ability of the human investigator to select among an infinite range of possible hypotheses the fruitful ones.

The belief that the human mind has "knowledge" of universal grammar is no more incompatible with scientific or experimental empiricism than that it has "knowledge" of the laws of logic, if "knowledge" refers to powers, innate powers of discriminating, comparing, remembering, etc., which constitute learning. But I do not see any justifiable ground for characterizing such knowledge as "perfect." I sometimes get the impression, on the basis of Chomsky's rather offhand dismissal of the theory of evolution, that it is not so much empiricism that he regards as intellectually baneful as it is naturalism. I wonder whether lurking behind his animadversions against empiricism there is a hostility to naturalism whose source is an unqualified Cartesian dualism that takes man and/or the human mind outside the order of nature.

7

On Culturlogism

PAUL KURTZ

University of Buffalo

THIS SYMPOSIUM brings together philosophers, anthropologists, and linguists. It is therefore appropriate to ask, what is the relevance of anthropology and linguistics to philosophy and in particular to the philosophical investigation of language? Does one commit a culturlogism by relating philosophical analyses to a cultural-linguistic framework?

It has been virtually an article of faith of contemporary analytic philosophy and phenomenology to insist that empirical questions concerning the origins of languages, their psychological, social, and cultural roots and functions, are not relevant to theories concerning the philosophy or logic of language. There are alleged horrors at committing the fallacy of "psychologism," "sociologism," or "culturlogism."

I have never been convinced that all philosophical questions concerning the theory or logic of language can be divorced from psychological, sociological, or anthropological inquiry, or indeed that philosophy can be strictly distinguished from science. As I examine many, supposedly "pure," philosophical analyses, I find psycho-socio-cultural presuppositions about language and man more often than not merely assumed without adequate empirical foundation or else based upon unverified conjecture and speculation.

What is the relevance of linguistics, anthropology, and the other sciences of man to theories of language? The chief point that I wish to make is that at least such inquiries are *not irrelevant,* as had been commonly maintained.

It is instructive in reading Professor Lounsbury's paper to find that the question of the commensurability or incommensurability of a language is related to the problem of cultural relativism or limited relativism. Whether or not there is a universal logical structure of language or universally shared fundamental prime concepts in human language may be ascertained in part by detailed comparative observations of the multiplicity of culture-symbolic systems. One aspect of the universality of the language question, according to Professor Lounsbury, involves kinship words and their classification. Is the concept of kinship universal in all cultures and do people in all societies have a common understanding of kinship relationships? No doubt complex problems of definition and meaning are involved, and one's overall bias in favor of cultural or limited relativism influences one's approach to the question. Still the message is clear for philosophers: before we can generalize on the basis of our limited Indo-European language stock about languages in general, we had better correlate our generalizations with hard anthropological data from different culture systems. Anthropology and ethnology thus have direct bearing on the basic philosophical problem of the nature of language.

Similarly, Professor Chomsky maintains that there is a close affinity between linguistics and philosophy. The concepts and conclusions of linguistics about the nature of language are directly relevant, he argues, to certain key questions of philosophy. Does Chomsky's paper violate one of the key principles of contemporary philosophy and commit a "psychologism"? For he is throughout concerned with providing an account of the origins of knowledge, learning, and perception. Chomsky indicates that if we wish to determine the relevance of linguistics to philosophy we must investigate the ways in which language is used and understood and the basis of its acquisition. He is concerned with how the child acquires knowledge of a language; and he attributes this to an innate schematism that restricts the choice of grammars. Clearly, Chomsky thinks that what he is saying is relevant to the classical arguments between empiricism and rationalism; it is not simply the *logic* of language that interests him, but its *psychological* foundations. I do not accept Chomsky's theory of innate structures. Moreover, as I view linguistics, it is closer to both anthropology and the behavioral sciences than he would apparently allow. Nevertheless, I think that what is significant in his paper is the fact that he believes that a genetic account is relevant to certain fundamental epistemological questions lying at the foundation of language.

In recent philosophy, problems of meaning have been translated into contextual questions concerning the uses of language. 'Use' and 'context' are helpful concepts that enable us to understand how language fits together and functions. What follows from this, it seems to me, is that if we are to fully explicate the nature of language we cannot restrict its contexts or uses to purely linguistic or formal content, but should be involved also with the relationships that languages have to behavior and culture.

Many things are no doubt meant by the terms "psychologism," "sociologism," and "culturlogism." Clearly one cannot simply identify or equate a logical or formal structure with a psychological or sociocultural process; nor may the validity of an argument or proof be warranted by reference to its psycho-socio-cultural origins — this would be the genetic fallacy at its worst. Yet insofar as general philosophical theories about the nature, purposes, and uses of language are involved, these cannot be isolated from the findings of linguistics, anthropology, and the other sciences of man. Such findings are at least relevant to our unraveling of the complexities of language, and they enable us to clarify how language grows out of and is related to broader contexts of use. If language in a rather fundamental sense is a dynamic and active ongoing affair of human beings transacting in a linguistic community, then linguistic contexts should not be reified or abstracted from their roles in culture and life. Therefore, to make reference in philosophy to the broader transactional contexts of language should not in every instance invoke attributions of "logism."

8

Linguistics and Epistemology

THOMAS NAGEL

Princeton University

THERE IS some reason to believe that Chomsky's views about the innate contribution to language-acquisition have a bearing on epistemological issues: on disputes over the existence of a priori knowledge, for example. Certainly if he is right, grammar provides a striking example of strong innate constraints on the form of human thought, and a natural object of philosophical fascination.

I do not propose to discuss the correctness of Chomsky's view concerning the importance and size of that innate contribution, or the adequacy of the support offered for it. The object of this paper is to investigate what epistemological consequences Chomsky's empirical hypotheses about language-learning have, if they are *correct*. The discussion will divide into two parts. First, I shall consider how Chomsky's hypotheses are most appropriately formulated, and specifically how the concept of knowledge can enter into their formulation. Second, I shall consider the bearing of these hypotheses on the epistemological status of our knowledge of natural languages, and also what they suggest about other kinds of knowledge, particularly those sometimes thought to be a priori.

I

The following, from page 58 of *Aspects of the Theory of Syntax,* gives a clear, brief statement of Chomsky's position:

It seems plain that language acquisition is based on the child's discovery of what from a formal point of view is a deep and abstract theory — a generative grammar of his language — many of the concepts and principles of which are only remotely related to experience by long and intricate chains of unconscious quasi-inferential steps. A consideration of the character of the grammar that is acquired, the degenerate quality and narrowly limited extent of the available data, the striking uniformity of the resulting grammars, and their independence of intelligence, motivation, and emotional state, over wide ranges of variation, leave little hope that much of the structure of the language can be learned by an organism initially uninformed as to its general character.

I believe Chomsky means to assert that we have here a genuine case of innate knowledge. His references to the Rationalists suggest that he does. Moreover, the alternative to an organism initially *un*informed as to the general character of the structure of natural languages would seem to be an organism initially *informed* as to that general character. And elsewhere (p. 27) he speaks of ascribing tacit knowledge of linguistic universals to the child. However, for the purpose of this discussion, it is not necessary to settle the exegetical point. The fact is that Chomsky's contentions about language-acquisition will suggest to most students of epistemology, as they suggest to me, that we are presented here with an example of innate knowledge. It is this natural philosophical interpretation that I propose to examine, and I shall not in the remainder of this paper concern myself explicitly with Chomsky's philosophical views, but only with the philosophical implications of his linguistic views.

The first question, then, is whether the initial contribution of the organism to language-learning, alleged by Chomsky, is properly described as knowledge at all. Let us begin by considering what I take to be a natural but bad argument for a negative answer to the question. The argument has the form of a reductio.

It occurs to most philosophers to ask, at some point in their consideration of Chomsky's views, whether the decision to apply the concept of knowledge in this case would not also commit us to ascribing innate knowledge, perhaps even a priori knowledge, to the human digestive system (or perhaps rather to human beings in virtue of the behavior of their digestive systems). For without having to be trained, instructed, or conditioned, the individual is able to adjust the chemical environment in his stomach to break down the digestible food that is introduced, while rejecting, sometimes forcibly, what is indigestible. This formidable task of classification and variable response is carried out even by infants, so it cannot be learned entirely from experience.

Admittedly the infant is not consciously aware of the principles that govern his gastric secretions, nor is the adult, unless he has studied physiology. But this does not distinguish the case from that of language-acquisition, for neither a child, nor an adult who has not studied linguistics, is consciously aware either of the grammatical rules of his language or of the principles by which he arrives at the ability to speak the language governed by those rules, on the basis of his exposure to a subset of the sentences of that language. In light of these parallels, it might be thought that the same reasons which can be offered in support of the view that there is innate knowledge of the general character of linguistic structure would count equally well in favor of the view that there is innate knowledge of the proper chemical means of digesting various kinds of food. The consequence of this would be that either both are examples of innate knowledge, or neither is. And it would then appear that the latter possibility is the more plausible. This would allow us to say that in both cases there is an extremely important innate *capacity* — to discriminate among and digest foods, or to acquire command of natural languages having a certain type of structure — but it would not be called innate *knowledge* in either case.

The trouble with this argument is that it ignores the difference between the operations that we have in the two cases the capacity to perform. In the case of digestion, the operation is not an action at all (this is obvious even though we do not possess an analysis of action). Nor do the data on which the operation is based, i.e., the various foods introduced into the stomach, have to be brought to the awareness of the organism. In the case of language-learning, on the other hand, conscious apprehension of the data (limited as they may be) is essential; and what the individual can do as a result of his linguistic capacity is to speak and understand sentences.

Moreover, the exercise of the capacity involves *beliefs*: e.g., that a certain combination of words is, or is not, a sentence of the language. Someone who regurgitates a bad oyster, on the other hand, is not thereby said to believe that it is indigestible. Though we may not possess an adequate analysis of the distinction, it is clear that certain methods of response and discrimination warrant the attribution of beliefs and attitudes, while others do not. Only of the former category is it appropriate to consider whether they give evidence of knowledge. The phenomena of language use belong to that former category, whereas the phenomena of digestion do not.

It is clear then that such cognitive concepts are entirely appropriate to the description of linguistic capacity and performance on particular occasions. What must be settled, however, is whether the concepts of knowledge and belief can be applied at higher levels of generality and abstraction in the description of the individual's linguistic capacity, and ultimately in the description of his capacity to acquire that capacity.

We may distinguish the following two theses: (1) that the general capacity to produce a set of performances each of which provides an instance of knowledge is itself an instance of more general knowledge; (2) that the general capacity to acquire other capacities each of which is an instance of knowledge is itself an instance of still more general knowledge. The former thesis is more plausible than the latter, but both are needed to warrant the inferential ascent from cases of linguistic knowledge revealed in particular utterances to the ascription of a knowledge of linguistic universals on which language-learning is alleged to depend.

It will be useful if we try to ascend step by step from the

most specific and immediate case to more general capacities. It seems obvious that we can speak of linguistic knowledge whose object is not merely the grammaticality or meaning of a particular utterance, but something more general. (In fact it is doubtful that we could speak of knowledge in the particular case unless we could also speak of it on a more general level.) To take a very simple example, we can ascribe to the ordinary speaker of English, on the basis of countless particular performances and responses, the knowledge that the plural form of a noun is usually formed by adding 's,' and that among the exceptions to this is the word 'man,' whose plural is 'men.' Now we *might* verify this ascription by finding that the individual can actually state the rule; but it is important that this is not necessary. Someone can possess general knowledge of a rule of the language without being able to state it. He may never have heard the words 'plural,' and 'noun,' for example, and may be unable to formulate the principle in any other way. When we come to the more complicated principles to which grammatical English speech conforms, that will be the usual situation. Only professional grammarians will be able to state those rules, and sometimes even that may not be true.

Under what conditions can knowledge of a language governed by certain rules be described as knowledge of those rules? It will be instructive in this connection to consider another type of knowledge that cannot be explicitly formulated by its possessor, namely unconscious knowledge in the ordinary psychoanalytic sense. This is of course a very different phenomenon from knowledge of the rules of grammar, but it has an important feature that, as Saul Kripke has pointed out to me, may bear on the linguistic case. The psychoanalytic ascription of unconscious knowledge, or unconscious motives for that matter, does not depend simply on the possibility of organizing the subject's responses and actions in conformity with the alleged unconscious material. In addition, although he does not formulate his unconscious knowledge or attitude of his own accord, and may deny it upon being asked, it is usually possible to bring him by analytical techniques to *see* that the statement in question expresses something that he knows or feels. That is, he is able eventually to acknowledge the statement as an expression of his own belief, if it is presented to him clearly enough and in the right circumstances. Thus what was unconscious can be brought, at least partly, to consciousness. It is essential that his acknowledgment *not* be based merely on the observation of his own responses and behavior, and that he come to recognize the rightness of the attribution from the inside.

It seems to me that where recognition of this sort is possible in principle, there is good reason to speak of knowledge and belief, even in cases where the relevant principles or statements have not yet been consciously acknowledged, or even in cases where they will never be explicitly formulated. Without suggesting that knowledge of the rules of a language is in other ways like the unconscious knowledge revealed by psychoanalysis, we may observe that accurate formulations of grammatical rules often evoke the same sense of recognition from speakers who have been conforming to them for years that is evoked by the explicit formulation of repressed material that has been influencing one's behavior for years. The experience is less alarming in the former case, but nevertheless recognizably similar. It can happen even if the grammatical principles are formulated in a technical vocabulary that may require a certain amount of effort to master.

So long as it would be possible with effort to bring the speaker to a genuine recognition of a grammatical rule as an expression of his understanding of the language, rather than to a mere belief, based on the observation of cases, that the rule in fact describes his competence, it is not improper I think to ascribe knowledge of that rule to the speaker. It is not improper, even though he may never be presented with a formulation of the rule and consequently may never come to recognize it consciously.

If the condition of recognizability cannot be met, however, the ascription of knowledge and belief seems to me more dubious. And this casts doubt on the possibility of carrying the ascription of knowledge to any level of generality or abstraction higher than that involved in the specification of grammatical rules for a particular natural language. Even some of those rules are highly abstract. But when we consider the alleged innate contribution to language-learning, we pass to quite another level, and there is reason to doubt that the principles of such a linguistic acquisition device, when they have been formulated, could evoke internal recognition from individuals who have operated in accordance with them.

The rules of a particular grammar deal in part with recognizable expressions, and retain some connection, in their formulation, with the speaker's conscious experience of his language. The connection in the case of linguistic universals, of the kind that Chomsky suggests are innately present, is more remote. One example that he offers is the proposal that the syntactic component of a grammar must contain transformational rules. This highly abstract condition is supposed to apply to *all* languages, and to determine the way in which a child acquires knowledge of the grammar of his native language by being exposed to samples of speech. But is it supposed that he could in principle be brought some day to recognize such a principle as the proper expression of an assumption he was making at the time (once the proper principle has been formulated and its meaning conveyed to him)? This may be a possibility, but the conditions of explanatory adequacy that Chomsky accepts seem not to demand it. Explanatory adequacy is in itself of course a very strong requirement. But a hypothesis could be shown to satisfy it on the basis of observation of the language-learning feat itself. The additional test of asking the language-learner whether he can recognize the principle as one that was activating him all along seems irrelevant. It seems not to be required even that such internal recognition should *ever* be available or possible, no matter how much effort is expended on it.

I may have misconstrued Chomsky on this point; but in light of it, I am uneasy about extending the concept of knowledge, and the related concepts of belief and assumption, to the

description of those innate capacities that enable a child to acquire knowledge of a language — any natural language — on
the basis of rather minimal data. If this is correct, then not
every innate capacity to acquire knowledge need itself be an
instance of knowledge — even though its structural description
may be quite complex.

II

The difficulties raised so far about the ascription of innate
knowledge on the basis of language-learning ability are really
broader difficulties about the ascription of innate *beliefs* or *as-*
sumptions on the basis of language-learning ability. I wish now
to turn to the epistemologically more interesting question,
whether there is any possibility that the other main type of
condition for knowledge could be met in such cases. I refer to
the justification condition. There has been considerable controversy over the exact nature of this condition, but I hope it will
be possible to discuss the present issue without entering that
maze.

The problem is this. We can imagine almost any belief to
be innately present, or that there is an innate tendency to develop that belief as the result of certain minimal experiences.
That is not a sufficient basis for ascribing knowledge, however.
Not just any belief that one cannot help arriving at is ipso
facto justified, even if it should be true.

Suppose that someone discovered that he was able on request to specify the square root of any integer to four decimal
places, without reflection or calculation. The fact that his ability was innate would not of itself guarantee the validity of his
answers. The grounding of his knowledge of square roots
would be rather more complex: he and other persons could
verify by calculation in case after individual case that the
number which he unreflectively believed to be the square root
of a given integer in fact was the square root. In virtue of this
further evidence, his unreflective belief in any given case could
be taken as strong evidence of its own truth. In that sense it

would be self-justifying — not merely because of the innateness of the capacity, but because of its independently verifiable accuracy.

With knowledge of a language we face a very different subject matter, but certain features of the case are the same. Let us consider first an imaginary example analogous to the one just discussed — a case in which someone has an innate capacity that is not generally shared. Suppose someone discovers that he is able to extend his vocabulary merely by observing new species of plants and animals, because he finds himself able to say what they are called without being told. Again, the mere fact that he is innately disposed to call this bird a magpie does not guarantee that that is its name. But if it is discovered in case after case that his unreflective belief conforms to general usage, the belief itself will provide evidence for its own truth.

Now, the actual phenomenon of language-learning that Chomsky describes is different from this, because it reveals an innate capacity that we all share. All speakers of English, for example, reach agreement in an obedience to certain grammatical rules, and attain this naturally and without calculation after a certain amount of exposure to the language. Now, no one individual's innate propensity to arrive at these rules of itself guarantees that they are the rules of the language he is speaking. That depends on a more general conformity to those same rules by all speakers of the language, and this is guaranteed by the universality of those same innate propensities. Thus if any given individual knows that his own linguistic intuitions about sentences that he has not encountered before, and his own original linguistic productions, are in conformity with the linguistic intuitions of other speakers of his language, then he can regard his innate tendencies as providing strong evidence for their own accuracy. But that is simply because as a matter of natural fact they are in conformity with the linguistic propensities of speakers of the language in general, as determined presumably by a uniform innate contribution. I am not suggesting for a moment that we actually *do* step back from our linguistic intuitions in order to validate them in this way. I am suggesting only that it is because such a justification is *available* that we can plausibly describe what our innately governed linguistic propensities provide as *knowledge* of the language.

The point of all the examples is this: in each case, the fact that the tendency to arrive at a certain belief was innate, did not by itself make it a case of knowledge. In the special case of language, where the actual rules are simply those by which competent speakers generally are governed, a universal innate tendency to arrive at certain rules is enough to guarantee their accuracy; but any one individual must still know that he is in conformity with the universal tendency, in order to know that his linguistic intuitions are correct. And this is a matter that is open to empirical investigation. The crucial fact is that in any individual case the alleged innate contribution to language-learning can itself be assessed for its accuracy as a source of knowledge of the language. It may be that no one ever engages in this sort of assessment, and that the innate tendency to construct the grammar of one's language in a certain way also includes an innate tendency to assume that other speakers will construct it in the same way; in fact this seems likely. But that assumption too is open to epistemological assessment by other means.

The importance of all this is that the innate factor, which Chomsky argues must underlie our language-learning capacity, bears no resemblance to the sort of unquestionable, epistemologically unassailable foundation on which some philosophers have sought to base human knowledge, and which is generally referred to as a priori or innate knowledge. What has been sought under this heading is something that is not itself open to the usual varieties of epistemological assessment and doubt, something whose opposite is unimaginable.

But what Chomsky offers us is a system of innate propensities that we are conveniently stuck with. It is perfectly imaginable that we should be differently constituted, but we are not. A mere innate tendency to believe certain things or perform in certain ways, no matter how universal, is not a priori knowledge. Even Hume thought that we all share a natural propensity to believe that the sun will rise again tomorrow. To point out the natural phenomenon of human agreement, innately determined, is simply to turn aside the epistemological demand that motivates the search for a priori knowledge.

In fact, such a move is closely related to Wittgenstein's position [1] — the main difference being that Wittgenstein applies it much more generally, and not just to language-learning. He argues that if one follows any chain of epistemological justification far enough, one comes in the end to a phenomenon of human agreement — not conventional agreement, but natural, innately determined agreement — on which the acceptance of that justification depends. He supposes this to happen whether the justification is empirical or deductive. If he is right, the procedures by which we subject one innate contribution to epistemological assessment will themselves simply depend on another innate contribution. And if at every stage what we have reached is only a contingent feature of our constitution, then there is no unquestionable a priori foundation on which our knowledge rests. It depends on a network of innate responses and propensities; and they are simply there.

If this is so, then epistemology may be essentially impossible. Insofar as Chomsky's contentions about language suggest that similar innate contributions underlie other cognitive phenomena as well, they suggest that all knowledge is in similar straits: it lacks an unassailable foundation. Sometimes, as in the case of language, one can take further steps to justify one's confidence in the yield of one's innate mechanism. Evidence of this kind is available to any speaker who successfully uses the language to communicate with others. But the admission of such evidence may in turn depend on innate principles that, without guaranteeing their own justification, form part of one's basic constitution; [2] so the task of justification may be incompletable.

Though this is epistemologically unsettling, it has practical compensations. If we had to learn by trial and error, or by training, how to digest food, we should have a much harder time surviving. But fortunately we don't need to *know* how to digest food, for we do it in the right way automatically. Language-learning may be similar. We do not need to *know* how to construct the grammar of a natural language on the basis of our early childhood exposure to samples of it. We simply *arrive* at a command of the language after a certain period of exposure, and find ourselves convinced that other speakers are following the same rules.

It may be true in many areas of human activity and experience that if we had to rely on what we could come to know, by either empirical or rational means, we should be unable to survive. But if in these areas we are fortunate enough to possess an innate endowment that suits us to deal with the world awaiting us, we do not require the knowledge that it would be so difficult, or perhaps impossible, to obtain. We can be guided by our innate ideas instead.

NOTES

1. I am aware that Chomsky does not share this view of Wittgenstein. He has been kind enough to show me a forthcoming paper that defends another interpretation.

2. I believe that this is connected with Quine's thesis of the indeterminacy of translation.

9

On Knowing a Grammar

ROBERT SCHWARTZ

The Rockefeller University

I SHALL NOT attempt to present detailed arguments refuting Chomsky but rather I shall raise some points I find worth further investigation. Broadly speaking, I am interested in discovering what someone who has learned a language can be said to know.

Chomsky claims that the grammar of a language should be seen as a description of the linguistic competence of a speaker of the language. Chomsky stresses that we must be careful to distinguish between a speaker's competence and his performance, and it is the former of these that a grammar is supposed to describe. Now, there seems to me to be nothing particularly mysterious or peculiar to language in the distinction between competence and performance. Surely we must allow that someone can have a proficiency, skill, or competence to do something and that a description of it is to be distinguished from a description of his actual performance. For example, we might claim that any of the numerous axiom sets for addition and subtraction characterize a certain part of the mathematical competence of someone who knows or has learned arithmetic. This does not mean that the person can state these axioms, nor that he will ever carry out any particular addition or subtraction, nor that his performance will always satisfy these rules, for he may purposely violate them or just make a mistake. A given S's performance could be expected to satisfy the axioms describing his competence only under ideal conditions of motivation, memory, attention, etc.

There might even be some arithmetic problems that, for reasons such as the size of the numbers involved and the mortality of man, we can be quite sure no one will in fact ever work out.[1] To claim that the axioms represent S's competence would seem merely to claim that S has some "mechanism" that, like the various axiom systems, can generate the unlimited set of correct equations. If this, then, is the competence-performance distinction, I find it relatively clear and unobjectionable.

But Chomsky makes the further claim that the speaker knows or has an internal representation of the rules of grammar of his language. Chomsky admits that in this instance he is not using 'know' in the sense of *knowing that* nor in the sense of *knowing how,* but in a third sense — that of tacit or implicit knowing. He finds the traditional "knowing" dichotomy too restrictive. Clearly S does not have propositional-like knowledge of the rules of his language. On the other hand, to claim S knows how to speak a particular language, while true, does not go far enough. Tacit knowledge is brought in to explain this 'know-how.' Chomsky's claim seems to be that in order to know how to speak a language, S must know (tacitly or implicitly) the grammar of the language.

A correct interpretation of this notion of tacit knowledge is not immediately apparent. In addition to eliminating the possibility of an explication in terms of knowing that or how, Chomsky also warns that to claim S has implicit knowledge of a grammar is not to regard the system of generative rules as a point-by-point model for the actual construction of a sentence by a speaker. The grammar is not to be construed as a performance model but rather as a characterization of competence equally applicable to both hearer and speaker.

If we allow that knowledge of a grammar is neither knowing that or knowing how nor a description of the process of sentence construction, what sense can be given to the claim that S knows the rules? Several interpretations of this claim worth considering are: (1) the rules describe regularities in S's linguistic competence, (2) for each sentence in his language, S knows its structural description (S.D.), generated by the rules of the grammar, and (3) in order to understand, produce, or decide on the grammaticality of a sentence S must determine or generate its S.D.[2]

On the first interpretation, to claim S knows the rules is to claim that the grammar describes regularities in S's linguistic competence. If this means that S knows the regularities in his language specified by the grammar, then, taken literally, this is just another way of saying that S has propositional knowledge of the rules and is admittedly false. If, however, what is meant is merely that the sentences of S's language exhibit the regularities specified or specifiable in terms of the grammar, then the claim is obviously true but does not involve some radically new conception of knowing. Any true description of regularities of or within the set of grammatical sentences will tautologically be true of the output of S's competence. Thus the particular rule (or set of rules) that allows only transitive verbs to occur in the environment *NP* describes a regularity in S's language. S might be said to "know" this regularity but only in the sense that he will consider strings that violate this rule ungrammatical. Similarly, in terms of the rules, it may be possible to specify the class of sentences that have nominalizations. This certainly marks a regularity in S's language, i.e., that only sentences that have a certain structure (specified *by the linguist* in his grammar) will have companion nominalizations. S again might be said to "know" this regularity but only in the sense that he knows that certain strings are sentences and that he knows that nominalizations of some of these strings are also sentences whereas other attempted nominalizations are not grammatical. These regularities then are regularities true of what S knows (the class of grammatical sentences) and not regularities he knows.

The next interpretation claims that the S.D.'s the grammar assigns to sentences of the language describe what S knows, the intuitions he has about these sentences. To some extent this claim is certainly true. For example, in terms of the S.D.'s it is possible to specify such information as which strings are sentences, which ambiguous, and which part of a string serves as subject or object in the sentence (e.g., in the sentences 'John hit Mary' and 'Mary was hit by John' the S.D.'s can be used to indicate that John is the hitter and Mary the recipient of the brutality). Knowledge of this information, however, is best seen as just a variant of our old friend know-that. We would expect we could get S, perhaps with a little prodding, to assert or otherwise indicate that he knows whether a particular string is a sentence or is ambiguous. Furthermore, if S is to be said to understand the sentence, we would expect him to know who in the sentence did what to whom. Thus it is reasonable to claim in these cases that the S.D.'s codify some of S's intuitions about linguistic strings.

The S.D., however, gives much more information than this. The S.D. of a sentence contains its complete derivation from a basic axiom. It provides an analysis of an underlying structure in terms of hierarchical categorizations, subcategorizations, and selectional specifications, a transformational history, and an analysis of the sentence's surface structure. Clearly, it cannot be claimed that S knows this information in the same sense as he knows whether a string is a sentence, is ambiguous, etc. After all, at present the linguist himself doesn't have knowledge of this sort about the S.D.'s of all sentences in the language. Thus while some of the intuitions S actually has about strings can be defined or specified *by the linguist* in terms of the analysis provided in the S.D., it does not seem reasonable to claim that S has intuitions of this analysis.

This account of the relationship between competence and grammar goes back to our original interpretation. Here, however, we require that the grammar not only generate all sentences of S's language but that it also provide means for specifying some of the other things S knows about these sentences, such as matters of ambiguity or subject-object relations. The grammar will capture regularities in S's language and it is essentially in terms of some of these regularities that S's intuitions are specified, but again this does not mean that S knows the regularities, i.e., knows the structural analyses in terms of which the regularities are specified.

Our third interpretation provides for a stronger relationship between grammar and competence. On this account, if S is to understand, produce, or decide on the grammaticality of a sentence, he must determine (generate, recover, analyze, synthesize, or whatever) its S.D. This would imply that for each string he produces or perceives there would be some process or representation in S corresponding to a derivation of the S.D. of that string.

But I find this account most puzzling, for it seems to run together a specification of competence with a description of the structures underlying the competence. Consider some of S's other cognitive competences, his previously discussed arithmetic competence, for example, or his competence to recognize strings as well-formed formulas of the propositional calculus. Both of these competences could be specified by a set of formal axioms or rules. Now, while S undoubtedly employs assorted strategies and heuristics in these areas, no one, I think, feels impelled to claim that for S to judge or produce an equation or formula he must generate or recover its corresponding derivation in one of the customary formal systems.

The fact that we can specify S's competence in terms of a formal system of generative rules does not in itself imply that S has represented a *corresponding* system in him. In fact, the whole question of what would count as a corresponding system is a messy issue. An example may best make my point. Suppose we observe an input-output device that labels spheres '+' if their density is greater than 1.0 and '−' if their density is less. We could specify this output with the following equations:

$$\text{Vol. of sphere} = \tfrac{4}{3}\,\pi\,\text{radius}^3, \text{Density} = \frac{\text{weight}}{\text{volume}},$$
$$\text{Acceptable } (+) \text{ density} = > 1.0,$$

but the device might not employ a set of principles anything like this. It might never determine the individual sphere's radius, weight, or volume; instead it might merely contain a liquid of density 1.0 and label '+' any sphere that sinks in the liquid, and '—' any that floats. Would it be reasonable to claim that our equations are internally represented in this machine? Although in some sense the liquid in the machine could be held to "stand for" the equations, it seems less reasonable to claim that the analysis provided by the equations is mirrored in any interesting manner by the internal processes of the machine.

Similarly, consider how S balances himself on a bicycle. Even though what he does may be specified in terms of the laws of gravity, are there any grounds for claiming that S unconsciously computes the relevant differentials and solves the appropriate physics equations? My point is not merely that S does not have propositional knowledge of these laws, but that even the seemingly weaker claim of unconscious computations is subject to doubt, and as long as such doubt remains, care must be taken in interpreting the assertion that the laws of physics model S's bicycle skills or vice versa. By these examples I do not mean to suggest that S possesses some simple one-step mechanical device for processing sentences, but rather that nothing in the analysis provided by S's perceptual and cognitive processes need correspond in any straightforward way to the S.D.'s provided by the generative grammar.[3]

At present, then, I see no compelling reason to suppose that S must generate the S.D.'s of a Chomskian grammar in order to produce or understand sentences. Nor do I find the meaning of the claim that S has tacit or implicit knowledge of the grammar of his language at all obvious.

II

Chomsky's approach to language-learning combines an attack on traditional learning theory with positive proposals for a language-learning device whose most notable (or notorious) feature is its possession of innate ideas. It is only this latter issue I shall discuss here and at that one particular aspect of it.

Chomsky finds it necessary to introduce his innateness hypothesis in order to explain how, on the basis of a finite, fragmentary, and frequently degenerate set of instances, an organism acquires a particular way of handling new cases. As I see it, the psychologically interesting question is whether the factors that shape the learning of language are specific to language or whether they are general features of the learning apparatus. This most certainly is an empirical matter. However, it should be noted that the child develops many skills and competences, acquires knowledge or relationships and regularities in his environment, learns games and complex patterns of social behavior, etc. in essentially the same "untaught" manner he learns language. In most of these cases, too, it is difficult to see how his behavior can be accounted for in terms of simple stimulus-response chains, stimulus generalization, reinforcement, etc. Thus Chomsky's problem would arise in all of these cases, yet it would seem implausible to claim distinct innate schemata responsible for each.

Further, as a consequence of the innateness hypothesis, it is frequently claimed that a child would encounter enormous (if not, from a practical standpoint, insurmountable) difficulty learning a language not of the predestined form. Direct evidence supporting this claim is admittedly not available. On the other hand, I believe there are good reasons for believing no *interesting* version of this claim will prove true. For the child, before, during, and after he learns language, masters various other complex symbol systems that, as Chomsky himself points out, do not fit the natural language mold. In many of these cases, too, he does so without explicit instruction. Of course it could be claimed that any symbol system that violates the Chomskian canons is not a language and thus outside the scope of the claim, but this would only make the argument circular.[4]

NOTES

1. Thus we may want to further distinguish having the competence from actually being able to do something. In the arithmetic case, S may not "be able" to solve a particular problem due to its

length but may be claimed to have the competence to do so. Or someone who has learned to speak a language and then suffers damage to his vocal cords may not "be able" to speak, although he might still have the competence to do so and would be expected to be able to do so once his injury healed.

2. I am not claiming that any of these positions is Chomsky's, rather they represent my attempts to make sense of his claim that a speaker knows the grammar.

3. In fact, it is not at all clear to me what it would mean for S to represent rules, generate S.D.'s, etc. unless he does so in some language or symbol system, albeit internal. As far as I know, however, no account has been offered about what such a system would be like. But this issue takes us farther afield than is needed for my point.

4. I wish to thank Nelson Goodman and Margaret Atherton for discussing these issues with me.

10

Neorationalism and Empiricism

KENNETH STERN

Smith College

IN THE PAPER Professor Chomsky prepared for the colloquium, he begins by expressing considerable skepticism regarding the claim made by Vendler, among others, that transformational linguistics can be of very much help in providing techniques for dealing with problems that analytic philosophers are interested in, but argues, on the other hand, that

> . . . the study of language can clarify and, in part, substantiate certain conclusions about human knowledge that relate directly to classical issues in the philosophy of mind.

The main issue that Chomsky has particularly in mind is ". . . how knowledge is acquired and [whether] the character of human knowledge is determined by certain general properties of the mind." Chomsky holds that his conception of the nature of language can both clarify (in large part), or perhaps "reconstruct" in a Deweyan sense, what lay behind the famous altercation between classical continental rationalism and British empiricism concerning "innate ideas," and, granted that his conception of language is right, resolve the issue in favor of rationalism.

The prevailing philosophic temper being what it is, Chomsky's latter claim, namely, that the rationalists were correct with regard to the existence of "innate structures of the mind," put as baldly as that, is arresting enough. Nevertheless, it became clear in the course of the subsequent discussion, whatever else was not, that a good many of the stanch empiricists who took part in the colloquium argued not so much that Chomsky's theory of language was not correct, but rather that neither his theory, nor any of its implications were really incompatible with modern empiricism. Professor Quine, for example, in his comment on Chomsky's views remarked (as I recollect) that in his view every rational man was an empiricist. In the same vein of criticism, Quine further remarked that although Chomsky apparently held that empiricism denied the existence of innate ideas, behaviorism (one of Chomsky's primary empiricistic targets) "is up to its neck in innate mechanisms." It must strike anyone as peculiar that so much of the discussion revolved about whether Chomsky was correct in thinking that there was any real issue between his reconstructed rationalism and modern-day empiricism, rather than about the substantive questions concerning Chomsky's theory. At least part of the reason is that it would seem that Chomsky's critics are unclear as to just what it is that Chomsky is claiming concerning his version of the (allegedly) discordant claims of modern empiricism and Chomskian neorationalism. To recur to Quine's latter remark quoted above (from my notes), that "empiricism is up to its neck in innate mechanisms," I cannot recall that Chomsky explicitly addressed himself to this remark in his reply to Quine, but as exponent of Chomsky's views, Jerrold Katz has written: [1]

> The basis for the controversy is not, as it is often conceived in popular discussions, that empiricists fail to credit the mind with any innate principles, but rather that the principles which are accorded innate status by empiricists do not place any substantive restrictions on the ideas that can qualify as components of complex ideas or any formal restrictions on the structure of associations which bond component ideas together to form a complex idea. On the empiricist's hypothesis, the innate principles are purely combinatorial devices for putting together items from experience. So these principles provide only the machinery for instituting associative bonds. Experience plays the selective role in determining which ideas may be connected by association, and principles of association

are, accordingly, unable to exclude any ideas as, in principle, beyond the range of possible intellectual acquisition.

The view expressed in this passage from Katz is, from what I could gather from Chomsky's informal remarks, consonant with Chomsky's who said in his informal exposition that (I paraphrase), the "fixed schematism" that is in the mind sets a limit to possible hypotheses that the mind can construct from the input consisting of speech and other relevant "data of the senses," and so puts fundamental limitations on the admissible hypotheses which seem to "fit" the input. The issue then, if I understand Chomsky, is not whether empiricism admits the existence of innate structures, but rather whether these structures "dictate" the kinds of beliefs or hypotheses we can have concerning the world. According to empiricism, the limitations of these beliefs or hypotheses are dictated by the limitations of our sensory apparatus, ignoring as basically irrelevant intellectual differences among men. According to Chomsky, there are certain *further* fundamental limitations imposed by the innate schematism of the human mind; and that there *is* such an innate schematism is shown by an examination of the nature of language, for certain facts about human language, and its mode of acquisition, are explicable only by the postulation of such an innate schematism, again on the grounds that not all the possibilities are actualized, and what is actualized seems to be universal. Essentially, Chomsky's idea seems to be that one must account for the samenesses in human languages (i.e., linguistic universals), as well as the differences, and these former cannot be accounted for on empiricist principles.

If the above is a necessarily brief, but nonetheless correct, account of Chomsky's view, then the question that must arise is whether there is any part of it that is unacceptable to an empiricist of a Quinean sort. From what I have read of Chomsky and others who take his position, nothing they write would show that they support even to the smallest degree that part of traditional rationalism which holds that the human mind is in possession of a set of necessary truths "about the world" known independently of experience. It was, of course, this claim that traditional empiricism rejected. But, in any case, it is not at all certain, given Quine's views concerning the a priori, that he would be very much concerned to reject such a claim in that form. Chomsky's brand of rationalism is surely more akin to Kant than to seventeenth-century rationalism, as his emphasis upon the informing character of the structures he holds are innate, as well as his use of the terms "schemata" and "schematism," show. As has already been pointed out, these schemata, according to Chomsky, limit the judgments of hypotheses that we can formulate about reality, over and above the limitations already present due to the limitations of our sensory apparatus. But why should there be anything in this claim that is intrinsically inimical to an empiricism that does not have as part of it the classical Humean view that all of our concepts in *form* as well as *content* are determined by what can be received passively through our senses? It seemed to me from Quine's remarks during the discussion that his view is that empiricism should be viewed as a method rather than a doctrine, so that if good evidence supporting the existence of these internal structures could be offered by Chomsky, he would be quite willing to accept their existence. So long as these "ideas" could be "externalized," and made sense of in terms of public testing, he could find no reason to reject the notion that they existed. Another problem, it is true, is involved here, for it is unclear how we are to understand these innate structures. Are they to be understood as simply dispositions, i.e., capacities and abilities, or as, potentially at least, actual neurophysical structures in the nervous system? Quine, who in his remarks held that modern empiricism permits any amount of innate ideas, just as long as they are made sense of in terms of publicly testable readinesses to behave, also insists in another place [2] upon the "promissory-note" character of the use of dispositional words, in that in addition to their preliminary redeemability in terms of publicly observable data, there ought also to be some real hope of "eventually redeeming them in terms of an explicit account of the working mechanism." [3] Chomsky, as I recall, does contend that it may very well be that physioneurological structures may be found as explanations for these abilities and capacities, although he is somewhat vague about this matter. Still, since he does, it is again not clear how his view is incompatible with a modern empiricism.

But let me now turn to an issue that really might promise to mark a difference between Chomskian rationalism and empiricism. Earlier on, I quoted a passage where Katz contends that empiricism does not allow for any principled limitations upon the range of complex ideas that can be acquired by human minds. As a preliminary remark, let me say that I should suppose that Katz and Chomsky would want to hold, perhaps *contra* Kant, that they are only speaking of human minds as presently constructed, and that they are not disallowing the possibility that changes in the structure eventually occur. The important question here, however, is trying to make "empirical" sense of this contention. The obvious, perhaps simple-minded question to be asked here is what sort of evidence could be presented for the contention that there are some complex ideas (hypotheses) that cannot be formulated? [4] This contention is, of course, reminiscent of Kant who maintained that there were certain necessary categories of rational understanding, and seems to me to be subject to the same difficulties. For what empirical meaning can be accorded to the contention that there are possible hypotheses that would fit the data of language or, following Chomsky's extrapolation from his linguistic investigations, data in general, which are, given the innate structures of the mind, unformulable? Perhaps it is here that Chomsky does part company with empiricism. But here empiricism is surely to be understood as a particular view concerning the verifiability of putatively scientific hypotheses, rather than an alternate view concerning the structure of the mind. If there is any dispute between Chomsky and Quine, then it would seem it lies in the question of whether Chomsky's contention that there are limits set by the structure of the mind upon formulable hypotheses, that, given the data, possible hypotheses are unformulable.

Connected with what I have just said is another difficulty

that I find in Chomsky's theory. Chomsky makes exciting claims that extend beyond even those he makes for the nature of language, for, as I understand him, it is his contention that not only are there fundamental restrictions imposed on the nature of language by the internal structures he postulates, but that similar ones also impose limits upon the nature of all knowledge and its acquisition. The question I should like to ask concerns Chomsky's extrapolation from what may be true about language to human knowledge in general, viz., even allowing the centrality of language in human nature, what evidence is there that what may hold true in the case of language also holds true for all of human psychology? Language *is* no doubt very central, but it is also quite special. Animals have been accorded the ability to have knowledge of the world comparable, at least in kind, with human knowledge, although it is conceded that they have nothing like language in any human sense.

Connected with the previous point, I should find it interesting if sometime Chomsky would discuss how his theory of language, and its implications for human psychology and epistemology, fits into, or rather does not fit into, the theory of evolution. The general direction of his claims appears to be that language and its acquisition and human rationality itself are a unique phenomenon in the natural order. Indeed, it is here that Chomsky displays his greatest affinity with Descartes, who held that language as the essence of rationality was what made a distinction *in kind* between man and other animate things. Seen in this light, Chomsky sets himself against Hume who (in the section in his *Inquiry* titled, "Of the Reason of Animals") ascribed diminished powers of inference to animals, but maintained they were analogous to those of human beings. It is in this area that Chomsky's views have the most remarkable implications, for his attack on behaviorism, and especially his attack on the behavioristic theory of language as "verbal behavior," seems to me, if substantiated, to have the most far-reaching implications for the modern "humanistic" view of the world so widely accepted. Chomsky's theories have so far provoked a great deal of discussion, but given their implications, no amount of investigation into their truth would be too much.

NOTES

1. *The Philosophy of Language* (New York: Harper & Row), pp. 240–41.
2. *The Ways of Paradox* (New York: Random House), pp. 48–56.
3. *Ibid.*, p. 52.
4. Chomsky in his remarks spoke of a limitation on possible hypotheses.

11

Is Linguistic Rationalism a Rational Linguistics?

MARVIN ZIMMERMAN

University of Buffalo

NOAM CHOMSKY, in criticizing Locke and others for attacking a crude form of the doctrine of innate ideas, is likewise obliged to avoid attacking a crude form of empiricism. He speaks critically of those empiricists who invoke some process of generalization or abstraction that functions along with association and conditioning to account for language-acquisition. He believes that empiricist accounts of language-acquisition are inadequate and thus require postulation of innate mental structure. He suggests that to refer to the processes involved in language-acquisition as processes of generalization or abstraction is to use these terms in a sense that has no recognizable relation to what is called 'generalization' or 'abstraction' in philosophy, ɲsychology, or linguistics.[1]

Chomsky implies that empiricists deny that the ability to generalize or abstract is innate, whereas what they deny is that the knowledge acquired by means of generalization, etc. is innate. In misinterpreting the position of empiricism, he is also equivocating on the meaning of rationalism in support of his own position. He relies on the fact that we are innately endowed with the ability to generalize, etc., to erroneously infer that the knowledge acquired by this means is also innate. The former claim is not what is at issue between rationalism and empiricism, but rather the latter, and, if all he intends to maintain is the former, then he has blurred the distinction between these two schools of thought. One of the difficulties is that his writings reflect shifts back and forth between these two positions.

If we permit him to infer the latter from the former, we would have to conclude that all knowledge, without exception, is innate, since all knowledge presupposes the use of processes and organs with which we are endowed at birth, such as, sense organs, brain, and other physical and psychological machinery. To suggest that empiricists deny such endowment would imply that empiricists make no distinction between the ability of human beings to learn, and other organisms and indeed inanimate things in nature.

If innate ideas are latent in that they require experience to bring them out, then they are not like being endowed with legs and arms and breathing apparatus, which we can observe and distinguish as functioning and operating at birth. This raises the need to make quite clear how the claim of innate knowledge as a hypothesis is distinguishable from the claim of empiricism. For if experience is stipulated as a necessary condition for exhibiting both innate knowledge and principles, as well as acquired knowledge, we need criteria for choosing between these two hypotheses. The rationalist will have to show that the particular experiences he believes necessary for eliciting innate knowledge cannot, without assuming the existence of innate knowledge, account for the knowledge he claims is innate. Otherwise, there is no reason to believe that this knowledge is innate rather than acquired. This will also necessitate spelling out more precisely what constitutes the innate knowledge allegedly unaccountable for on an empirical basis.

Since both allegedly innate knowledge and acquired knowledge must be within our capability, and both may be dispositional in being exhibited under specified conditions, neither the criteria of being within our capability nor being dispositional can be used to distinguish innate from acquired knowledge. In addition, dispositional knowledge cannot be equated with potential knowledge (if this means no more than possible knowledge), since the former constitutes actual knowledge, whereas the latter merely constitutes the possibility of knowledge. The point is that there must be some way of distinguishing between knowledge already possessed by the individual (for example, in his memory) which may be exhibited under specified conditions (dispositional knowledge), and knowledge not possessed by the individual and thus not qualifying as knowledge unless and until exhibited under specified conditions (potential knowledge). Since both dispositional and potential knowledge may be characterized as knowledge exhibited under specified conditions, describing innate knowledge as knowledge exhibited under specified conditions does not show that the allegedly innate knowledge is dispositional rather than potential. Thus, anyone describing innate knowledge as being 'latent' and thus exhibited under specified conditions is required to show this to be dispositional not merely potential. A claim to innate knowledge that turns out to be a claim to potential knowledge is a claim to no knowledge at all.

Chomsky asks "how on the basis of the limited data available to him, the child is able to construct a grammar of the sort that we are led to ascribe to him, with its particular choice and arrangement of rules and with the restrictive principles of application of such rules." Of course, he does not mean that the child is able to consciously spell out the grammatical rules and applications but that he exhibits a recognition of what is 'grammatical' and what is not, without having learned the grammar. If we restrict learning to formal instruction, then we have to account for those children who show recognition without formal instruction. But if Chomsky wishes to defend 'rationalism,' he will have to deny, as he does, that the child's knowledge of grammar can be explained by any kind of learning process, informal as well as formal. To show this, it seems, would entail careful investigations of the learning process almost from the moment of birth.

Chomsky seems to attribute to some kind of innate structure or principles or schema knowledge of grammatical structures. But this knowledge, though not entirely explicable on a basis of direct instruction, may be accounted for by the use of imagination, memory, reasoning as well as a wide range of data from all levels of experience not limited to language-acquisition. If Chomsky restricts the source of data too narrowly to instruction in language, he may be overlooking other sources of knowledge.

Chomsky states that the normal use of language involves new sentences that bear no point-by-point resemblance or analogy to those in the child's experience. This suggests an innate endowment to account for the new sentences not explicable by sentences previously acquired in the child's experience. But since complex ideas can also be conceived that bear no resemblance to anything found in experience, though these ideas may be broken down into elements traceable to experience (this is, of course, characteristically Lockean and Humean empiricism), it is not clear why similar explanations cannot also be made for new sentences. One does not expect Chomsky to deny that the semantic and syntactic elements making up the new sentences are empirically derived, and that the grammatical and logical forms of new sentences have been previously encountered. Since the doctrine of empiricism encompasses combining and abstracting elements of experience into new, more complex forms, this also applies to combining and abstracting elements of sentences into new, more complex sentences.

In attempting to refute the view that the output of grammatical sentences can be identified with the input of observed sentences, Chomsky tries to show that statistical studies of language have no direct relevance to the problem of determining the set of grammatical utterances. He attempts to give examples of grammatical utterances we are able to produce and recognize that we have never seen before and that therefore cannot be based on statistical approximations and the like.[2] But approximations can be formulated on a basis of frequency of 'sentence type' rather than frequency of 'sentence.' We can account for the production and recognition of a grammatical sentence as an instance of a 'sentence type' previously encountered, though the particular sentence may have not been previously encountered. Thus the output data can be explained on a basis of input data empirically and inductively, without any need to postulate innate principles or knowledge of grammar.

For example, Chomsky contrasts the sentence [(1) colorless green ideas sleep furiously] with the sentence [(2) furiously sleep ideas green colorless]. Though both sentences have probably never occurred in English discourse, we recognize the former as grammatical and the latter as not. Chomsky takes this to show that the notion of 'grammatical in English' cannot be identified with statistical approximations. But when we examine the 'sentence type' of sentence (1) above and compare its frequency with 'sentence type' of sentence (2), there is little doubt about the disparity in frequency of occurrences. Thus, contrast the frequency of 'sentence type' (1) with the subject (ideas) preceded by its modifiers (colorless, green) and followed by the verb (sleep) followed by its modifiers (furiously), with the frequency of 'sentence type' (2) with subject following the verb, and the modifiers following the subject. Examples of the first type are too numerous to list, whereas examples of the second type appear difficult to find.

At first glance, one may be overwhelmed and justifiably impressed by the power and intricate subtlety of transformational generative grammar, by the derivations linking 'surface' structure with 'deep' structure. Chomsky suggests that knowledge of the specific properties of grammatical transformations presupposes innate knowledge, since it cannot be plausibly shown that this knowledge was acquired through explanation or instruction. Of course, 'explicit' knowledge of the specific properties would normally be expected to require some kind of explanation or instruction. In fact, Chomsky's own writings have played an important role as forms of 'explanation and instruction' in acquiring explicit knowledge of the principles of transformational grammar. When he suggests that the language-learner has somehow established the facts for himself without explanation or instruction, he cannot be referring to 'explicit' knowledge of the specific properties. Otherwise, it would not square with his own admission that no one was aware of these principles until recently. Chomsky has contributed significantly to the recent awareness.

But if the knowledge to which he alludes was not acquired by explanation or instruction, then he must be referring to 'implicit' knowledge rather than explicit knowledge, i.e., to grammatical knowledge in general rather than technical familiarity with transformational grammar. In that case, invoking innate principles appears unnecessary, since knowledge derived from experience, including learning, thinking, analysis, imagination, etc., seems adequate to account for implicit knowledge of the specific properties.

The principles of transformational grammar seem to be formalized generalizations of linguistic usage, subject to continual revisions on a basis of new evidence. Knowledge of this grammar can be explained on an empirical basis without reference to any innate principles of grammar. The recognition that two sentences with different surface structures may have similar depth (underlying) structures, and vice versa, can be explained on empirical grounds. Thus, the recognition that the active and passive forms of a statement have the same depth structure, though different surface structures, can be accounted for by the data given in experience of the cognitive synonymity of these forms. The transformational rules with which we can generate the active and passive forms (surface structures) from the depth structures are themselves arrived at by empirical means, by generalizations of linguistic usage.

The recognition that two sentences [(1) John is certain that Bill will leave, (2) John is certain to leave], the former predicating certainty of an individual, the latter of a proposition, have different depth structures, is explicable in terms of prior experience with similar grammatical structures and vocabulary. That nominal phrases can be formed corresponding to deep structures but not to surface structures can be easily understood and explained on empirical grounds, on a basis of knowledge of the similarity in meaning and use of the nominal phrases and their corresponding deep structures. When we attempt to pin down what Chomsky means by innate knowledge and principles of transformational grammar, we discover that the examples, though reflecting varying degrees of technical and manipulative complexity, seem to be susceptible to empirical explanation.

A leading exponent of Chomsky's view of innate ideas, Jerrold J. Katz, has attempted to spell out the doctrine of linguistic rationalism.[3] He defines the observable grammatical features (input data) of a sentence in terms of what is directly predictable from final derived phrase markers (surface structures), whereas unobservable grammatical features are defined in terms of what can be predicted from its underlying phrase markers (underlying structures). Thus input data are restricted to surface structures, whereas output data contain allegedly innate elements found in the underlying structures, not in the surface structures.

Katz argues that any hypothesis about how the rules of language are acquired must explain how the semantic content contributed by unobservable grammatical features becomes part of the full meaning of sentences. Otherwise, the hypothesis fails to explain how a speaker knows what sentences with unobservable grammatical features mean. It turns out that examples used by Katz to illustrate his position seem to be explicable on empiricist grounds, and that what lends plausibility to his position is his restriction of input data exclusively to surface structures. The point is that if one can show that the elements found in the underlying structure are also derivable from the input data, then no innate principles are required.

Thus, the case of a 'you' subject in normal English imperative sentences, the case of a second verb phrase in comparative sentences, or the case of the subject-verb and object-verb relations are not cases of unobservable features (as Katz maintains), in the sense that they are explicable in terms of input data broadly understood. The doctrine of empiricism takes into account the broad context of experience, so that one can account for the knowledge of the so-called unobservable features, on inductive, empirical grounds. Thus, conditions under which one normally utters an English imperative sentence will make it inductively clear that a 'you' is understood. Likewise, ambiguity resulting from the absence of a second verb phrase in comparative sentences will normally be resolved on a basis of context, which is inductively determined. The problem of subject-verb and object-verb relations will depend on past experience with different contexts, lexical meanings and sentence frames, making up part of the input data.

Chomsky maintains that the "child's ultimate knowledge of language obviously extends far beyond the data presented to him." This presupposes that we know the data available to the child and that we can specify what the child's ultimate knowledge of language is. He also suggests that the ultimate knowledge is uniform, if not fixed, even if the original data is not. But this raises the problem of the distinction that Chomsky draws between competence and performance. Competence represents a measure of the child's ultimate knowledge of language, since Chomsky equates competence with what the speaker actually knows, whereas performance represents what the speaker reports about his knowledge (the actual use of language in concrete situations).[4] Chomsky feels that "a person who knows English may give all sorts of incorrect reports about the knowledge that he actually possesses and makes use of constantly without awareness." Of course, performance may not always measure up to competence, but since competence is ultimately dependent on overall performance, there must be a sufficient number of correct performances (reports) to justify the claim of competence. Otherwise, the alleged gap between the data presented to the child and his ultimate knowledge may not be as wide as Chomsky believes, and thus, his rationalist thesis would be less plausible.

Chomsky grants that the problem for the linguist is to determine from the data of performance the underlying system of rules that has been mastered and put to use in actual performance.[5] He concedes that actual performance does not directly reflect competence, and that a record of natural speech shows numerous false starts, deviations from rules, and so on. He talks about an ideal speaker who knows the language perfectly and is unaffected by such grammatically irrelevant conditions as memory limitations, distractions, shifts of attention and interest, and errors in applying his knowledge of the language in actual performance.[6] This raises the danger that deviations of performance from alleged competence may be erroneously explained as due to grammatically irrelevant conditions, and thus may mistakenly sustain the claim of competence. What is more significant, this may erroneously confirm the view that the child's ultimate knowledge extends far beyond the data presented to him, a view that is crucial to Chomsky's defense of innate knowledge.

Even output data that can be accounted for on empiricist grounds will not always be identical with input data, so that the mere fact of difference between input and output data will not support the claim of innate knowledge. Furthermore, given the empiricist psychological machinery (Chomsky will surely grant that the models of Locke and Hume would qualify), which includes the construction of complex from simple ideas and impressions, generalizations, abstractions, imagination, reflection, and reasoning, the difference between output data and input data would be expected to be so vast and varied (virtually unlimited) that the burden of showing that the output data cannot be accounted for on empiricist grounds is a formidable one.

One must also distinguish between being unable to account for the output data on empiricist grounds, and being able to show that the output data cannot be accounted for on empiricist grounds. The former would reflect the failure to prove the empiricist claim, whereas the latter would prove that the empiricist claim is false. To argue from the former to the latter would be to commit the fallacy *ad ignorantium,* for this would be to suggest that since the empiricist claim has not been shown to be true, it must be false.

NOTES

1. Chomsky, N., *Cartesian Linguistics* (New York: Harper & Row, 1966), p. 110.

2. Chomsky, N., *Syntactic Structures* (Mouton & Company, 1965), pp. 15–17.

3. Katz, J. J., *The Philosophy of Language* (New York: Harper & Row, 1966), pp. 240–82.

4. Chomsky, N., *Aspects of the Theory of Syntax* (M. I. T. Press, 1965), p. 4.

5. *Ibid.*

6. *Ibid.*, p. 3.

12

Language-Learning Models

LEO RAUCH

New York University

I SHOULD LIKE to call attention to a certain descriptive model that is often used — implicitly or explicitly — when we talk about language. It is my contention that the model has failed to account for the important differences between language-learning and language-use. Further, the model has blurred the distinction between the way we learn our native language and the way we learn a second language.

The model describes all language-learning as a process wherein the learner is shown an object, is told a word for it, is asked to say the word, and then has his correct response approved for future use.

There is a well-known story about a chauvinistic Englishman. He tries to establish the thesis that English is the best of all possible languages by arguing as follows: "Now consider some of the foreign words for knife. In French a knife is called a '*couteau.*' In German it's called a '*Messer.*' But in English, you see, it's called a knife — and that's exactly what it *is*!"

This story exposes one of the weaknesses of the model, namely, that it cannot apply to all language-learning. At age eleven or twelve, say, when he was learning French, our Englishman could understand that the word '*couteau*' means knife, since he already knew the word "knife." But how could he have grasped at age two, say, when he was "learning" English, that the meaning of the word "knife" *is* knife, if he did not know the word with which to name the object? He learned the meaning of a French word by referring it to an object plus its English name; but he could hardly have learned English in this way, since there was no other language in which he could name the object.

(We might ask: Is it not enough for the meaning of the word to stand for the object alone? No, since the child does not thereby learn the use of either. When I learn that *"couteau"* means knife, I immediately know something of how the word *"couteau"* can be used, because I already know how the word "knife" can be used. As Wittgenstein [1] would put it, it is part of the grammar of the word "knife" that *this* is what we call "to cut with a knife." Dewey holds a similar view in his approach to words as instructions.)

The faulty model of language-learning to which I have alluded (i.e., learning to name an object by being shown it, plus hearing its name, etc.) I shall call the Translation-Model. And I maintain that although the model may serve as an adequate description of the way we learn a second language, it does not describe adequately the way we learn our first language. The ground for my criticism of it is that the model involves a "translation" of the word being learned into the learner's native language, and that such "translation" cannot occur in the learning of the native language itself.

Perhaps the fundamental problem here is the enormously complex one about the relation between thought and the learning of language. There is an advertisement for Berlitz, showing the face of a Chinese four-year-old; over the picture there is a caption that reads: "If he can learn to speak Chinese in four years, so can you!" The advertisement ignores the fact that the child's way of learning is not at all like our adult learning. That is to say, *we* learn Chinese on the basis of the Translation-Model; the Chinese child does not. We learn words whose meaning we grasp by translating them into our native language; he "learns" something entirely different, namely, the correct use of his intelligence, in word-use, in word-plays, in word-moves. When we (in studying Chinese as adults) advance beyond the rudimentary vocabulary, we learn to construct sentences in conformity with certain rules. The child, however, does not learn the grammar of his language by being told its rules and obeying them in conscious conformity. Rather, when he succeeds in speaking his language with a certain degree of correctness, his utterances conform tacitly to grammatical rules. The rules may be said to guide his word-play, even govern his word-play, but their guidance or governance is invisible.[2]

All this is too well known to need elaboration. What is not known so well is that the sharp difference between learning a second language and using it with fluency is a difference sufficient to make the model useless for describing the latter. A recent article on bilingualism [3] indicates that speakers fluent in two or more languages are capable of switching among linguistic codes without having to take thought about the process. They do not find it necessary to translate to themselves the words of their second language into the words of their native language. This is remarkable when we realize that their use of a second language involves not merely the employment of grammatical rules different from those of the native language, but that word-order and case-endings may be different as well. Moreover, the languages can be as different as, say, an inflective language is from an agglutinative language, without there being a need for conscious translation from one to the other. Accordingly, the Translation-Model must be restricted even further, so as to apply only to the *learning* of a second language, but not to its fluent *use*.

Nor does conscious translation occur in the fluent use of certain nonverbal "languages," wherein we go from input in one sensory form to a restructured output in quite another sensory form. Consider the taking of Morse code; consider also the reading of music. Only the novice "translates" — i.e., by hearing the auditory signal, scanning his mental code-bank, finding the correct alphabetical correspondent, then writing it. Rather, the competent reader of Morse code writes the output without such conscious translation — usually a whole paragraph after the input! The same occurs when a competent musician plays his instrument: he reads the music some six or eight bars ahead of his playing; there is no process of conscious translation, even though the input involves the reading of a visual sign and the output an act of the voluntary muscles.

Users of the Translation-Model assume — either explicitly or implicitly — that ostensive definition and translation are two distinct processes, the former equating a word with a thing, the latter equating a word with a word. It is my view that the two processes are quite similar if not identical: in both there is a process of equating, and it is a conscious process.

Most philosophers in the past — particularly Mill, Schlick, C. W. Morris, and the early Wittgenstein — explain the original learning of language as a process of ostensive definition. They thereby make the mistake of equating words with things, a mistake due, I think, to the unconscious modeling of the process of learning a first language on the translation-process of learning a second language.

It makes no sense to equate a word with a thing — a mistake aptly characterized by Ryle as the "Fido"-Fido fallacy, the fallacy of regarding each word as a surrogate for the object it names. It is better to follow Dewey here, who holds that words do not stand for things, nor that they are images of things, but that they are rather instructions for dealing with things. In this way, at least, the difference between a word and a thing is retained.

Nor, for that matter, ought we to call a word a "picture" of an object, as the early Wittgenstein does. Indeed, it is more likely that we might take an *actual* picture as the object's surrogate — e.g., the lover kissing the picture of the absent beloved — than that we should ever take the *word* as the object's surrogate; that would be a confusion approaching insanity, like trying to smoke the word "pipe."

If we had to choose, therefore, between ostensive definition and translation, it would have to be the latter — the word-word relation — as our choice of the one coming closer to describing the learning of language. But then our former problem presents itself: into what word can a word be translated if there is no prior language to provide such a word? Accordingly, both processes, ostensive definition as well as translation, must go by the board.

Although Wittgenstein points out, quite frequently, what may be considered to be certain weaknesses of the Translation-Model, he also falls victim to other weaknesses of the same model. It is this that accounts for some of his difficulties regarding "symptoms" and "criteria." [4] Wittgenstein claims,[5] for example, that when we learned the use of a phrase, we were directed to certain behavior as explaining that phrase, e.g., "so-and-so has toothache" was equated with this or that behavior in another person. (Why the phrase should be so associated with the behavior of another, merely because it is so associated with my behavior, is held by him to be an unanswerable question.)

Let us suppose, however (adapting one of Wittgenstein's examples),[6] that a child were being raised among a tribe of American Indians who hold it to be one of their most cherished tenets that one must never give external expression to pain; if a man has a toothache he must not wince or cry aloud. Could the child learn what the phrase "having a toothache" means? Under the Translation-Model the answer would be No. Since he could never be shown the symptoms of a man in the grip of toothache, the child could never establish for himself the criteria for the phrase "has a toothache." Any sentence with that phrase would be a "novel" sentence for the child, and he would be incapable of understanding it if it were told to him, or of producing it himself. Such circumstances *should* render the moral code of his tribe unteachable. No fatherly Indian could tell the child, "Whenever thou hast a toothache, thou shalt show no signs thereof" — and expect the commandment to be understood.

Nevertheless, the teaching of such a code, even in so exceedingly taciturn a society, would not involve a self-contradiction, nor a factual impossibility. First of all, having a toothache and being shown the symptoms of toothache in another person are two entirely different experiences. What I experience of another is *behavior* that may be described as a symptom of pain; what I experience in myself is pain itself. So when the child began to experience toothache and began to wince and cry aloud, he could be told to stop behaving in that fashion, without the cessation of such behavior in any way diminishing his experience of pain. Secondly, even if the child were prevented, by some sort of posthypnotic suggestion, from experiencing his own toothache, the terms "tooth" and "ache" would be learned by him in that amorphous way in which, as Chomsky has reminded us, the wide body of language is learned, and under which circumstances alone the production of novel sentences is possible. So the Wittgensteinian skeptic is probably wrong, and we *can* learn the criteria for the proper use of a phrase without the necessity of experiencing (in ourselves or others) the symptoms to which the phrase refers.[7]

This more elastic view of language-learning is adopted by Wittgenstein himself, on the page following his statement of the more rigid view.[8] He warns us that it is one-sided to regard the use of language as though it were the use of a calculus, i.e., according to strict rules. Nor, he adds, are we taught the language according to such rules. He appears, therefore, to observe a distinction between learning and use, although he blurs the distinction because he does not go on to distinguish between the learning and use of a second language as against the learning and use of a native language.

NOTES

1. L. Wittgenstein, *The Blue and Brown Books* (New York, 1958), p. 24; J. Dewey, *Logic: The Theory of Inquiry* (New York, 1938).

2. Cf. N. Chomsky, "A Review of Skinner's *Verbal Behavior*," reprinted in J. A. Fodor and J. J. Katz (eds.), *The Structure of Language* (Englewood Cliffs, N.J., 1964).

3. P. A. Kolers, "Bilingualism and Information Processing," *Scientific American*, CCXI, 3 (March 1968).

4. See R. Albritton, "On Wittgenstein's Use of the Term 'Criterion,'" reprinted in G. Pitcher (ed.), *Wittgenstein: The Philosophical Investigations* (New York, 1966).

5. *Loc. cit.*

6. *Philosophical Investigations* (New York, 1953), Pt. I, par. 257.

7. C. S. Chihara and J. A. Fodor, "Operationalism and Ordinary Language," in G. Pitcher, *op. cit.*, especially pp. 413, 416, 419.

8. *The Blue and Brown Books,* p. 25.

13

Depth Grammar and Necessary Truth

RAZIEL ABELSON

New York University

DUALISMS DIE HARD, and the dualism of kinds of truth is no exception. It has enjoyed and survived more lives than a cat. From Plato's distinction between knowledge and opinion, through Aristotle's essential and accidental predications, the truths of fact and truths of reason of the Middle Ages, the adventitious and innate ideas of Descartes, Kant's a-posteriori and a-priori judgments, and the synthetic-analytic Procrustean bed of the logical positivists, some distinction has been preserved between corrigible and incorrigible knowledge, although all these attempts to define the difference have ended in failure. There is, I think, good reason for the persistence of the distinction, and equally good reason for our misgivings about it. I hope to bring both reasons to light in the following discussion of Chomsky's account of innate ideas.

Professor Noam Chomsky's paper in this volume, continuing in the direction sketched in his *Cartesian Linguistics,* maintains that contemporary theoretical linguistics has an important bearing on the epistemological dispute between rationalism and empiricism. He claims that the discovery of the difference between surface grammar and depth grammar explains vindicates and confirms the seventeenth-century rationalist doctrine of innate ideas. Consideration of Chomsky's thesis may shed some light on what went wrong with all the classical attempts to define the difference between the two kinds of knowledge.

The classical definitions of the distinction foundered on

one fundamental mistake that, I think, Chomsky tends to repeat, namely, the mistake of explaining a difference in type of knowledge in terms of a difference in the psychological process of acquisition, when the latter difference, in turn, can only be explained by the former. An epistemological difference is explained by a psychological one, the psychological difference in turn is explained by the ontological difference in the types of objects of knowledge, and this finally is and must be explained by the difference in the kind of knowledge we have of those objects. Why is some knowledge necessary and other knowledge contingent? Because one is acquired by pure thought and the other by observation. But how do we know whether observation is needed or not? Because the objects of the one type of knowledge do not require observation to be known. And how do we know this? Because our knowledge of those objects is indubitable. And so we go around a circle.

For example, Plato distinguished knowledge from opinion, explaining the difference by the type of experience leading to their acquisition (intellectual vision vis-à-vis sense perception). Aside from the literal worthlessness of the metaphor of the "mind's eye" that was responsible for the subsequent mythology of introspection, Plato could only explain how and why we employ one mode rather than another in terms of the type of objects known (forms vis-à-vis sensible objects) and the criterion of this distinction was, inevitably, that forms are known with certainty and sensible objects are not. Aristotle similarly explained the difference between essential and accidental predication in terms of the psychological processes of perception and abstract vision, and these in terms of their objects — essences and accidents, which in turn are identifiable only by the certainty or uncertainty of our knowledge of them.

Descartes and Leibniz, whom Chomsky hails as ancestors of transformational linguistics, tried hardest to avoid a psychologistic account of necessary truth, but they too failed, a fact that Chomsky seems to consider a virtue. He praises the Cartesians for postulating innate ideas that are clear and distinct to all knowing subjects, and he interprets these as principles of organization of thought and language, programmed genetically into the brain, and accounting for the rules of depth grammar universal to man. Now, it seems to me that there are two serious flaws in this interpretation of the doctrine of innate ideas.

1. Innate ideas, for any consistent rationalist, and certainly for Descartes and Leibniz, are necessary *truths*, not just necessary beliefs, that is, not ideas that could conceivably be false but that, for neuropsychological causes, the human species is compelled to hold. The issue here is the criterion of "necessary" with respect to necessary truths. The rationalists were looking for a criterion much stronger than any neuropsychological condition, since the latter cannot possibly guarantee the *truth* of an innate idea. The phrase "innate" is, of course, misleading, since it suggests the kind of psychological necessity that Chomsky considers confirmed by his linguistic theory, but, as Locke rightly pointed out, any such empirical criterion is open to disconfirmation by the behavior of children, idiots, and lunatics, not to speak of hippy poets. What the Cartesians meant by "necessary" was something considerably stronger than physiological or psychological constraint, something approaching logical necessity (whatever that is). For this reason, Leibniz rightly accused Locke of missing the point about innate ideas, the point being that they cannot be disconfirmed by empirical evidence. Descartes suggested clarity and distinctness as criteria of innateness, and these in turn were explained as precision and definability in terms of primitives. Whether these criteria are themselves sufficiently clear is, of course, highly doubtful, but the point is that they were intended to carry the force of logical necessity. That they fail to do so, and collapse into psychological conditions, is, from Descartes' viewpoint, a fatal defect.

Leibniz offered a criterion of clarity and distinctness that successfully avoided psychologism, but at the cost of proving useless in application, namely, the reducibility of innate ideas to identity propositions, taking identity propositions as paradigms of necessary truths, and thus charting the direction for the development of logicism in the foundations of mathematics. This project eventually proved unworkable even in mathematics. But the point is that it led to Frege, and not to Mill, Brentano, or Quine.

The rationalists were quite right to eschew any Chomsky-type criterion of innateness. For among the innate ideas, the most prominent are the truths of logic, and how could the ironclad necessity of logical truths be grounded on the weaker necessity of neurological causation? To attempt to do so is not to *explain* necessary truth, but to deny it, as J. S. Mill realized. Such an account is not a vindication of rationalism, but rather the most extreme form of empiricism.

2. Professor Chomsky has replied to this criticism by insisting that he does not particularly care if his analysis satisfies the intentions of Descartes and Leibniz, since he is not offering a thesis in the history of philosophy, but has found suggestions in the writings of Cartesians that, intended or not, lead to his own theory of generative grammar. Of course, philosophical labels do not matter all that much, and whether Chomsky's view supports rationalism or empiricism is less important than whether it is in fact true or false. But the peculiarity of his account of knowledge is that it seems to support *both* philosophical positions, and thus suffers from incoherence, and this difficulty is not just a matter of terminology.

Consider how one could hope to confirm Chomsky's theory of universal rules of depth grammar, together with his theory of built-in neurological dispositions responsible for those rules. Presumably, one discovers the rules of depth grammar by the empirical methods of comparative linguistics. But, if Chomsky's theory of innate ideas is correct, then it must be impossible to find disconfirming instances on the deeper level. Any apparently disconfirming instances must be relegated to the level of surface grammar by the very way our minds work. Thus the theory of depth grammar is empirically unfalsifiable, it is itself an innate idea, rather than a confirmation of the doctrine of innate ideas, a fact that should lead us to suspect that the support of one by the other is not only nonempirical, but circular.

In saying this, I am not criticizing the theory of depth grammar, for which I have great respect, but am only questioning its claim to be empirically confirmable. The question of whether a particular rule of transformation belongs to our universal depth grammar might, perhaps, be decidable by the number of observed instances of language usage it explains, but surely the assumption that there are such rules is not an empirical hypothesis, but a kind of pragmatic a-priori principle (Kant's regulative rule of reason), since it is only on this assumption that we can even begin to try to understand other languages than our own. I suspect that the theory of depth grammar, instead of providing confirmation for the doctrine of innate ideas, is simply a modern, more precise, but on the other hand more limited, form of the doctrine of innate ideas itself. What, after all, does the claim amount to that all men have innate ideas except that we are all gifted with the capacity to learn and understand and make sense to each other, i.e., that we have the capacity to be logical and grammatical? So the theory of depth grammar appears to be a linguistic application of the doctrine of innate ideas. In this respect, Chomsky is indeed the heir of Descartes, but he underestimates his debt to his ancestor. For instead of finding empirical support for Cartesian rationalism in linguistic theory, he has recast linguistic theory on the basis of rationalistic assumptions. It is the postulate of innate ideas or universal principles of understanding that supports the theory of depth grammar, and not the other way around.

But if the presuppositions of Chomsky's linguistic work are rationalistic, how does this square with his radical empiricist reduction of innate ideas to neuropsychological dispositions? The answer is, it doesn't. For how could we confirm his neuropsychological theory unless we already presuppose that we have these universal principles of understanding, in virtue of which we can match rules of depth grammar (and depth semantics) with neuropsychological dispositions? If we are to match people's brain states with their thoughts, we must first understand their thoughts, and for this we must presuppose rules of depth grammar.

These considerations bring me back to the theme with which I began. The reason why some distinction between two kinds of knowledge has survived a long succession of inadequate attempts to explain it has now emerged from this discussion: if some rules of thought were not universal and a-priori, there could be no transcultural understanding. But the reason why all attempts to explain the necessary truth of these rules in terms of some theory of the structure of being or in terms of neuropsychological processes must fail is that any such theory must already presuppose the very principles it is intended to explain, and thus commit both the fallacy of circular explanation, and the fallacy of reducing a strong sense of "necessary" to a weaker sense.

PART III

Logic and Language

A

Natural and Formal Languages

PAUL ZIFF

University of Illinois

THAT A FORMAL LOGIC is itself a language, of a sort, is today a common view. The articulation of such a view may rightly be considered one of the significant achievements of contemporary logical and linguistic research. But there is a posture from which formal logic is seen not merely as a language of a sort but as the ideal and proper form of language, the exemplar to which those evolutionary products that we call "natural languages" constitute at best abortive approximations. So viewed, a natural language, such as English, cannot help but take on a bad ambiguous topsy-turvy look. This world will, after all, look upside down if one stands on one's head.

Characteristically a formal language is constituted by a precisely specifiable set of expressions and various perfectly precise rules for their manipulation, combination, and interpretation. In consequence, in contrast with any natural language, a formal logic and formal languages in general appear to have the undeniable virtues of precision and clarity. But these virtues are purchased at a cost: the cost is the utter inutility of the formal language as a language with which to communicate in the world in which we find ourselves.

Characteristically the use of language calls for a physical transaction between distinct complexly structured organisms in a complexly structured context. I prefer to think and shall here speak of speakers and hearers as automata of a sort (organic rather than mechanical). The speaker-automaton puts out a certain set of linguistic data that is transmitted acoustically to the hearer. Some subset of the data is then received by and constitutes an input to the hearer-automaton. Generally the hearer will receive other sensory inputs at the same time. The input data is then processed in some way in accordance with the program, state, and structure of the hearer.

The realities of this complex linguistic transaction go and must go unheeded, ignored, if one is to dwell in the somewhat mythic and certainly myopic reaches of a formalism.

To begin with, the familiar forms of formal logic and formal languages are not equipped to cope with noise. And in the presence of noise the much vaunted absolute precision of a formal logic is apt to prove illusory. Yet in this world there is always noise.

The requirement that a formal language be perfectly precise can be and usually is expressed in terms of "effectiveness." Thus, for example, it is usually required that the rules and expressions of a formal language be such that the definition of a well-formed formula be effective in the sense that "there is a method by which, whenever a formula is given, it can always be determined effectively whether or not it is well-formed." [1] Effectiveness can be construed in terms of their being an algorithm or a method of computation for determining whether or not something is so. To say, for example, that the specification of well-formedness is effective is to say that there is an algorithm or a method of computation for determining whether or not a given expression is a well-formed expression of the language.

But the existence of an algorithm neither confers certainty nor guarantees absolute precision.[2] Consider, in particular, the difficulty of determining whether or not an expression formed by the combination of several million symbols is a well-formed expression of the language. The existence of an algorithm merely guarantees that there is a method of computation. But it is still necessary to perform the computation if one is to determine whether or not the expression is well-formed. Unfortunately even the best of computers is, in the final analysis, fallible, as is anyone else. The reason is of course that any physical signal is subject to distortion, owing to noise or error or some sort of disturbance or failure in transmission: noise-free error-proof channels of communication are not to be had. The question whether or not an expression formed by the combination of several million symbols is a well-formed expression of the language in fact admits of only a probabilistic sort of answer.

Problems of distortion, noise, error and the like are generally ruled out by assumption in the specification of a formal language.[3] However, Von Neumann's probabilistic logic provides an example of a formal language devised to cope with problems occasioned by a failure of transmission.[4] Such a system, in contrast with more familiar logics, thus constitutes a somewhat more perspicuous representation of an actual language.

In contrast with the familiar forms of formal language, a natural language, such as English, is and is bound to be distinctly noise-oriented. The realities of a linguistic transaction are such that a successful use of language to communicate is possible only if a variety of strategies is available.

Redundancy is the principal device for coping with noise, transmission failures, and the like. But redundancy has many forms. The utterance uttered by a speaker in the course of a speech transaction may itself be redundant; thus the plural affix '-s' is redundant in 'He has eight books.' This sort of redundancy constitutes a form of multiplexing and is available in connection with formal languages and computing machinery. But there is another form of redundancy frequently to be encountered in actual linguistic transactions and this form is not available in connection with formal languages or with computing machinery not programmed for pattern recognition.

Consider a speaker and a hearer both of whom are seated together at a dinner table; the speaker, holding up a piece of bread, turns to the hearer and says 'This bread tastes terrible.'

A redundant aspect of this transaction is to be seen in the fact that, in that context, the speaker probably would have communicated the same information if in fact he had said 'this bed tastes terrible': the phonemic contrast between 'bed' and 'bread' is rendered redundant by the perceptual features of the situation.

More generally, in the actual use of language the relevant inputs to the hearer need not be simply those corresponding to the linguistic output of the speaker during the course of the particular linguistic transaction. In particular, speakers often supply, or rely on the fact that the hearer is supplied with, various visual data.

Formal languages ignore the realities of the perceptual situation in a wholehearted manner: not only do they make no concession to the existence of perceptual difficulties, they eschew all reliance on perceptual strategies and abilities. But such reliance is characteristic of the use of a natural language and successful communication would be virtually impossible without it.

Consider the singular descriptive phrase employed as subject of the sentence 'The pen on the desk is made of gold.' By the use of such a phrase in an appropriately structured context one may well succeed in singling out a unique referent even though of course the English phrase 'the pen on the desk' does not have a unique referent. But from a purely formal point of view, a use of the phrase 'the pen on the desk' is apt to be deplored: since the expression does not in fact have a unique referent, the sentence 'the pen on the desk is made of gold' is formally classed either true, or false, or neither true nor false, depending on the system in question, but regardless of the actual truth or falsity of what is actually said in everyday discourse.

It is sometimes supposed that one could avoid the use of such phrases by making explicit what is merely implicit in the context of utterance.[5] But that is not true. For example, instead of the short phrase 'the pen on the desk,' one could perhaps find a long elaborate descriptive phrase presumably referring to the same referent, say, 'the pen on the desk in the study of the house at 3415 Black Hawk Drive in Madison, Wisconsin, at 8:00 A.M. on January 26, 1968.' But such a phrase does not make explicit what was merely implicit in the context. For no conning of the context of utterance need enable one to glean the information that the house in question was located in Madison, Wisconsin, that the date was January 26th, and so on. Furthermore, there is no way in which the factors serving to render the use of the short phrase efficacious in context can be made explicit. The hearer who understands what is said and who can determine what the referent of the phrase is does so by relying not simply on supplementary information but on the exercise of all sorts of perceptual and conceptual strategies. In particular, an exercise of the abilities required for pattern recognition is obviously called for.

To employ the long descriptive phrase rather than the more familiar short one would not be a matter of making explicit what was only implicit. Neither could it in any sense be said to exemplify an increase in precision. If anything, a use of the formally preferred long phrase would, in the actual use of language, contribute to imprecision, vagueness, and uncertainty since it would undoubtedly serve to increase the probability of error: seeing the gold-colored pen on the desk before him, the hearer need have no difficulty in locating the referent of the phrase; but what the date is is apt to be a matter for conjecture.

                                                    •   •   •

For a speaker to supply or rely on nonlinguistic inputs to the hearer is a commonplace in the use of a natural language. It is equally commonplace and equally essential for a speaker to be able, on occasion, to rely on a hearer's having a special program. The distinction between input data and a program is not a formal distinction: the program is simply data that serve to define a function to be computed by the automaton. In consequence, if a speaker wishes to minimize reliance on the program of the hearer, he can put out a more explicit linguistic datum. Conversely, if greater reliance on the program of the hearer is feasible and desirable, the speaker's linguistic output can be considerably compressed.

In all discourse, save that in which the speaker is attempting to communicate with a hearer that the speaker believes not to understand the language, the speaker relies on the hearer's having a specific linguistic program peculiar to the persons who speak or understand the language in which the discourse takes place. But speakers generally rely on the hearer's having a further special program as well, where this special program corresponds to specific information, knowledge, beliefs, and so forth pertaining to nonlinguistic matters. For example, relying on the fact that the hearer knows that alligators do not wear shoes, a speaker may say 'I bought a pair of alligator shoes' and expect to be understood. Again, a speaker may say 'I saw a man trying to stand on his head' and expect to be understood as saying that he viewed a man who was attempting a headstand, not that he uses a saw on people and not that the man in question was attempting to decapitate himself and then stand on the decapitated head. (Possibly the compound 'alligator shoes' may be held to have a special linguistic structure that serves to block the reading 'shoes worn by alligators,' but the other sentence would certainly be ambiguous were it not for the hearer's special program. There is no sharp line to be drawn between the specifically linguistic program and the special nonlinguistic program of a person who understands a particular dialect.)

From a purely formal point of view, a speaker's reliance on a hearer's special program is to be anathematized insofar as it sanctions implicit rather than explicit qualification.

Consider a situation in which a doorkeeper of a theatre after a performance reports to the manager 'No one got in without a ticket'; implicit to this discourse is the qualification that employees and players are not in question. Thus the doorkeeper is not saying that no person whatever, including himself, who entered the theatre did so without a ticket. From a formal point of view, the more explicit report 'No one, other than employees and players, got in without a ticket' would appear preferable to the implicitly qualified 'No one got in without a ticket.' But in point of fact, the explicit qualification would serve no purpose in the linguistic transaction we are supposing to have occurred; the explicit qualification would neither facilitate communication nor increase precision. On the contrary, discourse would tend to break down under the strain of explicitness. It is not merely that the resulting prolixity would be aesthetically unbearable: there would be a general failure of communication.

Consider, for example, the plight of an officer who wishes to order a private to shut a door. He might say to the private 'Shut the door!' The private then replies 'Yes, sir' and does nothing. The officer might then resort to the more explicit 'Shut the door now!,' whereupon the private shuts the door for a second and then opens it as it was. For he was not told to shut the door and leave it shut. And if he were told to shut it and leave it shut, there would then be the question how long was he to leave it shut? Or consider the maze one maunders in in attempting to make explicit the simple request 'Please tell me the time.' Where? Here. When? Now. According to what standard? Eastern Standard Time. With what tolerance? Plus or minus two seconds. In what language? English. What dialect? East Coast American. In how loud a voice? How quickly? (Yet if we are ever to make a conversational robot we shall have to make our way through such a maze as this.)

That speakers characteristically rely on hearers having special programs is of a piece with the fact that communication is characteristically an intramural affair and fares badly when cultural lines are crossed. And it is in the reliance on special programs that the different dialects of a natural language have their provenance.

In the use of language a speaker may rely on the hearer's receiving nonlinguistic inputs and on the hearer's having a specific program and structure. But the speaker's principal resources are to be found in his own program and structure. To speak one must use words (or their equivalents) and so the speaker must have or must find words to use: he must have some sort of a vocabulary. The profound differences between a formal language and a natural language take their loci in the respective vocabularies of each language.

A vocabulary may be thought of as constituted by a finite explicit store of words together with a set (possibly null) of morphologically productive devices. Consider a formal language, the words of which are '*x*', '*x* '', '*x* '' ', . . . , thus an infinite number of words. The vocabulary of this language is then constituted by an explicit store of one word, '*x*', and a recursive device for the further production of infinitely many words; thus the language has an explicit store of one word, an implicit store of infinitely many.

For the sake of definiteness, consider not the English language, which is as it were a vast slow perhaps soon to be completed process, the vocabulary of which obviously cannot conceivably be effectively specified, but rather the speech of a single speaker at a fixed moment of time, say some person's idiolect here and now. The vocabulary of this speaker can then be identified with the products of a set of morphologically productive operations over some given explicit store of words.

(The processes of lexical production are enormously varied, complex, and variously operative. Some productive lexical processes are virtually uniform throughout the language, for example, those by which plurals, past tenses, thus the familiar inflectional forms, are formed. Some processes are only fairly regular, for example, that process by which a set of adverbs can be produced from a set of adjectives by suffixing '-ly' ['quickly' from 'quick']. Another fairly regular production is exemplified by an operation over a domain of adjectives that consists in suffixing '-ish' and producing an adjective. Thus the operation over 'green' yields 'greenish,' and over 'greenish,' 'greenishish,' and so on. Or consider a pair of operations, one being that of suffixing '-ness' to an adjective yielding a noun, the other being that of suffixing '-ish' to a noun yielding an adjective. This pair of operations then produces 'quickness,' 'quicknessish,' 'quicknessishness,' and so on. [Although operations yielding infinite sets of products may seem somewhat counterintuitive and certainly are productive of lexical curiosities, there is no need to be excessively squeamishish about the matter. Contemporary transformational grammar has analogous progeny, as for example, 'The old old old old old old old old old old old problem is ever with us.'] Some productive lexical processes appear to have a more limited scope. The operation of suffixing '-er' to a verb to form a noun ['walker' from 'walk'] is of considerable importance though one does not have *'fatherer' from 'father,' *'rainer' from 'rain,' *'horser' from 'horse,' and in point of fact, 'peddle' is a back-formation from 'peddler.' And then there are such limited processes as those that have given rise to 'beatnik,' 'peacenik,' 'noodnik,' to 'telethon,' 'sellathon,' to 'cinerama,' 'Christorama,' and so on.)

The vocabulary of a formal language may be either finite or infinite. In either case the vocabulary of a formal language is effectively specifiable. In contrast, no nonarbitrary specification of the vocabulary of a natural language, or dialect, or idiolect can possibly be effective.

Presumably a word is in the vocabulary of a person at a fixed moment of time if and only if, at that time, first, he is able to use it correctly, given appropriate conditions for doing so, and second, an inability to understand a sentence in which the word is used is not attributable to a difficulty with the word in question. (The second condition has been invoked here to rule out the following sort of case: a person may be able to use the word 'buccal' correctly in that if he were presented with a substance identified as 'hirudin,' he could rightly say of it 'It is an anticoagulant extracted from the buccal glands of a leech.' But he need not be able to understand the question 'Are they buccal?' asked in reference to certain glands, and this inability could be directly attributable to his not knowing what 'buccal' means. In consequence, in accordance with the second condition, 'buccal' could not be classed a word in his vocabulary. If, however, one wished to insist that even so 'buccal' is a word of his vocabulary, the second condition could simply be deleted.)

The specification just provided of a person's vocabulary at a fixed moment of time is clearly not effective in any plausible sense of the word. There neither is nor does it even seem plausible to suppose there could be any sort of algorithm for determining either which words a person is able to use correctly or when an inability to understand a sentence in which the word is used is attributable to a difficulty with the word.

One might suppose that a way of determining whether or not the first condition is satisfied is as follows: take a biggish lexicon, say *Webster's Third International;* with respect to each word, test to see if the person is able to use it correctly. First, unfortunately and without a doubt there will be words of his vocabulary that are not in that dictionary; 'peacenik,' 'hippy,' 'greenishish,' 'squint-eyedishness.' Second, and more important, one finds that under such test conditions a person may fail to identify words that, given an appropriate occasion for use, he would use unhesitatingly and with ease. That it is not possible to specify a person's vocabulary effectively is hardly surprising when one realizes that no one, not even the speaker himself, has altogether free access to his vocabulary.

Thinking of a speaker as an automaton and of his vocabulary as a partially implicit and partially explicit store of words (the implicit store being that derivable by morphologically productive techniques), an educated speaker of English is bound to have a remarkably large and varied explicit store of words. In consequence there are bound to be remarkably complex storage arrangements serving to insure reasonably adequate access to storage.

Perhaps the most inscrutable aspect of an ordinary person's ability to use words is displayed in the ease and swiftness with which he finds the words to use: an ordinary speaker is a word-finding device par excellence. Ask him to describe the scene before him and at once the right words flow forth. Evidently given an appropriate occasion for use he has almost instant access to storage. Ready access to storage given an appropriate occasion for use is of course required if one is to speak a language with ease. But there is no reason at all to suppose that there either is or should be free and ready access to storage apart from an appropriate context and cues. What purpose would it serve? (But of course people differ with respect to ease of access, which is part of the reason why some are better than others at doing crossword puzzles.)

In considering the vocabulary of a speaker what is important, however, are not just the words he is able to use but rather what I propose to speak of as the "word-senses" that he is able to use. If two speakers both use the verb 'cool,' but the first uses the word in two senses ('Cool the meat' and 'Cool it, man!') while the second uses it in only one, then in an important sense the first speaker has a larger vocabulary than the second. I shall say that the first speaker has (so far) a vocabulary of two word-senses, the second only one.

That no one, not even the speaker, has altogether free access to word storage is only one reason why it is not in fact possible to provide a nonarbitrary effective specification of a speaker's vocabulary. The fact of the matter is that a natural language, or a dialect or an idiolect, does not ever have, not even at an arbitrary moment of time, a static fixed store of word-senses. The vocabulary of word-senses of a natural language is a continuous creation.

The expressions of a formal language are characteristically (but not invariably) required to be monosemous, and this of course to comply with the general requirements of effectiveness. In contrast, polysemy is a characteristic feature of any natural language. For example, with respect to a standard moderate-sized dictionary such as *Webster's Seventh New Collegiate,* an educated guess would be that of the 70,000 entries listed, at least 40,000 have at least three reasonably distinct meanings and thus are triply polysemous. *Webster's Seventh* is then a lexicon of 70,000 words but of at least 150,000 word-senses.

From the point of view of a formalism, pronounced polysemy can be seen only as a cancerous proliferation of meanings, calling for swift excision. The operation could be performed but nothing would be accomplished thereby; the proliferation would inevitably continue and, what is worse, there would be an immediate price to pay for the surgical insult. To eliminate even the evident homonymy and polysemy from a lexicon of a natural language would mean at least doubling the number of entries. And this would mean an enormous increase in the probability of error in the transmission and reception of signals. For instead of n phonemic patterns to be stored and rendered available for the appropriate processing, $2n$ such patterns would have to be so dealt with.

Though polysemy and homonymy can give rise to ambiguity in the use of words, by and large the ambiguity is merely potential. Syntactic, discourse, and contextual factors all serve as effective palliatives. There is no ambiguity of the sentence 'I can't bear to live with a bear in the house' that is attributable to the word 'bear' despite the fact that the word is both homonymous and polysemous. Here syntactic and discourse factors suffice to preclude an ambiguity. 'Put it on the table' is not apt to be ambiguous in the appropriate perceptual situation despite the fact that 'table' is distinctly polysemous. Again, there is not apt to be anything ambiguous about 'He just refused that dish' when said of a workman standing in front of the fusebox of a paraboloid microwave antenna. Reliance on a plurality of factors is the rule, not the exception, in the everyday use of language. But even if polysemy were the plague, there is nothing for it: it is an inevitable by-product of the successful use of words to communicate with in the sort of world we are in.

As I have elsewhere maintained,[6] a word's having meaning in a language can be thought of in terms of the word's having associated with it a set of conditions, where a condition is taken to be that which is expressed by an open sentence, a predicative expression, or that which can be explicitly stated by employing a nominalized predicative expression. For example, the word 'brother' has associated with it (at least) the two conditions of being male and of being a sibling. But owing to the complex character of the contexts in which words are used and the purposes for which they are used, one finds that inevitably the set of conditions associated with a word is subject to constant variation. The continual modulation of meaning is characteristic of all discourse in a natural language.

If the set of conditions associated with a word admits of a reasonably clear bifurcation into two virtually exclusive proper subsets, such that in the contexts in which the word is used the members of either one subset or the other are relevant but not both, then the word is polysemous having at least two relatively distinct meanings. For example, the word 'division' has associated with it a subset of conditions pertaining to army groups and a subset of conditions pertaining to arithmetic matters. Although there are cases in which 'division' is used such that both subsets of conditions are relevant, such cases are rare and such a use of the word takes on the character of a pun, as in 'I want to see Lt. George's division' meaning both his army group and his arithmetic.

If the set of conditions associated with a word does not admit of any clear bifurcation into exclusive subsets, it may still be the case that in certain contexts only certain proper subsets are in fact relevant. If so, such a word is not polysemous in that it does not have distinct meanings, but it is akin to a polysemous word in that it has a plurality of senses. For example, the word 'brother' has associated with it not only the conditions of being male and of being a sibling but also the condition of behaving fraternally. The first two are but the third is not relevant in connection with the utterance 'Does he have a brother?,' whereas the third is but the first two are not relevant in connection with the utterance 'He has been a brother to me.' On the other hand, there are unpunlike common cases in which all three conditions are relevant, as in 'I wish I had a brother.'

Neither polysemy nor a plurality of senses need be confused with generality, though the distinction is subtle. I can here do no more than indicate the direction in which the distinction is made. The word 'tiger,' for example, has associated with it the condition of being striped. Should one encounter a creature *sans* stripes, one could nonetheless characterize it as "a tiger," albeit a freakish one. In so doing, one need not be using the word 'tiger' in a special sense. The difference between this sort of case and the cases of the distinct senses of 'brother' is related to the fact that the condition of being striped is relevant in connection with the question 'Is that a tiger?' even if it should prove to be the case that the condition is not satisfied, whereas the condition of being a sibling is irrelevant in connection with the question 'Has he been a brother to you?.'

One can distinguish between polysemy and a plurality of senses and generality but only as one can distinguish between segments of a varying continuum, a constantly shifting spectrum. For the sets of conditions associated with the words of a natural language do not stay put. They could if the world would but it won't and so they don't.

I can supply no effective catalogue of the means of modulating the meaning of words. But some of the ways are obvious and familiar. Thus one uses a word in a restricted sense when one wishes to slough off unwanted conditions. To restrict the set of conditions is to put what Empson has called "a depreciative pregnancy" on the word.[7] One can also use a word in an expanded sense; when Hamlet said of his father 'He was a man,' he was putting "an appreciative pregnancy" on 'man,' thus adding the condition of being courageous to the set associated with 'man.' A use of a word in a shifted sense occurs when one speaks of "baking bread" for of course one bakes dough that becomes bread on the completion of the process (and thus 'digging a ditch,' 'winning a race,' 'building a house'). When a novel set of conditions is associated with a word only for the immediate occasion of use, the word is said to have "a nonce sense.' And then there are such classical devices as irony, metaphor, metonymy, and so forth.

The inevitable upshot of the constant modulation of meaning under the pressures of usage is the appearance of polysemy in a language. Owing to the nature of the phenomena dealt with, the use of a word in a natural language must take on something of the character of an operation with an analogue device. In contrast, the vocabulary of a formal language can readily be digital in character.

One could attempt to abort the birth of polysemy in a natural language by expanding the language's explicit vocabulary as follows. First, if a word w_o has a set of conditions δ associated with it, and δ has n elements, then form the power set of δ, call it 'P'; w_o may then be dropped from the vocabulary of the language and replaced by distinct words $w_1, w_2, \ldots, w_2n - (n + 1)$ (where the deletion of $n + 1$ elements is required to avoid the immediate production of unnecessary synonyms) where to each w_i there corresponds one and only one element of P (excluding the null set). Thus there will be no occasion ever to restrict the sense of any word. However, this will still not account for the use of a word with an expanded sense, or in a shifted sense or in a novel sense. Hence secondly, we shall have to find some means of constructing a complete vocabulary so as to obviate the need for expanding and shifting and creating senses. There is excellent reason to suppose that neither of these steps is at all feasible.

Consider, for example, the sentence 'It was a fine drive' and the various matters that may be in question: a backhand drive in tennis, a drive in the country, a cattle drive, the army's drive on the eastern front, sexual drive, the garage drive. *Webster's Seventh* implausibly lists some 40 senses of 'drive.' One may plausibly suppose that anyway at least 6 conditions can be associated with the word. Were one then to introduce a separate word for each combination of conditions according to the indicated formula, one would have to introduce 57 distinct words to replace the single word 'drive.' It should be evident at once that the cure for polysemy would be worse than the disease. For how could one store the resultant prodigious number of words in such a way as to insure reasonably adequate access to storage? (The problem here is analogous to that one would encounter were one to attempt to replace a useful analogue device such as a slide rule with a digital device such as a table of correlations corresponding to all discriminable positions of the slide on the body.) The enormous utility of a single word's having a plurality of senses is to be seen in the fact that the word then constitutes a coding device serving to insure reasonable access to the stored plurality of senses. (Although all formal languages in fact rely heavily on coding devices and would be utterly unintelligible without them, the devices, namely abbreviative definitions, are officially disclaimed and denied formal status.)

A complete vocabulary, in the sense intended here, would be one that obviated the need for further modulating the meaning of words. Thus it would comprise all the words anyone could ever devise. But the question whether a given vocabulary is so complete makes sense only if one could effectively enumerate all possible conditions that a human being could conceive of as obtaining in the universe. Whether this is possible would appear to depend on the neurophysiological structure of the human brain. If its structure were analyzable in terms of discrete states, perhaps such an enumeration could be effected. But there appears to be little reason to suppose that the brain is so analyzable.

                                              •   •   •

Formal logics and formal languages are bright, shiny conceptual instruments of great beauty and precision. They permit of operations more delicate than could be performed by even the finest surgical laser. But they are unsuitable for use as languages to communicate with in this world. Being bound to the requirements of effectiveness, they are bound to lose luster when exposed to the corrosive forces of actual discourse.

In discussing the requirements of effectiveness Church has said:

> The requirements of effectiveness are (of course) not meant in the sense that a structure which is analogous to a logistic system except that it fails to satisfy these requirements may not be useful for some purposes or that it is forbidden to consider such — but only that a structure of this kind is unsuitable for use or interpretation as a language. For, however indefinite or imprecisely fixed the common idea of a language may be, it is at least fundamental to it that a language shall serve the purpose of communication. And to the extent that requirements of effectiveness fail, the purpose of communication is defeated.[8]

English fares badly on this account. For the requirements of effectiveness are flaunted by a natural language and in every quarter. There is no algorithm for determining which expressions are well-formed and which are not. There is no algorithm for determining which expressions are words of the language and which are not. And when one speaks in a natural language there is always room for conjecture whether one has managed to communicate anything at all.

If Church is right and I am right too, then perhaps nothing is suitable for use as a language. But that is no reason to quit talking: we are all going to do that anyway.

NOTES

1. A. Church, *Introduction to Mathematical Logic* (Princeton, N.J.: Princeton University Press, 1956), p. 51.

2. See Church, *op. cit.*, p. 53, for what appears to be a contrary view.

3. See Church, *op. cit.*, p. 51.

4. See J. Von Neumann, "Probabilistic Logics and the Synthesis of Reliable Organisms From Unreliable Components," in C. E. Shannon and J. McCarthy (eds.), *Automata Studies* (Princeton, N.J.: Princeton University Press, 1956), pp. 43–98.

5. See W. V. O. Quine, *Word and Object* (New York: John Wiley & Sons, 1960), p. 183.

6. See P. Ziff, *Semantic Analysis* (Ithaca, N.Y.: Cornell University Press, 1960), pp. 171 ff.

7. See W. Empson, *The Structure of Complex Words* (New Directions Book).

8. *Op. cit.*, p. 52.

B

Language, Logic, and States of Affairs

RODERICK CHISHOLM

Brown University

1. MR. ZIFF WRITES: "That a formal logic is itself a language, of a sort, is today a common view. The articulation of such a view may rightly be considered one of the significant achievements of contemporary logical and linguistic research." But what does it mean to say that "a formal logic is a language" or (what Mr. Ziff does not say) that "logic is a language"? Presumably it doesn't mean merely that the truths of logic can be expressed in a language or that one may construct rather special languages just for the purpose of expressing these truths. For in that sense of "is a language," one could say with equal justification that "astronomy is a language" or that "biology is a language." If "a formal logic is a language" is intended to express something of philosophical interest, what it would be intended to tell us, I suppose, is that to know what the subject matter of logic is, what logic is about, we should consider some of the relations between logic and language. But what relations between logic and language? And is this way of looking at logic more plausible than its alternatives?

These questions and others like them, it seems to me, are among those that should have been discussed in a conference on philosophy, logic, and language. Let us try to recall, at least, what some of the basic issues are.[1]

Broadly speaking, there are three ways of looking at the subject matter of logic. We may speak of the "metaphysical" view, the "psychologistic" view, and the "linguistic" view.

2. According to the metaphysical view, as I interpret it, there are certain abstract, propositional entities that constitute the subject matter of logic. These entities have been called by very different names, among which the most common at the present time would seem to be "states of affairs" and "propositions." [2] They are said to be *propositional* entities in that they have a form or structure analogous to that of sentences. States of affairs may be conjunctive or disjunctive, for example, and for each state of affairs there is another state of affairs that is its negation. And they are said to be *abstract* entities in that they bear a certain analogy to attributes. Thus attributes may be divided into two groups, those that are actualized or exemplified and those that are not; and states of affairs, according to the present view, may be divided into two analogous groups. But there are rather different ways of referring to these two groups. Using the term "state of affairs" and not "proposition," one may put the distinction by saying that some states of affairs are actualized and that other states of affairs are not actualized. (There being horses, for example, would belong to the first group, and there being unicorns to the second.) Or one may say that there are states of affairs, some of which exist and some of which do not exist. Or again, that there are possible states of affairs, some of which exist and some of which do not exist. Or, to avoid saying that there *are* certain (possible) things some of which do not exist, one may use "is exemplified" in place of "exists" and say simply that states of affairs are like attributes in that some of them are exemplified and others of them are not.[3] Or, finally, using "proposition" instead of "state of affairs," one may put the same distinction by saying that some propositions are such that they are true and other propositions are such that they are false.

According to this metaphysical conception of logic, then, the theorems of logic are necessary truths about states of affairs. Consider, for example, the theorem expressed by "$\sim (p \mathbin{\&} \sim p)$." This may be construed as telling us that, for every state of affairs p, that state of affairs which consists of p in conjunction with the negation of p is a state of affairs that, necessarily,

is not actual (does not exist, is not exemplified). And analo-
gously for the other theorems of logic.

To do justice to this metaphysical conception of logic, we
should consider how one might defend the thesis that there are
such entities as states of affairs. Thus the metaphysician may
well reason as follows. Actual or exemplified states of affairs
are the terms of the relation of causation ("*a*'s being F was
caused, in part, by *b*'s being G") and also the terms of the relation of before and after ("Aristotle refuted that view long before Smith had thought of it").[4] Nonactual or unexemplified
states of affairs, as well as actual or exemplified states of
affairs, may serve as the objects of belief, desire, and other
propositional attitudes ("There is something that both Jones
and Smith hope to see realized, but their hopes will be unful-
filled"). They are what we refer to when we discuss what it is
that people say or assert ("Jones meant something by that sentence, but I don't know what it is"). They may also be the
"bearers of value." Thus if we ask what sorts of things are good
in themselves ("What are the things that would matter
most?"), our reply may well refer to states of affairs that do
not exist (e.g., "There being a just distribution of pleasure").
Some metaphysicians will also say that states of affairs, exemplified and unexemplified, are needed to explicate the concepts
of truth and falsity. The following is one possible explication:
"A sentence is true, in a certain use, provided the belief it
would express if it were interpreted in that use is a belief that
is true; and a man may be said to have a belief that is true, i.e.,
he may be said to believe something correctly, provided, first,
he believes with respect to a certain state of affairs that that
state of affairs is exemplified,[5] and provided, secondly, that
that state of affairs *is* exemplified.[6] And finally, the metaphysician may argue, we cannot give an adequate account of the
truths of logic without reference to such entities as states of
affairs.

3. "Psychologism" was the view that logic has to do with
thinking or, more exactly, with believing or judging. Let us re-

call briefly the difficulties that this view involved, for then we will know what to look for in the case of "logic is a language."

Consider once again the theorem expressed by "$\sim(p \mathbin{\&} \sim p)$." One has only to formulate the possible psychologistic interpretations of this theorem to see that they are inadequate. The simplest version was: "For every proposition p, there is no one who accepts both p and the negation of p at the same time." On this interpretation the theorem becomes false. A more cautious version was: "For every proposition p, no one who understands both p and its negation accepts both at the same time." On this interpretation the theorem is problematic and, even if true, contingent. Other psychologistic interpretations seemed to be empty; or, at any rate, they were as much applicable to the truths of astronomy, say, as to those of logic, and so they failed to mark out any special subject matter for logic. Consider, for example, the following three: (a) "For every proposition p, there is no one who believes p correctly and who also believes the negation of p correctly"; (b) "If you wish to have no false beliefs, then, for every proposition p, don't believe both p and the negation of p!"; and (c) "For every proposition p, don't believe both p and the negation of p!" (On the second and third of these interpretations, the theorem is taken to be a "rule of thought," on the second, a hypothetical imperative, and on the third, a categorical imperative.) To the extent that these were plausible psychologistic interpretations of the logical theorem expressed by "$\sim(p \mathbin{\&} \sim p)$," the following are equally plausible psychologistic interpretations of the astronomical truth expressed by "There are exactly 9 planets": (a) "There is no one who believes falsely or incorrectly that there are exactly 9 planets"; (b) "If you wish to have no false beliefs, then don't believe that there are not exactly 9 planets!"; and (c) "Don't believe that there are not exactly 9 planets!" Finally, all the versions of psychologism seemed to presuppose the being of the abstract, propositional entities to which the metaphysical theory refers; for the "propositions" of psychologism are the "states of affairs" of the metaphysical theory. If there are such entities, what is wrong with the metaphysical interpretation of logic?

4. "Logic is a language" may be construed as telling us that there is still another way — a "linguistic" way — of looking at these matters. Some versions of "linguisticism" seem to me to be more confused than psychologism and more obscure than the metaphysical theory. But other versions of it may be neither confused nor obscure. Thus there is the view according to which the theorems of logic may be construed as pertaining to concrete linguistic entities ("mounds of ink") and need not be construed as pertaining to abstract entities of any sort. I would say that the philosophically important questions about the relation of logic to language have to do with the status of this type of view and with whether there are plausible linguistic alternatives to it. Among the questions to which such a view gives rise are the following:

(1) How would we interpret the theorem "$\sim(p \mathbin{\&} \sim p)$" if we construe it as pertaining to sentence-tokens? Would it be sufficient to say: "For every x, if x is a sentence-token, then the sentence-token formed by conjoining x with the negation of x is false"? Or would it be necessary to relativize the interpretation to a language — say, as "For every x, if x is a sentence-token in any language L, then the sentence-token formed in L by conjoining x with the negation of x is false in L"? And in such a case, could the expression "a language L" be construed as pertaining just to concrete things and not to abstract objects of any sort?

(2) Would the theorems of logic, if construed as pertaining to sentence-tokens, be true in a world in which there were no sentence-tokens? If not, would they then be contingent rather than necessary?

(3) Would this version of "linguisticism" be any more successful than was psychologism in marking out a special subject matter for logic? Or would it be equally applicable, say, to astronomy? ("What 'There are 9 planets' really tells us is that

all sentence-tokens in the English language, which begin with a 'T,' followed by an 'h,' an 'e,' an 'r,' an 'e,' a space, an 'a,' an 'r,' an 'e,' a space, a '9,' a space, a 'p,' an 'l,' an 'a,' an 'n,' an 'e,' a 't,' in that order, and then ending with an 's,' are true.")

(4) Is it possible to say what it is for a sentence-token in an ordinary nonformalized language to be *true*, or to be *false*, without presupposing the being of the metaphysician's states of affairs? Or would there be a way of avoiding "true" and "false" that would be more successful than were the "rule" maneuvers of psychologism? ("For any x, if x is a sentence-token, do not write what would be the result of conjoining x with its own negation except as part of a longer sentence-token!")

(5) Are there more plausible versions of "Logic is a language"?

(6) In view of the considerations to which the metaphysician appealed (above), is it unreasonable to suppose that there are such things as his states of affairs? If there are such things, is it unreasonable to construe the theorems of logic in the way in which the metaphysician proposes? And finally, is his way of construing them any less plausible than "Logic is a language"?

I do not profess to know the answers to all these questions. But it seems to me important at least that someone raise them in a conference on philosophy, logic, and language.

NOTES

1. I should note that I do not disagree with Mr. Ziff's principal thesis (that for purposes of ordinary communication our natural languages are more efficient than any formalized language) and I have no reason to question any of his particular observations about natural languages. Since I have been given the option either of commenting upon the details of Mr. Ziff's paper or of discussing more generally whatever philosophical questions his paper may suggest, I have taken the second course in the hope of keeping certain fundamental issues alive.

2. "State of affairs" has been used by C. I. Lewis in this way,

and "proposition" by Russell. Other terms have been: *"Satz an sich"* (Bolzano), *"Gedanke"* (Frege), *"Urteilsinhalt"* (Brentano and Marty), and *"Objektive"* (Meinong).

3. But this may be to push the analogy between attributes and states of affairs too far. There is a clear answer to the question "What sorts of things are attributes exemplified *in*" (viz., "Everything"), but to find something for states of affairs to be exemplified in we may have to multiply entities beyond necessity. Thus some have said that states of affairs are exemplified in *the world,* and others have said that they are exemplified in *concrete events;* but one may well wonder whether there is such a concrete thing as the world and whether, *in addition to* actual (or "exemplified") states of affairs, there are also such things as concrete events. And it is relevant to note that, even if there weren't any concrete things, there would be actual states of affairs; e.g., there being no unicorns. (This footnote, which was not included in the original paper, was added in order to throw light upon problems that were raised by Professor Ezorsky; see final paper in this volume.)

4. What we sometimes call "events," on this conception, will be a subclass of actual or exemplified states of affairs. If the metaphysician accepts the suggestion made in the previous footnote, he will not say that states of affairs are exemplified *in* events (for he will not say that they are exemplified *in* anything). And since "proposition," when used to refer to what is, according to the metaphysical theory, the subject matter of logic, is used synonymously with "state of affairs," as that expression is now being used, he will say that events are a subclass of propositions — a subclass of true propositions. If it seems paradoxical to say "all events are true propositions," the reason lies, not in the view that is being expressed, but in the fact that "proposition" is readily taken in senses other than that intended here (for example, as referring to a mental act or to a sentence). Thus Frege could say, "A fact is a thought that is true," since he used the word "thought [*Gedanke*]" as we are now using "state of affairs." See "The Thought: A Logical Inquiry," as translated in *Mind,* LXV (1956), 289–311; the quotation is on p. 307.

5. The point of the first clause of the definition is to avoid paradoxes about "true" and "false" by providing for the possibility that some beliefs are *not* beliefs with respect to any state of affairs that that state of affairs is exemplified; e.g., your belief and mine,

if what you now believe is that what I now believe is false, and if
what I now believe is that what you now believe is false.

6. Where "proposition" is used in place of "state of affairs,"
and "true" in place of "exemplified," such a definition will seem
less interesting, and the metaphysician may be led to say, as Russell
once did, that truth and falsehood are "incapable of analysis"; see
"Meinong's Theory of Complexes and Assumptions, III," *Mind*,
XIII (1904), 524. But "exemplified" and "unexemplified" (or "actual" and "nonactual," or even "existent" and "nonexistent"), in
place of "true" and "false," may suggest at least this much of an
"analysis": when we say of a proposition (state of affairs) that it
is true (exemplified), we are saying something analogous to what
we are saying when we say of an attribute or property that it is
exemplified.

C

On Ziff's "Natural and Formal Languages"

RICHARD M. MARTIN

New York University

THE VIRTUES of a formalized language-system — and this is Professor Ziff's main contention — are purchased at the cost of their "utter inutility" as instruments of communication "in the world in which we find ourselves." But surely in this world we do in fact often communicate in terms of formal systems, e.g., in a formalized arithmetic- or set-theory, perhaps even in basic English. What Professor Ziff says here thus seems to me false. What he wishes to say is, perhaps, that we do also communicate in a natural language, and that natural languages are in various respects richer in modes of locution than most formalized languages, and that communication itself is a very complex affair in need of analysis. But these are mere truisms, at least prima facie. What Professor Ziff does *not* say, but, it seems to me, *should* have said, is that much progress has been made in studying the complex facts of communication by means of the study of formalized languages, and that such study likewise promises to contribute much to both the syntax and semantics of natural language. But more about this later.

"The realities of . . . complex linguistic transaction," he tells us, "go and *must go* unheeded, ignored, if one is to dwell in the somewhat *mythic* and certainly *myopic* reaches of a formalism [italics added for emphasis]." But *must* these realities go unheeded? What kind of a 'must' do we have here? Is Professor Ziff making a prognosis that never, never, never will the complexities of linguistic transaction be studied using the notions of logic and formalized languages? Well, the fact is that they have been and are being, to some extent at least.

Formalized languages are *mythic,* or normative, in a non-pejorative sense, in the way in which arithmetic or geometry are. Or classical particle-mechanics, or relativity theory. And are not the rules even of generative grammar mythic in essentially the same sense? Perhaps arithmetic too is *myopic* in Professor Ziff's view. Surely the arithmetic of integers is myopic with respect to the real numbers, not being strong enough to accommodate them, and that of real numbers myopic with respect, say, to relativity theory. In each case the formalized language can be extended, however, to incorporate a wider domain of theory. The myopia here is not something intrinsic to formalized languages. Let us beware lest *we* be myopic of them, of what they are, and of how they function in inquiry, more particularly, in linguistic inquiry.

The myopia Professor Ziff speaks of is traced back to the "requirement that a formal language be perfectly precise," and this requirement in turn to the demand for "effective" linguistic rules. This demand has been clearly stated by Alonzo Church.[1] A linguistic structure lacking effective rules is for him "unsuitable for use . . . as a language." I am inclined to agree with Professor Ziff in thinking this demand too strong, but disagree with him as to the reasons. Some very interesting formalized languages have been, or can be, put forward, lacking effective specification of all of their rules. All of them are languages, however, in terms of which we can surely communicate. Three examples will suffice.

Consider Gentzen's celebrated proof in 1936 of the consistency of a certain formulation of elementary number theory. The proof requires the noneffective principle of transfinite induction of the order of Cantor's least epsilon number ε_0. The proof can be given in a language, surely, in which we can communicate. Or consider arithmetic augmented by the addition of Hilbert's rule, to the effect that if some property is provable of 0, of 1, of 2, and so on, it is then provable of all natural numbers. The use of this rule surely does not take us beyond some language in which communication is possible. Or, finally, consider the Hilbert-Bernays method of introducing Russellian descriptions of individuals – the method echoed by Strawson. Here one must first prove the existence and uniqueness of the object described before the description is regarded as a significant term. Thus here a syntactical definition by simultaneous recursion must be given of 'theorem' and 'term.' But the notion 'theorem' is not necessarily effective in the strong sense – in essentially the wording of Church – of there existing a method by which, given a formula, it can always be determined in a finite number of steps, whether or not it is a theorem – for there may be no certain method by which we can always either find a proof or determine that there is none to be found. We can conclude, I think, that Church's requirement of effectiveness is too strong. On this point, it seems to me, Professor Ziff is throughout most of his paper battling a windmill.

Effectiveness is construed in terms of an "algorithm or method of computation for determining whether or not something is so." But "the existence of an algorithm," Ziff goes on, "neither confers certainty nor guarantees absolute precision." This may well be so, pending clarification of how 'precision' and 'certainty' are construed here. Perhaps they are *pragmatical* terms – it is *we* who in given contexts of utterance or assertion are certain or precise. But no matter. Professor Ziff's *argument* on behalf of this point is what concerns us at the moment. "Consider," he says, "the difficulty of *determining* [italics added] whether or not an expression formed by the combination of several million symbols is a well-formed expression of the language. The existence of an algorithm merely guarantees that *there is* a method of computation. But it is still necessary to perform the computation if one is *to determine* whether or not the expression is well-formed . . . [italics added for emphasis]." Is Professor Ziff not confusing here a question concerning the existence of a method of computation with a question concerning a result of using the method in a particular instance? Is he not confusing a question of what exists with a question as to what we know? An expression containing several million symbols may be well-formed, of course, without our knowing, or being able easily to determine, that this is the case. Our knowledge is fallible, of course, and admits of degrees of probability. Professor Ziff extolls Von Neumann's probabilistic logic, designed to cope with problems arising from "noise" or a failure of transmission. The moral to be drawn is to design new logics — or rather to apply existing logic — to "problems of distortion, noise, and error and the like," rather than to berate all logic and formalized languages. Develop better methods of determining with higher accuracy whether the expression containing several million symbols is well-formed or not. Professor Ziff's argument here is supposed somehow to be against formalized languages but, as such, seems to me to fail to make its point.

"Formal languages ignore the realities of the perceptual situation in a wholehearted manner: not only do they make no concession to the existence of perceptual [or communicative] difficulties, they eschew all reliance on perceptual strategies and abilities." Now, in the words of Malvolio, what employment have we here? To bring in the realities of the perceptual situation, resort may be had to a pragmatics. Many alternative pragmatical metalanguages have been studied in some detail in recent years, but Professor Ziff remains silent thereon. In pragmatics the user of language is brought in fundamentally as well as suitable locutions by means of which his relations to language may be studied. Here due consideration can be given to perceptual difficulties and there need be no neglect of the speaker's strategies and abilities.

Consider now the example 'The pen on the table is made of gold.' "Now from a purely formal point of view," we are told, "a use of the phrase 'the pen on the desk' is to be deplored: since the expression does not have a unique referent, the sentence 'The pen on the desk is made of gold' is formally classed either false [by Russell] or neither true nor false [by Hilbert-Bernays and Strawson]." The way out of this difficulty is, we are told, the exercise of all sorts of perceptual and conceptual strategies. Here, it seems to me, there is confusion between a matter concerning syntactic or semantic structure and one concerning communication. It is a commonplace that in communication all kinds of "perceptual and conceptual strategies" may be used on the part of both speaker and hearer. But such strategies need not be read into syntactic or semantic structure. According to Zellig Harris, "grammatical utterances are, in fact, rather awkward carriers of . . . face-to-face communication. . . . What is special to grammatical utterance . . . is not that it has meaning, expresses feelings, communicates, or calls for a relevant response . . . , but that . . . it is socially *transmissible*." [2] In short, it seems that Professor Ziff has confused communication with transmissibility, and he goes on to suggest, incorrectly, some differences in this regard as between a natural and formalized language.

"For a speaker to supply or rely on nonlinguistic inputs to the hearer is a commonplace in the use of a natural language. It is equally commonplace and equally essential for a speaker to be able, on occasion, to rely on a hearer's having a special program." I fail to see why it is not equally commonplace to say the same of a speaker of a formal language. But no, we are told. "From a purely formal point of view, a speaker's reliance on a hearer's special program is to be anathematized insofar as it sanctions implicit rather than explicit qualification." Give the explicit qualification and "the resulting prolixity would be aesthetically unbearable: there would be a general failure of communication." The example of the officer commanding a private 'Shut the door!' is a case in point.

It seems that here too Professor Ziff is confusing matters concerning purely linguistic structure, i.e., syntactical and semantical features of language, with those concerned with communication. It is surely a commonplace to note that all manner of nonlinguistic factors enter into the latter, e.g., in the words of Colin Cherry,[3] "little movements of the hands and face, . . . nods, smiles, frowns, handshakes, kisses, fist shakes, and other gestures," including grunts and groans and sticks and stones. We can handle communication in terms of linguistic *acts* or *events*, perhaps, not just in terms of transmissible expressions. An act of utterance, e.g., the act of person X's uttering sentence *a* at time *t* is a very complex act consisting of utterance, tone of voice, manner of utterance, context, etc., etc. If 'communicate' is a relational word with its arguments linguistic acts, or at least one of them a linguistic act, we can perhaps handle the various nonlinguistic factors in communication. But Professor Ziff offers no analysis of what communication is, or of *its* structure or grammar, or of the various factors that enter into it. The key notion of his paper thus, it seems, remains pretty much in limbo.

"The profound differences between a formal language and a natural language take their loci in the respective vocabularies of each language. . . . The vocabulary of a formal language may be either finite or infinite. In either case the vocabulary of a formal language is effectively specifiable. In contrast, no nonarbitrary specification of the vocabulary of a natural language, or dialect, or idiolect [of a some one person here and now] can possibly be effective." No proof is offered of any of these quite distinct contentions, and immediately we are told that "the specification of a person's vocabulary at a fixed moment of time is clearly not effective in any plausible sense of the word." But the notion that a vocabulary of a language, at least of a formalized language, is effective presupposes that that language have *primitive* terms and that these be effectively specifiable. As Church puts it, "the specification of the primitive symbols shall be effective in the sense that there is a method by which, whenever a symbol is given, it can always be determined effectively whether or not it is one of the primitive symbols." [4] Now, Professor Ziff's contention here is meaningless unless *all* the words of a natural language, or dialect, or idiolect, or whatever, are to be regarded as in some sense primitive. Perhaps they should be so regarded, but this we are not told. Suppose for the sake of argument that they are. Is there then only a finite number of them? Suppose for the sake of argument that there is. It is then contended that no effective tests can be devised for deciding whether or not, given a word, it is an item in the vocabulary. I for one would not wish to give such wholesale hostage to future research on this matter. Think of how clever some yet unborn fieldworker in linguistics may turn out to be in devising suitable behavioral or other tests for determining a speaker's vocabulary!

Professor Ziff conflates effective tests for determining a speaker's vocabulary with those for determining the total vocabulary of the language. But surely we should distinguish these rather sharply. Concerning the latter Zellig Harris has noted that "the set of arbitrary grammatical elements, including sound elements, vocabulary, rules of classification, and rules of combination, must be finite, or recursive with finite generators." [5] This description would not presumably apply to an idiolect, but only to a total language, natural or formalized.

There are of course many kinds of formal languages with differing syntactic and semantical structures. Professor Ziff lumps all of these together, somewhat as Strawson does, to create what seems to me a straw man. It is true that it is usually required of a formal language that its primitive vocabulary be effectively specifiable. Also it is usually required that its formulae be of finite length. But formal languages have been studied that admit expressions of infinite, even nondenumerable, length. It is not a far step to languages with a nondenumerable primitive vocabulary, although, so far as my knowledge extends, such languages have not been very much studied as yet. Professor Ziff of course must rule them out as impossible, therewith again giving hostage to future research. The variety of formal systems is so great that one of these days one may well turn up that will very closely approximate a natural language in crucial respects.

Now on to the comments concerning polysemy and monosemy. "From the point of view of a formalism, polysemy can be seen only as a cancerous proliferation of meanings, calling for swift excision. . . . To eliminate even the evident homonymy and polysemy from a lexicon of a natural language would mean at least doubling the number of entries. And this would mean an enormous increase in the probability of error in the transmission and reception of signals." But now surely Professor Ziff is putting forward here a strange view indeed. The presence of polysemy in a formal language is no "cancerous proliferation of meanings." But one can easily distinguish different meanings, e.g., by subscripts. Thus 'probability$_1$' can stand for degree of confirmation, 'probability$_2$' for statistical probability, and 'probability$_3$' for degree of credibility or belief. We have not tripled the number of entries, but merely subdivided the entries under one heading, much as a standard lexicon does. But if we do this, do we then increase the liability of error in the transmission and reception of signals? I should have thought it would be the other way around, in some types of communication anyhow. To speak of probability$_2$, when probability$_2$ is meant rather than probability$_1$ or probability$_3$, is surely to increase accuracy of what is said and hence to increase accuracy of reception. Consider some 4-way ambiguous sentence S with readings S_1, S_2, S_3, S_4. Taking Professor Ziff literally, there is greater likelihood of error in transmitting one of these readings than in transmitting S itself. Surely this view is somewhat quixotic, and a sentence containing words with too much polysemy may fail to communicate altogether.

The poet takes delight in the multiple ambiguity of words, and in using them in expanded and unexpected ways. But, as Paul Valéry has reminded us, "every true poet is much more capable than is generally known of right reasoning and abstract thought." [6] The poet chooses his words with great skill and exactitude, just as the mathematician chooses carefully the various successive symbols of a formula. I once had a long argument with John Berryman on this topic, and he argued forcefully that poetic language is quite as exact as that of mathematics. Of course the poet may use in some context a multiply ambiguous sentence or phrase rather than any of its more exact readings. But then it is this very ambiguity perhaps that is aimed at. To use a reading in its place would be less desirable — in fact might spell the difference between poetry and prose.

"Although all formal languages in fact," Professor Ziff goes on, "rely heavily on coding devices and would be utterly unintelligible without them, the devices, namely abbreviative definitions, are officially disclaimed and denied formal status." But this statement is surely not correct. Abbreviative definitions are not "officially disclaimed and denied formal status," on any reasonable rendition of this phrase. The list of abbreviative definitions is part and parcel of the notion of a logistic system, i.e., if such a list is actually given. Definitions are intimately intertwined with the axioms, as any worker with formal languages well knows. Change a definition ever so slightly and some change in the axioms may have to be made, and conversely. Definitions are theoretically dispensable, however, and thus no list of them need be given. If not, then everything one wishes to say must be said in terms wholly of the primitive vocabulary. Church being Professor Ziff's sole authority on all logistic matters, we can refer to the longish footnote 168 (pp. 76–77) in Church's book for corroboration.

What can we say now, more positively, about the use of formalized language-systems in linguistics? I recently asked an eminent linguist, who is also a thorough logician, why it is that linguists pretty much to a man have rejected the help that modern logic, including logical syntax and denotational semantics, have to offer. Most linguists toil on as though modern logic did not exist, and when they do discover some relevant point well known to logicians they regard it as their own discovery. The answer to my question was instructive. The reason is due in part, I was told, to the rather disparaging view logicians have tended to take toward natural language. From the point of view of the logician, a natural language has, in Professor Ziff's words, "a bad ambiguous topsy-turvy look." It is logically imperfect, its words ambiguous, inexact, and imprecise, etc., etc., as we have been told again and again. It needs overhauling and "regimentation," to use Quine's somewhat militaristic word.[7] Well, being a dove, I prefer not to use the terminology of hawks. Linguists contend, on the contrary, that a natural language is exactly what it is with no need for regimentation, and his aim is to study the complex phenomenon of

natural language *exactly as it is*. This is after all what he
studies, just as the physicist studies the complex, evanescent
phenomena of nature.

Ryle, in what seems to me one of his better metaphors,
has noted that the philosopher is to the formal logician what
the cartographer is to the geometer. The cartographer "finds
no Euclidean straight hedgerows or Euclidean plane meadows.
Yet he could not map the sinuous hedgerows that he finds or
the undulating meadows save against the ideally regular boundaries and levels . . . in terms of which alone can he calculate
out the relative positions and heights of the natural objects
which he is to record from the visual observations he makes.
The cartographer is one of the clients of geometry. The possibility of his map being approximately correct or precise is the
gift of Euclid." [8] But the geometer does not turn to the cartographer, or rather to the sinuous hedgerows and undulating
meadows themselves, and say: Oh you geometrically imperfect
entities, you, you are vague and imprecise and need overhauling. You must be regimented so as to become exact Euclidean
straight edges or planes! It is as though the wave-theorist were
to say to the undulating waves of the sea: You imperfect
waves, you. You too must be regimented so as to obey my exact equations!

Enough has been said to see, perhaps, that the linguist's
attitude toward the formal logician is, to some extent at least,
justified. But where do we go from here? Let us go back
twenty years, for a moment, and then lament with the late
Uriel Weinreich, that "decades have been wasted" [9] in linguistic study by the failure to utilize the resources of modern logic.

Just over twenty years ago, in Chapter VII of his *Elements of Symbolic Logic*, Reichenbach attempted "to apply
the methods of symbolic logic to an analysis of conversational
language." [10] The "conversational language" that Reichenbach
considered included a kind of unified language for science
augmented with such extra terms as science seems to need.
The attempt was indeed a serious one, perhaps the most detailed that had been made up to the time or that has been

made since. The chapter incorporates surely important insights and attempts bravely to extend logic into areas where extension is needed. Nonetheless much in the chapter needs revision or correction, or, more important, cannot be regarded as sound. What is now needed is a critique of Reichenbach's work based on the advances in philosophic logic in the intervening years. We could then go on to pave the way for an improved foundation for a "logistic grammar" of the kind Reichenbach envisaged. It has been said, by Reichenbach's critics, that he knew neither enough logic nor linguistics to carry his program very far. Perhaps so. But he made an important beginning, from which linguists can well profit, as Weinreich has pointed out.

This is not the occasion to attempt to carry on where Reichenbach left off. Instead, let us call attention very briefly to the many areas of logical theory of immediate interest to the study of natural language.

In the first place, there is the *calculus of individuals*. This calculus, or rather theory, is concerned primarily with such relations between individuals as *discreteness, overlapping, part-to-whole*, etc. Its origins go back to Leśniewski's *O padstawach matematyki* of 1927–31.[11] The significance of the subject for philosophy was well emphasized by Leonard and Goodman in 1936 [12] and for biology, more particularly for the theories of cell division and fusion, by Woodger in 1937.[13] Then in 1951 the subject came to the fore again in the "constructional" or "constitution" system of Goodman's *The Structure of Appearance*.[14] Despite these significant uses of the calculus of individuals, most philosophers, philosophic logicians, and linguists continue to ignore the subject altogether and therewith, it would seem, deprive themselves of a most useful logical tool.

Next, let us turn to *event-logic*, including the logic of *tenses*, this latter recently under intensive development in California, Oxford, and elsewhere. In event-logic a special ontology for events is explicitly admitted. The need for such an ontology has been forcefully pointed out in several recent papers by Donald Davidson.[15] Davidson's suggestions hark back to some extent to those of Reichenbach. The trick is to admit new variables ranging over events where variables over physical objects are already available. For Reichenbach, the new variables seem explained away, but just how is not too clear. And Davidson is content with using such variables to help gain suitable "logical forms" for statements of ordinary language, but without telling us what theory is needed to govern them.

In event-logic, the calculus of individuals is used to help gain what appears to be a suitable linguistic framework for talk of events, physical objects, and their interrelations. Hence a two-sorted language is employed. To have one kind of variable over events and another over physical objects seems a not unreasonable course, prima facie at least. Our common language contains an abundance of expressions for both, as do the specialized languages for the sciences. Even so we can unify the ranges of the two sorts of variables later if desired.

In event-logic a theory of tenses may be built up. Or, one can build this up independently, in the UCLA or Oxford manner. Strawson's complaint that formal logic cannot handle changes of tense is no longer justified, and indeed never was.

We can skip over logical syntax rather quickly, although its usefulness for the study of natural language has perhaps not been fully realized. Concerning semantics, denotation, the truth-concept, analytic truth, modal notions, belief, and the like, I have had my say elsewhere and need not repeat it here.

Pragmatics, however, is still in its infancy. In the words of Carnap, "there is an urgent need for a system of theoretical pragmatics, not only for psychology *and linguistics* [italics added], but also for analytic philosophy. Since pure semantics is sufficiently developed, the time seems ripe for attempts at constructing tentative outlines of pragmatical systems." [16] Such an outline would incorporate items upon which many contemporary logicians are working under such various titles as deontic logic, erotetic logic, the logic of commands, epistemic logic, the logic of belief and of knowledge, the logic of action, the logic of performatives, etc., etc.

Elsewhere thirty-seven atomic sentential forms for a kind of unified pragmatics have been discussed, and these need not be repeated here.[17] They include forms for *acceptance, rejection, preference* (in the cognitive sense), *indifference* (likewise cognitive), perhaps *quantitative acceptance, performance, intention* (with a 't'), *knowing that* and *believing that, assertion, utterance, asking, answering,* perhaps *commanding* and *exclaiming* also, various alternative forms for handling sentences concerned with *perception* of objects as well as of events, and finally, some tentative forms for handling *conception* along lines suggested by a certain interpretation of Frege.

A concluding remark now concerning logical form, a topic not mentioned by Professor Ziff. But it should have been, it seems to me, for logical form surely has a great deal to do with the depth grammar of natural language. Perhaps even the depth grammar of a sentence *is* its logical form, as Herbert Bohnert has suggested. Since no one seems to have told us very clearly just what depth grammar is, the suggestion here is perhaps as acceptable as any.

Presumably every logical form should be definable in terms of suitably chosen atomic ones. To give a logical form for a sentence of a natural language is one step. To paraphrase that form in terms of the acceptable atomic sentential forms available is another. The task of a logistic grammar is in part, I take it, to select suitable forms and then to formulate laws of paraphrase as between combinations of those forms and sentences of the natural language. We are far off of course from this goal, but progress is being made. And this much may safely be contended: many acceptable forms are available in the kind of unified pragmatics referred to — a modest contention indeed.

To put this matter in another way. It is a widespread opinion, and one more and more frequently being voiced, that linguists will be forced, internally as it were, to come to grips with the results of modern logic. Indeed, this is apparently already happening to some extent. By 'logic' is not meant here recursive function-theory, California model-theory, constructive proof-theory, or even axiomatic set-theory. Such areas may or may not be useful for linguistics. Rather under 'logic' are included our good old friends, the homely locutions 'and,' 'or,' 'if — then,' 'if and only if,' 'not,' 'for all x,' 'for some x,' and 'is identical with,' plus the calculus of individuals, event-logic, syntax, denotational semantics, and the various parts of pragmatics alluded to above. It is to these that the linguist, as well as the philosophic analyst, can most profitably turn for help. These are his tools. And they are "clean tools," to borrow a phrase of the late J. L. Austin in another context, in fact, the only really clean ones we have, so that we might as well use them as much as we can. But they constitute only what may be called "baby logic." Baby logic is to the linguist and philosopher what "baby mathematics" (in the phrase of Murray Gell-Mann) is to the theoretical physicist — very elementary but indispensable domains of theory in both cases.

Unfortunately Professor Ziff has written as though the riches of modern logic do not exist. The result is, it seems to me, that he has not given formal languages a fair hearing. He has based his entire paper on what seems to me a weak point due to Church. He has taken too narrow a conception of what formal languages are and has disregarded almost all recent advances. He has failed to grasp the relevance of the search for logical form for the study of language. Finally, the gravest methodological sin of all — by giving hostage to future research, both theoretical and empirical, he has blocked the road to inquiry.

NOTES

1. *Introduction to Mathematical Logic* I (Princeton, N.J.: Princeton University Press, 1956), p. 52.

2. *Mathematical Structure of Language*, MSS., p. 7.

3. *On Human Communication* (Cambridge, Mass. and London, England: M.I.T. Press, 1957), p. 4.

4. *Op. cit.*, p. 50.

5. *Op. cit.*, p. 11.

6. *The Art of Poetry* (Vintage Books, New York: Random House, 1958), p. 77.

7. In *Word and Object* (New York and London, England: Technology Press of the Massachusetts Institute of Technology and John Wiley and Sons, 1960), pp. 157 ff.

8. *Dilemmas* (Cambridge, England: Cambridge University Press, 1954), p. 123.

9. In "On the Semantic Structure of Language," in *Universals of Grammar,* 2nd ed., ed. J. H. Greenberg (Cambridge, Mass. and London, England: M.I.T. Press, 1966), p. 192.

10. (New York: Macmillan Co., 1947), pp. 251–354.

11. In *Przeglad filozoficzny* 30–34 (1927–31).

12. H. S. Leonard and N. Goodman, "The Calculus of Individuals and Its Uses," *The Journal of Symbolic Logic,* V (1940), 45–55.

13. J. H. Woodger, *The Axiomatic Method in Biology* (Cambridge, England: Cambridge University Press, 1937), including Appendix E by A. Tarski.

14. (Cambridge, Mass.: Harvard University Press, 1951).

15. Donald Davidson, "The Logical Form of Action Sentences," in *The Logic of Action and Preference,* ed. N. Rescher (Pittsburgh, Pa.: Pittsburgh University Press, 1967) and "Causal Relations," *The Journal of Philosophy,* LXIV (1967), 691–703.

16. R. Carnap, *Meaning and Necessity,* 2nd ed. (Chicago: University of Chicago Press, 1956), p. 250.

17. See the author's "On Some Relations of Pragmatics," in the *Festschrift* for Sidney Hook, *Sidney Hook and the Contemporary World* (New York: John Day, 1968).

1

On Formalized Models of Natural Language

HERBERT G. BOHNERT

Michigan State University

FORMALIZED LANGUAGES continue to be a focus of dissension among linguists, logicians, and natural-language philosophers. The nonmeeting of minds is often evidenced, as in this symposium, by the ineffectualness of the arguments brought forward as much as by more substantial differences. I should like to survey a few of both sorts, making distinctions along the way that may narrow some areas of difference, and then to sketch an approach to the use of formalized languages in natural-language studies and philosophy that may be less open to misunderstanding.

Paul Ziff, in his paper "Natural and Formal Languages," calls the view that "a formal logic is a language of a sort" one of the significant achievements of contemporary logical and linguistic research.[1] The trend of his argument, however, is to discount the relevance of formal languages to the study of natural languages, and especially to reject any view of formal languages as ideal exemplars to which evolutionary natural languages can only approximate. The argument, though touching on significant issues, is made ineffectual by his use of "formal language" in ways permitting, if not encouraging, such narrow readings that his points, when holding at all, hold trivially. Even he, presumably, did not intend (commentator) Roderick Chisholm's ultranarrow reading of "a formal logic is a language," i.e., as confining attention to pure logics without descriptive predicates. Such a reading would make the "ideal exemplar" view more preposterous even than Ziff suggests.[2] But

Ziff himself trivializes the matter almost as badly by limiting his consideration to formal languages patterned closely upon existing logic-based axiomatizations. He makes the limitation explicit by inserting qualifiers like "familiar" or "characteristic" in his charges. A charge that formal languages achieve precision at the cost of "utter inutility in communication" is inconclusive, to say the least, if directed only at systems in which communicative convenience has been deliberately subordinated to other system values.[3] A charge that formal languages "eschew all reliance on perceptual strategies and abilities" is, under such limitations, simply odd. The more critical question, clearly, is whether there is something about formal languages in a more generic sense that forces certain undesirable or unnatural features.

Before taking up such questions, it is worth noting that Ziff's charge, even as given, is overstated, since, as Richard Martin remarked in his commentary, people can, and occasionally do, communicate in existing formalized languages. Moreover, considerations of communicative convenience may enter into their construction, as can be seen in choices, e.g., between Polish and parenthesis notation, or between Sheffer stroke and more generous assortments of primitive connectives. Such choices, of course, incur no inevitable "cost" in precision. It should, indeed, be stressed that viewing a logical formalism (with nonlogical predicates) as a genuine language in which things can be said and communicated is no mere afterthought in the wake of a purely mathematical development. Van Heijenoort[1] tellingly spells out how fundamental the conception was in Frege's own development, as it was, of course, in Russell, Carnap, Quine, and others. In particular, he gives a revealing picture of Frege's concern with the problem of learning such languages, and of "catching on," given certain "hints." Presumably none of these logicians would have denied the communicative inconvenience of the easy-to-describe, hard-to-use syntax of their own constructions. That it did not disturb them suggests they had little difficulty in conceiving of harder-to-describe, easier-to-use formalizations.[4] And presumably they felt that such formalisms would not bar humans from communicating with fragments of well-formed expressions, aided by memory, visual cues, or, for that matter, from communicating even by ill-formed fragments, analogy, or metaphor, granted the Fregean powers of "catching on." [5] Precise specification or description of a language need not involve description of all the ways in which the language can be used, nor the abilities involved in such use, any more than precise specification or description of an automobile model need mention its possible use as a weapon, or refer to human response times.[6] Some of Ziff's more strange-sounding charges (e.g., about "perceptual strategies" not being taken account of) seem to stem, in part, from an urge to be holistically inclusive, with a corresponding disinclination to distinguish between language and language-using system or method. To be sure, such a distinction may involve a certain arbitrariness or be hard to draw in complete generality, but science seems to flourish on such distinctions. Those who reject them are less often rewarded by more realistic descriptions than penalized by inarticulateness.

But now let us turn from the possibility of "imprecise" use to questions concerning precision of specification. Earlier I remarked that selecting a notation with improved communication values need not entail a loss of precision. A natural question is "Must not formalized languages *always* be precise?" Without entering deeply into the issues such a question may suggest, we might note, to begin with, some respects in which the answer should be No, even with respect to the typical formalized languages Ziff has in mind. A Tarskian or Carnapian semantics, for example, can only be as precise, roughly speaking, as the metalanguage translations provided. While standard examples of such semantical systems may exemplify or aspire to precision in one or more senses, nothing inherent in the symbolism prevents choosing a universe of discourse such as Cultures, with predicates such as Nomadic, Hieratic, Urban, etc., all left as semantically imprecise as they appear in natural English, since English itself could be used as the metalanguage.[7] Besides this possibility of interpreting the imprecise by the imprecise, there are at least two senses in which even a formalized language cannot actually attain precision. I refer here to Quine's "inscrutability of reference," [8] which he traces to residual indeterminatenesses of the ostension process and the purely logico-mathematical limitations imposed, e.g., by the Löwenheim-Skolem theorem. If, further, one were to accept the notion of private languages with, e.g., inverted spectra (as Quine does not), this would suggest a third sort of irreducible "imprecision." It is worth remarking that without "artificial" formalizations the Löwenheim-Skolem limitation on precision could hardly have been conceived, and other sorts of inscrutability, e.g., associated with indirect ostension, mastering the individuating devices of a language, and so on, would be harder to analyze.

The preceding remarks concern only semantic precision. They still presuppose a precise syntax. Let us now turn to the question of a possible "overprecision" in syntax. The claim would not be, of course, that a syntax given by vocabulary and rule would be more precise than a native speaker could give, but rather that even if proposed by a professional linguist-observer, its sharp inclusion and exclusion of strings would be hard to justify as representing with significant faithfulness a native speaker's changing propensities to utter, recognize, understand, or forget particular words or constructions. Some of Ziff's remarks (in his attack on Church's effectiveness requirement) portray the problem vividly, as have discussions by others, e.g., Chomsky in his degrees of grammaticality. But a more faithful representation can hardly be attained by giving an *imprecise* syntax, whatever that would be, or by simply refraining from giving any, though this occasionally seems hinted at in extreme antiformalist discussions.

A first obvious step away from confusion is to note that mutability is not the same thing as imprecision. Change, indeed, cannot be noted except in terms of "before and after" characterizations. A direction often taken that avoids this confusion is to envision a given speaker as characterized by a momentary idiolect, any one such idiolect being specified by vocabulary and rules (whether in the logician's style or in that of the linguistic transformationalist). The speaker may even be viewed as characterized by a wide variety of such idiolects at a given moment, each one representing a different degree of grammaticality, or even quite distinct conceptions as to what is to count as language (gestures, intonations, pauses). The problem then arises of what should be said about the relation between an actual, laboriously constructed syntax and these rapidly varying hypothetical ones. One might be tempted to say that the actually given syntax has some statistically approximative relation to this hypothetical ensemble. Such a proposal has an attractive resemblance, at least at first, to the methods of physics, where, e.g., a hypothetical velocity-at-a-moment is assumed while any observed velocity represents an average. Certain related analogies suggested by Carnap [9] have been forcefully criticized by Chomsky,[10] though his critique seems to apply with equal force to his own syntactical representations.

Part of the difficulty is conceiving what an ascription of a momentary idiolect to a speaker is to mean. If a person is, at a given moment, mentally reciting the alphabet, what does it mean to count "Babylon" as part of his vocabulary at that moment? An extreme operationism that would attribute an idiolect only on the basis of time-consuming tests would tend to reject momentary idiolects. Chomsky, in his recent strong reversal of his own earlier operationistic attitudes, accepts theoretical concepts and takes his sort of grammar as characterizing a competence.[11] Since competences change, however, the approximation problem, as between an actually given characterization and the hypothetical changing ones, remains open. It is not, in particular, resolved by speaking about the competence of an *ideal* speaker-hearer, since that only shifts the approximation problem to an even more difficult level, i.e., as between actual and ideal speaker-hearer. Had such a ploy been suggested by Carnap, Chomsky's reaction can only be imagined.

The trend of the preceding two paragraphs has been to

suggest that the momentary-idiolect tack, while having an attractive formal clarity,[12] raises questions sufficiently difficult so that its scientific status can be viewed, at best, as that of a valuably suggestive *façon de parler*. (Whether viewing a formalized grammar as characterizing an ideal competence adds more than another, less suggestive, *façon de parler* need not be entered into here.)

Before proceeding to seek a less problematic role for formalized languages, certain further conceptual puzzles are best gotten out of the way.

Ziff rejects the idiolect concept or any other sort of purely syntactic representation of language, though not because of the difficulties mentioned, and in particular not on operationist grounds. On the contrary, he speaks not just of behavioral competences but of the internal state of the speaker, viewed as an automaton, with varying access to various parts of its storage. Such variation might seem only to call for some time-dependent weighting function over the vocabulary, but Ziff takes a more drastic stand: "The fact of the matter is that a natural language, or a dialect, or an idiolect, does not have, not even at an arbitrary moment of time, a static fixed store of word-senses. The vocabulary of word-senses of a natural language is a continuous creation." The words "static" and "fixed" indicate a Zeno-like confusion. Would the claim be improved if it spoke of a dynamic fixed store? Or of a dynamic unfixed store? And "continuous creation" seems only the equally confused Bergsonian contrary to the static and fixed. Even something like a "continuously creating" automaton need not lack at each moment an effectively characterizable vocabulary of words (or word-senses, if the phrase is to be given a clear meaning).

Actually, effectiveness is not the real target of Ziff's attack. It is clear from his argument that he would remain unsatisfied if the effectiveness requirement were softened to semieffectiveness, or to some nonconstructive but still logico-mathematically determined specification. What seems to disturb Ziff, and often others [13] concerned with natural language, is not so much the precision with which a formalized language's set of well-formed formulas is specified, but *that* it is specified, more exactly, that such a language is *defined* by referring only to signs and their concatenations, without reference to times or speakers. To be sure, such specification has its proper place, the critics agree, but the implied place seems to be elsewhere than in natural-language investigation.

In making such strictures, the critics appear to have primarily in mind the constructions of the logicians, but, like the earlier mentioned methodological objections to idiolects, they fall equally upon the syntactical constructions of the linguistic transformationalists. While Chomsky's own phrasings, at times, obscure the purely syntactical nature of his grammars,[14] he puts the matter plainly enough in several places.[15] In thus relocating the boundary under dispute, I am, of course, viewing formal languages and grammars in a more general way (essentially that of the automata theorist) than in typical logical presentations, but this generality seems entirely appropriate to the generality of the antiformalist's objections, i.e., to syntactical specification per se.

To the extent that misgivings center on this point, i.e., on syntactic definition of languages, it may be natural to expect that they stem in part from logico-linguistic snarls as much as from the mutabilities and "imprecisions" of human behavior. For instance, a critic might inquire as follows: "In what sense, if any, can a formalized language be said to *describe* a natural language? Descriptions are not typically viewed as analytic sentences but as synthetic ones, yet a sentence, e.g., asserting that a string S is a well-formed prepositional phrase of a defined language L will be logically determinate, not synthetic." At first glance this might seem to introduce the whole analytic-synthetic controversy, if, indeed, it did not establish the scientific sterility of formalized languages immediately. But, all that is required, I think, is a slight, not unnatural shift in point of view. The history of science is often said to exhibit an interplay between analytic and synthetic in which what had been taken as a law comes to be viewed as a definition, and vice versa. To the extent that we acknowledge a genuine interplay, we might also describe it in terms of a shift of "synthetic burden" from some assertions to others. In connection with a formalized language L, the synthetic burden may be viewed as shifted away from assertions, e.g., that such and such expressions are or are not wffs (well-informed formulas) of L, and toward assertions (about wffs of L) in which nonsyntactical terms enter. That such a shift is not problematic, or even especially strange, may be seen by considering a dictionary as defining a set of words. More concretely, consider a list of all the principal entries in Merriam-Webster's second edition (i.e., without definitions or other text) and suppose we ask "Does this list describe the vocabulary of English?" One answer (which, oddly, might occur more readily to a logician than to a linguist) is "The list expresses no proposition since it is not a sentence. Hence it describes nothing." An attempt at a more affirmative answer (assuming, perhaps, a tacit assertion about the list) would tend, with increasing care, to bog in detailed qualifications. But even in the midst of such frustration it would be odd to blame the list for being recursively or effectively given (a class given by a finite enumeration is, of course, recursive), or for the fact that any assertion of presence or absence of a given word on the list is not a synthetic one. A more proper target might be the phrase "the vocabulary of English." But conceding this, and along with it the propriety of the original question, it is then fair to reject the parallel question as to whether a given formalized syntax describes *English* (or English syntax).

What is called for, both in the case of the list and of any given formalized syntax, is no single claim, but many, variously qualified assertions, some more guarded than others, some concerning particular entries, or particular wffs, others about various subsets of the whole list or stringset. Assertions even about the whole list or whole stringset need not be unduly sweeping or unnaturally precise, e.g., "most Londoners over fourteen had, in the early sixties, some reading knowledge of, say, ten per cent of the words on the list, "Every word on the list was passed on by two authorities," "Some English words are not on the list." It should be stressed that information on single entries, such as is given by the actual Merriam-Webster, as opposed to the bare list, concerns *syntactically specified* strings. Thus syntactic specification ("without reference to time or speaker," and with its inevitable nonsynthetic assertions, e.g., " 'y' occurs in 'syntax' ") is seen as an essential ingredient in many typical synthetic assertions of linguistics. Even as assertion that a certain word has shifted in meaning, or that it appears understandable to a certain aphasiac only at certain moments requires reference to the word as a syntactic structure. It should be noted also that traditional dictionaries and grammars typically facilitate discussion of historical language change by being *inclusive* in a way that would bar them from being regarded as a "model," in any stringent sense, of any idiolect characterizing any particular person or group at any one time. Nothing in principle prevents formalized languages and their vocabularies from being used in the same way. Indeed, I view their proper role in linguistics as a straightforward extension of the methods of traditional dictionaries and grammars.

These reflections provide, I believe, the key to an escape from what might be called the "mathematical-model muddle in linguistics." Once we separate the analytic from the synthetic statements, as determined by the definitional structure of a formalized language, it becomes clear that the defined language need not be regarded as an all-in-one-piece mathematical model of anything that must be evaluated only by some overall measure of approximation to something. Instead, a formalized language can be viewed as providing a vocabulary (by recursive methods) with the help of which empirical assertions can be made, piecemeal, about any of an infinite variety of structures, with each separate assertion bearing its own qualifications and "imprecisions." It can be too inclusive to be regarded as a model of any actually used language, as already remarked, or it can be too underinclusive. The latter occurs when the investigator is interested simply in examining certain suggested grammatical rules by following them out in a rigorous way. Indeed, much of the "inadequate" appearance of logical studies, in the eyes of antiformalists, results from this specialized sort of investigation, e.g., where formalisms lacking any descriptive predicate at all are studied in order to focus attention on rules for a residual logical vocabulary. Similarly, certain of the investigations by natural-language philosophers into the "logical grammar" of some single problematic concept, such as intending or wishing, may be carried out in reference to variations in a limited fragment of syntax. Such fragments are typically characterized only informally, of course. My point is just that if formalized, even with all needed logical apparatus, the resulting formalisms would be too underinclusive to be viewed as modeling a language (in any except an already quite abstract sense).

In thus trying to separate the notion of mathematical model as it is used in physical science, with its accompanying conceptual sophistications, from the notion of a formalized language, I am aware that I am flying in the face of what may seem to some an almost tautological link between these two notions. The axiomatizations typically studied by logicians are, or are prototypes for, systems of laws describing physical systems in ways for which questions of precision and approximation can be sharply formulated and are of central importance. But, of course, *formulating* a description is not *being* a description. Typical axiomatizations *formulate* descriptions but few would say that the notation used *is* the description in any simple map-like sense. The concept of a formalized language itself *being* a model of something is thus not at all necessarily derivative from its use in formulating models.

It may be conceded that there is nothing intrinsically absurd in viewing a formalized language as being a model. It is in a sense a self-model, at least. And it could be regarded as a model of other formalized languages in various respects. But of course there are many respects and correspondingly many measures of resemblance, in sign designs, in overlapping vocabularies, in syntactic constructions, etc. But no one sort of correspondence (and approximation to it) has a dominating role comparable with that of semantic truth correspondence, which enters when a language is used as a language, rather than as a more map-like representation. For example, suppose a team of linguistics were to regard Sibeth's *Wörterbuch* [16] as a model of the vocabulary of the Mecklenburg-West Pomeranian dialect of low German and suppose that by a wondrous methodology, into which we need not inquire, they were to assign a highly reliable measure of the degree to which the "model" approximated the "actual vocabulary" of the dialect. I suggest that this figure would be of little help to someone wondering to what extent it might aid in reading the *Quickborn* poems of Klaus Groth, written in the Holstein dialect of low German. A quite independent approximation measure would be called for. Indeed, a single number however "accurate" would typically be of far less significance than many small tips on correspondences, e.g., that Mecklenburg "ei" becomes Holstein "ee." There is, clearly, no single problem of approximation. In languages, as in other complex entities, the sorts of resemblance that may be important to note and evaluate are manifold, and the evaluations are guided by purposes.

Perhaps enough distinctions have been drawn to permit safely what might otherwise seem a confusing return to a model-like viewpoint. That is, we may permit ourselves to acknowledge resemblances (in the diffuse, many-faceted ways spoken of above) among languages, as among human faces, and between words on a given list and words encountered in reading or listening. In particular, we need not deny that intended use and descriptive intention enter into the compiling of dictionaries, distinguishing pharmacological from commercial, unabridged from "collegiate," English from Twi. Similar intentions will be manifest in formalized grammars. If one wishes to use words such as "describe" or "model" to refer informally to such intentions, as we would in speaking of a *Hungarian* dictionary, confusion need not follow, if the distinctions of the sort here stressed are tacitly understood.[17] Even if a formalized syntax were presented in the form of a definition of the word "English," one need not take up arms to contend an empirical claim. Nor need one have an Orwellian fear that such a definition, through hidden powers intrinsic to definition itself, might suddenly acquire a legal, compulsive status, perhaps banishing real, culture-laden English to Nuspeak nonhistory.[18] The worst penalty such a move warrants is a grumble at the spectacle of yet another meaning being added to the burden of a word in common use, as various sciences have added meanings to "field" and "group."

I should now like to provide a more concrete illustration of various preceding remarks and for some still to come, in the form of two formalized languages, called English I and English II to distinguish them from English and yet to suggest a modeling intention in the way just described. The syntax need not be actually given here (that of English II takes two pages in its current form) [19] since the characteristics relevant here can be made sufficiently evident by informal characterization and by a display of some sentences generated at random from the given grammar by a computer.[20] The first remark we can consider these languages as illustrating is the one concerning the possibility of alternative logical formalisms more adapted to human communication needs. The claim that these languages represent an alternative *logical* formalism rests on the existence of algorithms that translate well-formed sentences of these languages into formulas of the first-order predicate calculus (based on a dictionary assignment of name and predicate symbols to the English words in a given dictionary). For sample translations, see Exhibit I. Logical relations among sentences of English I or II are defined to be just those among their logical translations. English I is less Englishlike than English II, e.g., in having logic-like variables, but it is more articulate, in that every predicate calculus form has an English I equivalent, while this is not true of English II. The claim that these formalisms are more adapted to human communication rests on a number of points. The most evident from the ran-

Exhibit I

5 ENGIGEN 20

NOT BOTH BOTH FIDO FALLS AND FOR EVERY X FOR SOME X1 EITHER FIDO LIKE
S FIDO OR NOT EITHER X1 BETWEEN X X1 OR FOR SOME X2 NOT FOR SOM
E X3 BOTH X BETWEEN LINUS X2 AND BOTH X2 HITS X1 AND EITHER CAT
HY BETWEEN X2 X3 OR FOR EVERY X4 X3 BETWEEN X2 X4 AND IF NOT CA
THY LIKES ALAN THEN NOT ALAN GIVES CATHY ALAN

BOTH ALAN LAUGHS AND FOR EVERY X IF DODIE BETWEEN X X THEN NOT NOT EI
THER DODIE RUNS OR EITHER IF X PUSHES TABBY THEN EITHER CATHY W
EEPS OR EITHER NOT LINUS GIVES X X OR NOT FOR EVERY X2 EITHER N
OT X2 KISSES X2 OR X WEEPS OR X WEEPS

FOR EVERY X BOTH X KISSES X AND BOTH X HITS CATHY AND EITHER FIDO HIT
S DODIE OR IF X WEEPS THEN EITHER X RUNS OR NOT NOT BOTH X HITS
X AND FOR SOME X1 FOR EVERY X2 BOTH X1 BETWEEN BOB X2 AND FOR
EVERY X3 IF IF TABBY LIKES X1 THEN IF X2 PUSHES X3 THEN BOTH X1
PUSHES X3 AND BOTH X2 LAUGHS AND IF X3 BETWEEN X2 X2 THEN X1 R
UNS THEN X1 HITS X2

BOB FALLS

CATHY RUNS

dom sentence exhibit may be merely the use of spelled-out English words instead of symbols. The claim here must be guarded, however, since communication has many aspects. What is easy to read may be laborious to write. What may be easy to read in a verbal sense may be hard to read in a conceptual sense, as witness the simplified overview provided by symbols of a mathematical equation whose English equivalent would be elephantine. Less superficial "improvements" can be noted in the more elaborate syntax of English I and II. The usual predicate calculus notation does not admit compound subjects or predicates, and it pays for the simplicity of its rules in the clumsiness of its sentence structure. Thus "George or Donald answered" must be changed to "George answered or Donald answered" before direct translation into, e.g., Ag v Ad, is possible. Something like an algebraic factoring law seems indicated: $A(g \lor d) \equiv Ag \lor Ad$. Actually, English I and II have fairly general factoring laws. The improvement in intelligibility and in writing effort may be glimpsed in exhibit II where factored and nonfactored versions can be compared. The nonfactored version is shown not in logical notation but in English I, which uses the words "both," "either," "if," and "not," as Polish groupers, as suggested most recently by Quine.[21] English II avoids the obvious pile-ups of groupers by a flexible system of precedences among connectives that need not be explained here but can be noted in some of the examples in Exhibit II.

In summary, I have tried to point out that objections to formalized languages too often rest on overnarrow conceptions of what a formalized language must be, e.g., that "precise" structure demands, in several distinct senses, rigid use. In particular, I have tried to point to certain pervasive but quite inappropriate assumptions as to the status of formalized languages as "models" of something that, on the antiformalist side, appear to bar adequate treatment of language imprecision or variation, and that, too often, on the proformalist side, are conceded to require, as justification, an overall measure of approximation as between the formalized language and the natural language of which it claims to be a model. I have tried

Exhibit II

20 ENG2GEN 4

IF CATHY SINGS THEN IF FIDO IS NOT YELLING THEN IF LINUS IS UNEASY THEN BOB IS NOT HOPEFUL .
SOME CHILD WHO WEEPS DOES NOT POUT .
ALAN IS YELLING OR DODIE CRIES AND FURTHERMORE LINUS LAUGHS AND ALAN DOES NOT POUT .
CATHY IS NOT TIRED OUT AND FURTHERMORE ALAN DOES NOT CRY .
ALAN IS NOT YELLING AND FURTHERMORE EVERY GIRL IS A CHILD .
FIDO RUNS AND FURTHERMORE TABBY IS NOT A BROTHER OF LINUS OR FIDO .
NO BOY WEEPS .
NO BOY IS NOT A CHILD .
FIDO IS NOT BESIDE A BOY WHO IS A GIRL .
ANY PET WHO SINGS IS NOT UNEASY .
DODIE IS BESIDE AND BESIDE LINUS .
DODIE IS A SISTER OF ANY DOG .
CATHY IS CHEERY OR TABBY IS HOPEFUL AND FURTHERMORE DODIE IS BRAVE AND FURTHER-
MORE DODIE IS NOT A GIRL .
IF CATHY DOES NOT FALL THEN DODIE DOES NOT SEND ALAN TO EVERY CAT .
DODIE IS NOT A SISTER OF ANY CHILD WHO IS A GIRL .
CATHY GOES FROM CATHY TO SOME PET .
TABBY IS A CHILD AND FURTHERMORE BOB IS NOT A CHILD OR BOY .
TABBY DOES NOT SIGNAL TO SOME BOY WHO SINGS .
IT IS NOT THE CASE THAT ALAN GOES FROM FIDO TO A GIRL .
FIDO IS NOT TALLER THAN EVERY GIRL WHO FALLS .

to indicate a way out of this "model muddle" by sketching a more natural, less problematic role for formalized languages in natural-language studies.

NOTES

1. For a fairer crediting, see J. van Heijenoort's "Logic as Calculus and Logic as Language," in *Synthèse*, September 1967.

2. There are, of course, other readings of "formal language," e.g., as "uninterpreted syntactical system," that would be warranted by the literature, but would even further trivialize Ziff's charges.

3. As by Church, *Introduction to Mathematical Logic I*, pp. 2–3, ". . . it is desirable . . . for purposes of logic to employ a specially devised language, a *formalized language* as we shall call it, which shall . . . reproduce the logical form – at the expense, where necessary, of brevity and facility of communication."

4. Some steps toward a more communication-oriented logical formalism will be described presently.

5. The possibility of such "free-wheeling" use of formalized languages was often stressed to me by Carnap.

6. Antiformalists often accuse the formal language tradition of "overlooking" all but the referential uses of language. But concentration on one use is not to overlook others, except in an obviously methodological way. Indeed, since the referential aspect of language is basic to most "word-games," its study is basic to their study.

7. Strictly speaking, a concession is called for here, involving *syntactical* precision. Since typical semantical formalization calls for syntactical distinctions, e.g., of predicate degree or type, which are not sharply drawn in English, the English used metalinguistically will tend to undergo some "adaptive" reinterpretation. Problems suggested by this remark can be bypassed, for present purposes, if we conceive, more hypothetically, of object and metalanguage being syntactically alike, except for the Tarskian requirement of stronger logic in the metalanguage, but with the descriptive terms of both still being imprecise in an appropriate sense.

8. W. V. Quine, "Ontological Relativity," *Journal of Philosophy*, LXV, 7, 1968.

9. R. Carnap, *The Logical Syntax of Language*, 1937, p. 8.

10. N. Chomsky, "Logical Syntax and Semantics," *Language*, XXXI (1955), pp. 36–45.

11. The troublesome double reading of this sort of phrase will be remarked upon presently.

12. The clarity of the momentary-idiolect notion mentioned here is just the one already indicated, i.e., distinguishing linguistic mutabilities from imprecision so as to admit, in principle, the possibility of syntactically describable, synchronic "snapshots."

13. The definitional aspect of formalized languages appears to confuse not only the critics but even some of the defenders. L. J. Cohen, in his *Diversity of Meaning* (Herder & Herder, 1963), distinguishes between *de jure* and *de facto* languages (more or less paralleling Ziff's formal-natural distinction) and attacks *de jure* languages in a spirit similar to Ziff's. J. Fodor, in a review (*Journal of Philosophy*, May 21, 1964), scores some sound points against Cohen but himself misconstrues the role of "rules" in formalized languages. He views them as explanatory rather than definitional. This leads him to forced misreadings of statements of Cohen that are unobjectionable on the definitional conception of *de jure* ("Presumably Cohen does not intend to be taken literally when he says . . ."). Only toward the end of his review does Fodor appear to contemplate the possibility of a definitional view of rules, and then only for some rules. Even here, such a "constitutive" view is credited only to a mimeographed paper of John Searles rather than acknowledged as typifying the formalized language tradition. It may be granted that the word "rule," e.g., as used by Carnap, may be a bit misleading, and that the "spread-out" format of some syntactical formulations in which each "rule" may appear to be a separate sentence or even a command, rather than a clause in a very long definiens, may disguise the definitional nature of the overall procedure, but it is not a very deep disguise.

14. On p. 4, *Aspects of the Theory of Syntax* (M.I.T. Press, 1965), we are told "A grammar of a language purports to be a description of the ideal speaker-hearer's intrinsic competence." Then on p. 9 we are warned "To avoid . . . a continuing misunderstanding, it is perhaps worthwhile to reiterate that a generative grammar is not a model for a speaker or a hearer." But the next sentence again raises doubt: "It attempts to characterize in the most neutral possible terms the knowledge of the language that

provides the basis for actual use of language by a speaker-hearer."
The next few sentences continue this odd vacillation, ending inconclusively.

15. "On the Notion 'Rule of Grammar'" in *The Structure of Language* (eds. J. Fodor and J. Katz), Prentice-Hall, 1964, pp. 119 et seq.

16. Sibeth, G. G., *Wörterbuch der Mecklenburgisch-Vorpommerschen Mundart von Mi.* Leipzig, 1876.

17. I shall, on occasion, use "describe" and even "model" in this unassuming sense, when confusion with more demanding, more genuine senses of these words is unlikely.

18. Cohen (*op. cit.*) cites a somewhat similar Orwellian anxiety and argues not only against it but against Orwell's own faith in language power. Cohen's moral is antiformalist. But the present argument should suggest that the moral is misplaced.

19. H. G. Bohnert and P. O. Backer, *Automatic English-to-Logic Translation in a Simplified Model: A Study in the Logic of Grammar.* IBM Research Paper, RC 1744, 1967.

20. The IBM APL/360 system.

21. Quine, W. V., "Logic as a Source of Syntactical Insights" in *Structure of Language and Its Mathematical Aspects* (ed. R. Jakobson), American Mathematical Society, 1961.

2

Effectiveness and Natural Languages

GEORGE BOOLOS

Columbia University

IN "Natural and Formal Languages" Professor Ziff is concerned
to point out certain differences between natural languages,
such as English, and formal languages, descriptions, and (oc-
casional) uses of which are to be found in books on formal
logic. Ziff argues that despite the undeniable precision and
clarity of formal languages, these are utterly useless as languages "with which to communicate in the world in which we
find ourselves," and mentions several important and hitherto
insufficiently emphasized ways in which what might appear to
be inelegancies and sources of misunderstanding in natural
languages will often serve to make one's mind known to others
more easily: redundancy, polysemy, sorts of inexplicitness and
imprecision, reliance on what speakers and hearers can per-
ceive and be expected to know, and what Ziff calls "modulation of meaning." With his contention that these features are
understandable and desirable in languages to be used by human beings like ourselves I have no wish to quarrel. It is to the
use Ziff makes of a certain technical, mathematical concept,
that of *effectiveness,* in describing how natural languages differ
from formal ones, that I want to take exception.

It is clear from his paper that Ziff regards the notion of
effectiveness as crucially important for understanding these
differences: ". . . the requirements of effectiveness are
flaunted by a natural language and in every quarter. There is
no algorithm for determining which expressions are words of
the language and which are not." "Being bound to the require-

ments of effectiveness, [formal languages] are bound to lose luster when exposed to the corrosive forces of actual discourse." "The vocabulary of a formal language may be either finite or infinite. In either case the vocabulary of a formal language is effectively specifiable. In contrast, no nonarbitrary specification of the vocabulary of a natural language, or dialect, or idiolect can possibly be effective." After providing this definition of a word's being in a person's vocabulary at a given time: "at that time, first, he is able to use it correctly, given appropriate conditions for doing so, and second, an inability to understand a sentence in which the word is used is not attributable to a difficulty with the word in question," he says, "The specification just provided of a person's vocabulary at a fixed moment of time is clearly not effective in any plausible sense of the word. There neither is nor does it even seem plausible to suppose there could be any sort of algorithm for determining which words a person is able to use correctly or when an inability to understand a sentence in which the word is used is attributable to a difficulty with the word."

To say that there could be no algorithm for deciding which words a person is able to use correctly at a certain time reflects a misunderstanding of the notions of *algorithm*. Of course there couldn't be an *algorithm* for determining whether a person can use a given word correctly. Any procedure for deciding that would involve examining him or his writings or utterances or his brain or what have you. But that there is such a procedure is not implied when it is said that the person's vocabulary at a given time is effectively specifiable. Saying this merely means that an algorithm exists that always gives either a "yes" or a "no" output, and that gives a "yes" ouput just when its input is a word in the person's vocabulary at the time in question. The existence of this algorithm is to be understood in the same, rather attenuated, mathematical sense as is used when it is (truly) said, for example, that if Goldbach's conjecture is false, a numerical (a finite sequence of digits) exists which denotes an even number greater than two that is not the sum of two primes. It is not required that there should be, somewhere in the universe, an actual inscription (token) of a description of the algorithm or of a computing machine that carries out the computation specified by the algorithm, nor, a fortiori, that we have recognized an actual inscription to be a description of the algorithm. All that is necessary is that *some sequence* of letters and punctuation marks *be* a description of an algorithm that gives the correct answer. The sequence, though, need not be one that anyone has ever written down or that is to be come across somewhere in the world.

Now it is clear that in this sense, there is an algorithm for telling whether a word is in a person's vocabulary at a given time, if the person's vocabulary is finite at that time. For if it is finite, there will be a (finite) list of all the words in it, and a sentence reading: "check to see whether the word given as input is one of the following words [here follows the finite list]; if it is, give output yes, if not, no, will be a perfectly adequate description of an algorithm of the desired sort.

It might be objected: To be sure, if (as we shall assume for the moment) his vocabulary is finite, there is such an algorithm-description. But, and this is the question you haven't yet answered, how do you tell which description is the *correct* one?

The short answer to this question is "it doesn't matter if I can't," but the question reveals a confusion that it is easy to fall into, which an example of a sort familiar to students of the theory of effective operations (recursive-function theory) may serve to dispel. The confusion gone, the short answer will be seen to be correct. Consider the following set, which we shall call G. G contains any even (natural) number that is less than every counterexample to Goldbach's conjecture. This conjecture, which asserts that every even number greater than two is the sum of two primes, is presently an unsolved problem of number theory. It is known only that if there is a counterexample, the smallest one will be quite huge, but it is not now known whether there is even one. However, in spite of our ignorance about the truth or falsity of Goldbach's Conjecture, the set G is effectively decidable! For either Goldbach's Conjecture is true, and thus G contains all even numbers, in which case it is effectively decidable (use the division algorithm with divisor 2), or it is false, and thus G is finite, in which case again it is effectively decidable. By the law of excluded middle, Goldbach's Conjecture is either true or false, and therefore G is effectively decidable. At present, however, we don't know *which* effectively decidable set G is! The point of this example is that *it is not necessary to know an algorithm for deciding membership in a set in order to know that the set is effectively decidable.* (Ziff may merely be claiming that we seldom possess or know an algorithm [as opposed to their being one] whose output is "yes" just when its input is a word in the vocabulary of a speaker at a given time. This is hardly surprising or interesting. We don't possess an algorithm whose output is "yes" just when its input is a word in any of the lost plays of Sophocles, either; this shows nothing about the effective specifiability of this set.) All that one needs to know is that *there is* an algorithm for deciding membership in the set.

Since algorithms are procedures, and since procedures pose the same kinds of problems of individuation as rules and propositions, in order to avoid an inessential complication, let us for the moment identify algorithms with sentences describing them and let us take sentences to be finite sequences of symbols. Then to know that a set is effectively decidable, all one has to know is that *there is* (in the thin mathematical sense described above) a finite sequence of symbols with a certain property. Now, although someone may have come to know this by recognizing a certain sequence described or presented to him to have the property, it is not necessary for him to have come to know it this way. He may have come to know it by somehow recognizing that not all sequences could lack the property, for example. Thus that we cannot at some moment tell which of a number of algorithms is the correct one for deciding membership in a set, or describe the correct algorithm in some useful way, does not mean that we do not then know that the set is effectively decidable.

Ziff's repeated assertions that a person's vocabulary is not effectively specifiable suggest that he requires that some algorithm be known which would correctly decide whether a word is in a person's vocabulary, if his vocabulary is to be correctly described as "effectively specifiable." To insist upon this is, as we have argued, to use the term "effective" in some other sense than the technical one. That Ziff does mean to be using the technical sense of "effective," however, is, I think, clear from the quotation from Church's *Introduction to Mathematical Logic* that Ziff gives and the gloss on it he immediately makes. Ziff may also be insisting that there be an algorithm which tells, for any given person, word, and time, whether the word is in the person's vocabulary at the time, if we are correctly to call any person's vocabulary effectively decidable. ("There neither is nor does it even seem plausible to suppose there could be any sort of algorithm for determining . . . which words a person is able to use correctly. . . .") Not only is it *not plausible* to suppose this; it is *impossible* that there should be such an *algorithm,* for what would the input of such an algorithm be? A word? A person? A word and a person? An ordered pair consisting of a word and a person? An algorithm is a "mechanical" procedure that an agent follows in operating upon sequences or arrays of *symbols.* Certain symbols are given to the agent (a person, an office of secretaries, a computing machine) as input. Following the algorithm, the agent writes down more symbols, possibly erases some, possibly does some prescribed side-calculations, goes on in this manner, and possibly stops. If he stops, the sequence or array that appears in the appropriate place is the output of the computation. Some examples of algorithms are the procedure for finding the product of two numbers, the truth-table method for determining whether a formula of the propositional calculus is a tautology, and the procedure sketched by Aristotle for telling whether a syllogistic inference is valid. If the procedure one is using to solve a problem is genuinely algorithmic, no intelligence or luck or magic is needed to arrive at the answer; all one has to do is manipulate symbols in accordance with the procedure until the procedure directs one to stop.

What sort of "algorithmic procedure" then could there be for telling whether a word is in (e.g.) Alfred's vocabulary? One sort has already been described: the input word is checked against the members of a finite list of words and a "yes" or a "no" output is given according as it is, or is not, one of them. This is not the kind of algorithm that Ziff seems to have in mind when he says that vocabularies are not effectively specifiable. He seems to want a routine or kind of inspection that involves interrogating or examining Alfred himself, for he writes, "That no one, not even the speaker, has altogether free access to word storage is only one reason why it is not in fact possible to provide a nonarbitrary specification of a speaker's vocabulary." No such routine is an *algorithm*, however, whatever else it might be, and to say that since such a routine is lacking a person's vocabulary is not effectively specifiable is therefore to commit a non sequitur. (Possibly Ziff has in mind an algorithm whose input is a word and some sort of standardized correct physiological *description* of a person, and which says "yes" just in case the word is in the person's vocabulary. But nowhere in "Natural and Formal Languages" does Ziff say that this is what he means, nor is there any argument in the paper that such an algorithm couldn't be found.) Presumably Ziff would want to say that it was possible to provide a nonarbitrary effective specification of the set of words tattooed across Alfred's chest, for, after all, there is a routine for determining membership in the set if Alfred is cooperative. But the absence of a peeking procedure in the case of Alfred's vocabulary is entirely irrelevant to the question whether his vocabulary is effectively specifiable or not, for the answer to it depends solely on *what words are in fact in Alfred's vocabulary* and not on how that vocabulary is described or referred to.

It is important to realize that "I don't know" is a perfectly possible answer to a question of the form "Is the set which . . . an effectively decidable set?" The (correct) answer to any such question will be a function of the *set* being asked about. If different descriptions are used to refer to the same set, the corresponding questions will have the same answer.

though it is possible that someone not know that they have the same answer if he does not know that the descriptions do refer to the same set. The inference: "A is an effectively decidable set. A is identical with B. Therefore, B is an effectively decidable set," is a perfectly valid one, for the dots' position in "... is an effectively decidable set" is a *referentially transparent* one. Thus if the set of words in Alfred's vocabulary is in fact coextensive (and hence identical) with some set described in a way that makes it possible for us to see that it is effectively decidable, then the set of words in Alfred's vocabulary is in fact an effectively decidable set, even if we do not know, or cannot recognize, that it is one. The idea that a set might be effectively decidable "under one description but not under another," which may lurk behind some of what Ziff says, is a confusion. How a set is described cannot in the least affect the answer to the question whether it is effectively decidable once what the members of the set are (and hence what the set is) is fixed; it can, however, affect what we *know* about the set, including the answer to that question. Ziff seems to miss the distinction between a question's having an answer and its being known what the answer to the question is when he writes, "The question whether or not an expression formed by the combination of several million symbols is a well-formed expression of the language in fact admits only of a probabilistic sort of answer." While it is perfectly true that we may never know with full certainty what the correct answer to the question is, it can hardly be denied that if the *correct* answer to it is "yes," then it *admits of* the answer "yes." We may not be able to tell whether a statement of the form "The set which ... is effectively decidable" is true, but it certainly does not follow from this alone that the set which ... is *not* effectively decidable!

Up to now we have considered only cases in which we assumed that the person's vocabulary was finite and, hence, effectively decidable. Ziff gives examples, of the "anti-anti-anti-anti-Communist" variety, which indicate that we should be as willing to say that a person's vocabulary is infinite, and willing to say it for much the same reasons as we are to say that the set of grammatical sentences in his language is infinite. Since there are sets of words that are not effectively specifiable (e.g., the set of words formed by prefixing n "anti-"s to "Communist," if n is the Gödel number of a true sentence of arithmetic), it might seem possible for a person's vocabulary not to be effectively specifiable, if, as Ziff suggests it typically will be, it is infinite.

The vocabulary of a single speaker at a fixed moment of time can, according to Ziff, be identified with "the products of a set of morphologically productive operations over some given explicit store of words." Presumably, though Ziff does not say so, the operations are effective, and the set of them and the store of words are both finite sets. Now, though there are finite sets of operations over some given finite store of words the set of whose products is not effectively specifiable (cf. the theorems of a standard axiomatization of the predicate calculus), an argument, that seems to me to be at least fairly convincing, can be given for thinking that the "morphologically productive operations" over a *speaker's* store of words nevertheless yield an effectively specifiable vocabulary: it seems more or less plausible to suppose that an algorithm could be devised to calculate an upper bound to the number of times the morphologically productive operations have to be applied to members of the store of words in order to produce any given word. If so, one could then check through all sequences of applications of the operations with fewer members than the output of the algorithm (since there would be only finitely many such sequences) and see whether the given word was the product of one of those sequences. That such an algorithm could be devised (knowledge of the store of words and the set of operations being assumed, of course) seems plausible, because (roughly) it certainly seems credible that one could construct an algorithm to calculate an upper bound to the number of different sequences of phonemes or letters that occur in the shortest production of a word that don't appear in the word, and this seems credible, because it seems incredible that, whatever my vocabulary and the morphologically productive operations yielding it may be, there is a word in it, a description of whose production requires mention of sequences of phonemes containing a million times the cube of the number of phonemes in the word itself. In order to tell that "anti-anti-anti-anti-Communist" is a word in my vocabulary, I don't believe that I or any sensibly designed machine that enumerates my vocabulary would have to look at sequences fourteen billion phonemes long, and that the same goes for any other sequence of phonemes. Somewhat hesitantly, then, I conclude that even if speakers' vocabularies are infinite, it is a good guess that they are effectively specifiable, and therefore remain unconvinced that the notion of effectiveness, as used by Ziff, has anything to do with the differences between natural and formal languages.

3

A Note on Metaphysics and Language

GERTRUDE EZORSKY

Brooklyn College

IN HIS "Language, Logic, and States of Affairs," Professor Chisholm suggests that the notion of abstract entities that he calls "states of affairs" can clarify certain issues in philosophy of language. According to this position (which I shall call the metaphysical view), there exists a state of affairs corresponding to every significant sentence. Thus, there are, corresponding to "The earth is round" and to its denial, two states of affairs, only one of which is exemplified in something actual. While that which exemplifies a state of affairs is actual, the state of affairs itself has being.

Professor Chisholm writes: "Where I have used 'exemplified' others (e.g., Meinong and Lewis) have used such terms as 'actual.'" He suggests that the notion of a true or false sentence taken in ordinary language presupposes "the *being* of the metaphysicians' states of affairs." (Italics added).

The metaphysical view is offered as a hypothesis that is supposed to resolve some problems in philosophy of language. For example, this view is supposed to provide an answer to a puzzle that arises out of such sentences as "There is something that both Jones and Smith want to see realized and their hopes will never be fulfilled." The objects of Jones's and Smith's desire is, of course, not anything actual. But surely a desire must have some object. The metaphysical view supplies such an object, an unexemplified state of affairs, having being, but not actuality.

Professor Chisholm does not argue that any alternative to

this view is necessarily false, only that the metaphysical view can clarify some issues in the analysis of language. Since the metaphysical view is not necessarily true, then its denial, "There are no states of affairs," must be significant. But according to the metaphysical view, this is a state of affairs corresponding to every significant sentence. In that case, there must be a state of affairs corresponding to the significant sentence, "There are no states of affairs," namely, the state of affairs, such that there are no states of affairs. But surely that state of affairs is paradoxical. Can the paradox be resolved, in familiar fashion, by positing a hierarchy of orders of states of affairs? No, it cannot. Consider the following: Given a hierarchy of states of affairs, the paradoxical state of affairs would become a second-order state of affairs, such that there are no first-order states of affairs. Hence the paradox would disappear. But this move, positing such a metaphysical hierarchy, is not open to those who hold the metaphysical view described by Professor Chisholm. Here is why: If there were such a hierarchy, there would be a second-order state of affairs, such that there are first-order states of affairs. This second-order state of affairs would be exemplified in first-order states of affairs. But according to the metaphysical view, what exemplifies a state of affairs is something actual. Hence, first-order states of affairs, since they exemplify a second-order states of affairs, must be actual. However, states of affairs are not supposed to be actual but merely to have being. Moreover, the hierarchy cannot be topped by second-order states of affairs, since they presumably exemplify the third-order state of affairs, such that there are second-order states of affairs. Thus, by parallel argument, second-order states of affairs are actual too. And so on, upward and onward. States of affairs fall into actuality and the distinction between being and actuality disappears.

Index